A Complete Field Guide to
Nests in the United States

↗↗↗↗↗↗↗↗↗↗

BOOKS BY
    RICHARD HEADSTROM

The Living Year

Birds' Nests, A Field Guide

Birds' Nests of the West, A Field Guide

Adventures with a Microscope

Adventures with a Hand Lens

Adventures with Insects

Adventures with Freshwater Animals

Garden Friends and Foes

Nature in Miniature

The Story of Russia

The Boy's Book of Lizards (in preparation)

A COMPLETE
FIELD GUIDE TO
NESTS IN THE
UNITED STATES

Including Those of
Birds, Mammals, Insects, Fishes,
Reptiles, and Amphibians

ˁˁˁ

BY RICHARD HEADSTROM

IVES WASHBURN, INC. , NEW YORK

⁄ A COMPLETE FIELD GUIDE TO
NESTS IN THE UNITED STATES

LIBRARY OF CONGRESS CATALOG CARD NUMBER: 70-96287

MANUFACTURED IN THE UNITED STATES OF AMERICA

VAN REES PRESS • NEW YORK

111 To My Wife 111

Preface

In 1949 I published *Birds' Nests, A Field Guide* as an aid in identifying the nests of our eastern birds. At the time I felt it might be useful and would fill a need. The favorable reception accorded the book led me to publish, two years later, in 1951, the companion book, *Birds' Nests of the West, A Field Guide,* which served the same purpose.

As both books have demonstrated their usefulness over the years, the need for revising and enlarging the material has become increasingly more evident. It appeared that they would serve the user even better if combined in a single volume. The thought also occurred that data on the nests of other animals, such as the mammals, insects, and fishes, should be added and would be equally useful.

For nests are not the prosaic things that many seem to think—they are interesting facets of animal behavior. The study of nests can be a rewarding and fascinating pastime in itself and, perhaps more importantly, provide us with insights into the habits of the animals that make them.

Hence it is hoped that the present book, *A Complete Field Guide to Nests in the United States,* may not only be as welcome as the two previous guides, but also be the means of developing a broader interest in our wildlife, as well as leading to many enjoyable and profitable hours outdoors.

✓✓✓ ACKNOWLEDGMENTS ✓✓✓

I want to express my grateful appreciation to Dr. Olin Sewall Pettingill, Jr., and Mr. Torrey Jackson for permission to use their photographs and to my wife who ably assisted in the preparation of the manuscript.

Contents

✔✔✔✔✔✔✔✔✔✔✔✔✔✔

✔✔✔✔✔ PART ONE

NESTS OF BIRDS EAST OF THE ONE-HUNDREDTH MERIDIAN

Nests On or In the Ground

xi

⁊⁊⁊⁊⁊ PART TWO

NESTS OF BIRDS WEST OF THE ONE-HUNDREDTH MERIDIAN

Nests On or In the Ground

Nests Above the Ground

Nests Above the Ground

⚡⚡⚡⚡⚡ PART FOUR

NESTS OF MAMMALS WEST OF THE
ONE-HUNDREDTH MERIDIAN

Nests In the Ground or In Burrows

Nests Above the Ground

✓✓✓✓ **PART FIVE**

NESTS OF INSECTS

⸊⸊⸊⸊⸊ PART SIX

NESTS OF FISHES

✔✔✔✔✔ PART SEVEN
OTHER NESTS

Photographs follow page 214

Drawings of insect nests follow page 406

Introduction

The surest way to identify a nest is when it is occupied by its maker. This is not always easy, for many birds build their nests in inaccessible places. In the summer when the trees and shrubs are in complete foliage we often pass them by or overlook them.

When October and November arrive and the brisk autumn winds clear the trees and shrubs of their leaves, many nests, which were artfully concealed only a few weeks before, become exposed in the most unexpected places. Along the roadside we discover the nests of the orioles and goldfinches, in the shrubbery about the garden the nests of the mockingbird and catbird, in the nearby thicket the nests of the chat and towhee, and in the fields and woods the nests of birds too numerous to mention.

These nests may not be in such perfect condition as when they were newly completed, but it is surprising how well they can withstand the buffeting of the elements and endure even into the following spring without losing their identity. Even though at times there may be considerable variation in the nests of the same species, there are certain general characteristics as to the material used, location, and size, which make most nests possible to identify. The chipping sparrow usually lines its nest with horsehair, the barn swallow and bush-tit with feathers, the scissor-tailed flycatcher with cotton, and the goldfinch with thistledown; the catbird may be expected to use grapevine bark in the main part of its nest, the hooded oriole Spanish moss; while the hummingbird, wood pewee, olive warbler, and Coues's flycatcher will cover the exterior with lichens.

The variety of materials used by birds in building their nests is sometimes astonishing. Many, like the grasshopper, field, and sage sparrows, use grass, while others, such as the hawks and herons, employ sticks and twigs. The red-eyed vireo selects strips of bark, bits of dead wood, paper, and the down of plants for its nest, the kingbird weed stems, plant fibers, rootlets, wool, and string. The robin, phoebe, and magpie find mud a most serviceable material. The parula warbler weaves a nest of Usnea hanging from a tree limb.

When the materials with which the birds normally construct their nests are not available they substitute other substances. Thus, a chipping sparrow will use fine wire instead of the customary horsehair and the crested flycatcher and blue grosbeak will utilize discarded cellophane or plastic wrappers in place of cast snakeskins. Birds display a great deal of ingenuity in nest-building. They readily adapt themselves to varying environmental conditions. In a place subject to strong winds, the red-winged blackbird will build a much deeper nest than in a sheltered location. The chimney swift now builds in chimneys in preference to the hollow trees in which it formerly nested and the Vaux's swift will do so occasionally. The barn swallow and phoebe today make use of man-made structures instead of building nests on rocks as they did originally.

Some birds display remarkable skill and craftsmanship in building their nests. The robin builds a bulky, compact, thick-walled structure of mud, reinforced with grass and straw; the hummingbird a dainty, trim affair covered with lichens; the oriole an exquisitely woven nest. Not all birds go to such lengths; the mourning dove, for instance, puts together merely a loose platform of twigs. The yellow-billed cuckoo does slightly better and yet its nest is little more than a shallow, frail platform, so loosely constructed that the eggs appear to be in danger of falling through the interstices.

Many birds make only a slight pretense at building a nest. The killdeer, spotted sandpiper, upland plover, prairie chicken, and California quail deposit their eggs in a crudely lined hollow in the ground. The whip-poor-will does not even deign to scoop out a hollow, but simply lays its eggs among dead leaves as if aware that they so closely resemble the color and pattern of the forest floor that they will generally remain undetected. For much the same reason woodpeckers place their eggs in natural holes in trees or in cavities that they excavate, having discovered, perhaps, that in such hiding places their eggs are comparatively safe—except against such enemies as squirrels and snakes. Finally there are the birds, such as the cowbird, that lay their eggs in the nests of other species and leave the raising of their young to the foster parents.

Since birds build nests in which to incubate their eggs and to serve as cradles for their young until they no longer need protection, it is not surprising to find that they select nesting sites with the greatest care and build them, as a rule, in inaccessible places or where they will be most completely hidden. Some go to extreme lengths to conceal them, such as the meadowlark and some sparrows that arch their nests over with growing vegetation, or the ovenbird that covers its nest with dry leaves from the forest floor. The hummingbirds and wood pewee are usually adept in the art of camouflage and cover their nests with lichens so that they appear to be excrescences on the branch of a tree.

Nests are placed in almost every conceivable location. The song sparrow may build its nest beneath a tuft of grass, the great blue heron in the tallest tree, the yellow warbler in a low bush, the black-capped chickadee in a decaying stump, the woodpecker in a hole in a tree, the kingfisher in a burrow in a sandbank, the chimney swift in a chimney, the phoebe on a bridge, the house sparrow in an electric-light hood, the osprey on the crossbar of a telephone pole, and the house wren in the most unlikely places —in an old tin can, a flowerpot, the fold of a blanket hanging on a clothesline.

But in the choice of a site, individual birds often depart from the general species rule. A blue jay was found building a nest on a tree root projecting from an overhanging eroded bank instead of in the usual pine tree, a song sparrow used a horse's skull instead of the usual grass tussock, and a pair of black phoebes built a nest for two consecutive years in a well four feet below the surface. Flickers have been known to drill their nesting holes through the outer wall of icehouses and to deposit their eggs on the sawdust insulation between the outer and inner walls. Birds that commonly nest on the ground may choose a low shrub or brier bush or vice versa.

Such instances, however, are rare. For the most part birds follow a fairly consistent pattern in nest-building, in use of materials, in size and shape, and in location. Except in unusual instances, when only a specialist might attempt to identify a nest, most of them can be identified with reasonable success.

Most birds nest singly, but a few, like the purple martin and some of the swallows, herons, terns, and gulls, nest in colonies. To these might be added the bobolink, the red-winged blackbird, and the marsh wren, which nest in somewhat scattered communities. As a rule, birds build their nests for just one season. Usually the birds that survive the winter return the following season to the same nesting site, but only a few species use the same nest year after year. Certain owls are known to use the same hole for years in succession, and crows and hawks often rebuild their old nests.

How to Use
This Book

The first step to consider in identifying a nest is to determine what kind of an animal built it. This should present no problem except in one or two instances when a mammal's nest may resemble one built by a bird. Having decided what sort of animal built it, the second step is to look in the section of the book dealing with nests made by the animal and others like it, such as birds, mammals, insects, and so on.

To illustrate, let us take two hypothetical birds' nests and determine their identity. Our first nest is one we find on the ground while walking through a field. Turning to the section on birds' nests, we select the division Nests On or In the Ground and, more specifically, the subdivision I. In Fields or Pastures. We have a choice between A. Open Nest and B. Closed Nest. Observing that our hypothetical nest is of the open type, we next have to note its exact site, and on doing so find that it has been built in a brier growth. We therefore go to a(4) where we have two possibilities. On comparing our nest with the descriptions given for the nests built by the clay-colored sparrow and the field sparrow and noting that our nest contains weed stems and rootlets, materials mentioned in the description of the field sparrow's nest, we conclude that it was made by this bird.

We find our second hypothetical nest in a small sapling while strolling through the woods. Again we turn to the section on birds' nests, this time turning to the division Nests Above the

Ground, which we find has nine subdivisions. Since our nest is not built on a building or in a hole, and since it is neither a hanging or a semihanging one, it is necessary to examine the materials of which it is made. We can see that it is not covered on the outside with lichens, does not contain a layer of mud, and is not made of cottony materials or twigs and sticks. Therefore we now have to choose between V and VI. We reexamine our nest and see that it is made chiefly of bark strips and rootlets, with some fibers and a few twigs. Our choice is V. We now have to measure the inside diameter of our nest, which we find is less than two inches. We have to decide between a(1) and a(2). As our nest is not built in a conifer we turn to a(2), where we have three possibilities. On comparing our nest with the descriptions and noting that our hypothetical nest is "decorated exteriorly with corky bits of wood" and that it contains "bits of dead wood in the bottom," we conclude that its builder was the black-throated blue warbler.

Since identification is based, in part, upon measurements, a tape measure is essential and should be taken on all field trips, as well as a pencil and notebook for recording pertinent data.

As the measurements of a nest of a given species vary slightly, those in the key are average and not definitive. Moreover, as the size and particularly the depth of a nest vary with its state of preservation, the measurements apply only to nests that are fairly well preserved.

The breeding ranges as given are not necessarily complete but are limited to the eastern and central United States east of the One-Hundredth Meridian and western United States west of the One-Hundredth Meridian.

Since subspecies are known by various names in different states or regions, names that differ from the species name are listed beneath it to avoid confusion in identifying a nest where an unfamiliar name is also given as the maker's.

In the cross-references, the first reference refers to a description of the nest while the secondary references refer to other situations in which the nest is apt to be found.

PART ONE

↗↗↗↗↗↗↗↗↗↗↗↗↗↗↗

NESTS OF BIRDS
EAST OF THE
ONE-HUNDREDTH
MERIDIAN

↗↗↗↗↗↗↗↗↗↗↗↗↗↗↗

Nests On or In the Ground

I

↑↑↑↑↑↑↑↑↑↑↑↑↑↑↑

In Fields or Pastures

A. Open Nest

a(1). *In or under a tussock of grass*

  1. See III A a(2) 2.

Mallard

  2. Of grass, leaves, bark strips, pine needles, and moss; lined with fine rootlets or pine needles and grass; outside diameter, 3 inches; outside height, 1¾ inches; inside depth, 1 inch. Sometimes sunken and sometimes placed in a tussock of sphagnum and often embedded in moss; well concealed. Usually where pastures are overgrown with scrub; also swampy woods and open woodlands and slashings. See also II A a(2) 3.

     Eastern and central United States south to Connecticut, northern New Jersey, West Virginia, northern Illinois, and Nebraska.

Nashville Warbler

  3. Bulky, cup-shaped, constructed principally of dried grass, with some leaves, weed stems, rootlets, and shreds of corn husks; lined with fine grass or horsehair. Usually placed on ground sheltered by a tuft of grass but sometimes placed in a small bush or tree. Outside diameter, 4¾ inches; outside height, 2½ inches; inside

9

diameter, 2½ inches; inside depth, 1¾ inches. See also Nests Above the Ground VI A a(1) 3 and VI B b(1) 5. Open fields of dense vegetation and open brushland with scattered trees.

Northwestern Minnesota, southern Michigan, and western Ohio south to southern Texas, southern Mississippi, central Alabama, and northern Georgia.

Dickcissel

4. Loosely built cup of grass, rootlets, and fine weed stems; lined with fine grasses and plant down. Inside diameter, 2¾ inches; inside depth, 1¾ inches. Grasslands and cultivated clover fields.

Western Minnesota and eastern Nebraska.

Lark Bunting

5. Bulky, cup-shaped; of dried grass; lined with fine grass, hair, or rootlets; outside diameter, 4½ inches; outside height, 3 inches; inside diameter, 2 inches; inside depth, 1¾ inches. Usually sunken and well hidden; sometimes placed in or under a cluster of wild or cultivated plants, such as strawberries or potatoes. Old pastures, hayfields, and worn-out farmlands, and, in southern parts of range, palmetto and oak scrub. See also I B b(1) 2.

Southern New Hampshire, Minnesota, North Dakota south to northern Georgia, southern Louisiana, and Texas; also prairies of central Florida.

Grasshopper Sparrow

6. Loosely woven, cup-shaped; of grass; lined with finer materials, hair often being used. Well hidden. Outside diameter, 3 inches; inside diameter, 2 inches; inside depth, 1 inch to 2 inches. Grassy and bushy fields, open grasslands with a mixture of tall tufted grasses, tall weeds, and scattered small woody growths.

Southern New Hampshire, New York, South Dakota south to North Carolina, West Virginia, and northern Texas.

Henslow's Sparrow

7. Well-built, cup-shaped; of grasses, weeds, bark, and leaves; lined with finer materials, sometimes with rootlets or hair. Outside diameter, 4¼ inches; outside height, 2⅜ inches; inside diameter, 2⅜ inches; inside depth, 1¾ inches. Sometimes built in a dense bush or tree (often a conifer) up to 4 feet above the ground. Cutover lands, abandoned farmlands, neglected fields, shrub-fringed woodland lakes, and the vicinity of human habitations. See also II A a(2) 8 and Nests Above the Ground VI A a(2) 7 and VI B b(1) 8.

Eastern and central United States south to coastal North Carolina, southern Virginia, northern Georgia, southern Illinois, and Missouri.

Song Sparrow

a(2). *In tall grasses*

1. See Nests Above the Ground VII C c(4) 5.

(Eastern) Ground Dove

2. Cleverly concealed. Of grasses, weed stems, and rootlets arranged in a circular form and lined with similar materials, but finer; sometimes placed at the foot of a tuft of grass or bush. Outside diameter, 5 inches; outside height, 2 inches; inside diameter, 2 inches; inside depth, 1¾ inches. Grassy fields.

Eastern and central United States south to New Jersey, West Virginia, Illinois, and northern Missouri.

Bobolink

3. A slight, flimsy arrangement of grass and sometimes moss; lined with finer grass, hair, or rootlets; almost always placed in shallow hollow or depression. Out-

side diameter, 4 inches; outside height, 2 inches; inside diameter, 2 inches; inside depth, 1½ inches. Brush fields or neglected pastures and hayfields adjoining tidal marshes.

Eastern and central United States south to northern Iowa, northern Indiana, Pennsylvania, Long Island, and the New Jersey coast.

Savannah Sparrow

4. A shallow cup-shaped cavity scratched in the dry earth among the short prairie grass in exposed places. The upper edge is sometimes rather thick and turned inward while the bottom is loosely and thinly laid; flimsy. Lined chiefly at the rim with bits of bleached grass and fine weed stalks. Inside diameter, 2½ inches; inside depth, 1¾ inches. Dry grassy fields; interior plains.

North Dakota south to central Kansas, eastern Nebraska; also western Minnesota.

Chestnut-collared Longspur

a(3). *Under a thistle, small bush, or weed stalk*

1. See II A a(2) 7 and II A a(1) 14.

Rufous-sided Towhee

2. Rather bulky, thick-rimmed, well-cupped but not tightly woven; of dried grass and rootlets; lined with fine grass, rootlets, and hair. Outside diameter, 4½ inches; outside height, 1¾ inches; inside diameter, 2 inches; inside depth, 1½ inches. High dry uplands, such as short grass, hayfields, or pastures.

Eastern and central United States south to North Carolina and Kentucky, Missouri, and Nebraska.

Vesper Sparrow

a(4). *Under low, thick bushes or growth of sprouts and briers*

1. Bulky; of fine grasses; lined with hair. May also be built in a shrub or small conifer. Outside diameter, 4¼ inches; outside height, 2¾ inches; inside diameter, 1¾ inches; inside depth, 1½ inches. Brushy grasslands or clearings in northern forests. See also Nests Above the Ground VI A a(1) 5.

   Northern Nebraska, northwestern Illinois, and north-central Michigan north to Canadian border.

                                          Clay-colored Sparrow

2. Cup-shaped, well-made; of coarse grasses, weed strips, and rootlets; lined with finer grasses and hair. Often placed in a low bush, such as huckleberry, or in a brier patch, only a few feet above the ground. Outside diameter, 5 inches; outside height, 2½ inches; inside diameter, 2 inches; inside depth, 1½ inches. Brushy pastures, abandoned farmland, woodland borders, and cut or burned over woodlands. See also II A a(1) 16 and Nests Above the Ground VI A a(1) 6.

   Eastern and central United States south to northern parts of Gulf States.

                                          (Eastern) Field Sparrow

a(5). *In a depression of the ground*

1. See III A a(3) 2.

                                                Gadwall

2. A slight hollow in the ground; lined with rushes, straw, grass, or stubble and brown down with whitish centers. Usually in grass of prairies or beneath a bush with little attempt at concealment; invariably on dry ground, sometimes as much as a mile from water though often near water.

   Canadian border south to Nebraska and Iowa and casually east to western Pennsylvania.

                                                Pintail

3. See III A a(3) 6 and III A a(4) 2.

Shoveller

4. A slight depression in the ground; thinly lined with grass and a few feathers; sometimes the nest lining is little more than the bent over blades and weeds growing about the structure. In or among grass tufts or bushes; usually vegetation is thick about nest and effectively conceals it. Open prairie country or bushy grasslands.

Canadian border south to Illinois, Missouri, and Arkansas and east to Michigan and Indiana.

Prairie Chicken

5. A hollow in the ground; lined with grasses and dead leaves. In grass in fields and waste lands.

Locally in various eastern states and in Upper Mississippi Valley.

European Partridge

6. A slight natural hollow in grass or grainfield; lined scantily with leaves, grass, and straw.

Mainly north of Mason-Dixon Line (Delaware, northern Maryland, southern Ohio, southern Indiana, Missouri, northern Oklahoma) and north to southern Maine, northern New York, southern Michigan, and Minnesota.

Ring-necked Pheasant

7. Usually a slight hollow scooped out in the ground; sometimes lined with chips of stone or wood, a few pebbles or some weed stalks; or these may be scattered over small area surrounding nesting hollow. Hollow may vary from a shallow, saucer-shaped depression to 1 or 2 inches deep by 3 inches in diameter and may also be a cup-shaped depression among crushed stones or on bare rock without lining. Gen-

erally 4 eggs (1.4 inches by 1.1 inches); pale buff, blotched, and streaked with blackish markings. On grass-covered or bare, gravelly ground in open situations that afford the bird an extended view.

Florida and Gulf of Mexico north to eastern and central United States.

Killdeer

8. Usually a mere depression, 4 to 5 inches in diameter and 2 to 3 inches deep, scratched in the concealment of grass from 7 to 10 inches high; lined with dried grass. Four eggs (1.9 inches by 1.4 inches); olive with few large gray spots. Pasturelands, wide open grassy fields, and flat prairies.

Southern Maine, Michigan, and Wisconsin south to northern Virginia and southern Illinois, southern Missouri, and Oklahoma.

Upland Plover

9. Normally built in upland location, but in proximity to water. A saucer-shaped depression, usually slightly lined with dry grasses but sometimes with weed stalks or mosses; occasionally in cavity under a large rock. Usually 4 eggs (1.3 inches by 0.9 inch); buffy, spotted, and heavily blotched with browns. Margins of ponds and shores of streams.

Eastern and central United States south to northern South Carolina, Alabama, and southern Louisiana.

Spotted Sandpiper

10. Of coarse stems and leaves; lined with finer materials, often with thistledown and a few feathers; woven solidly to withstand the strong winds of early spring. Outside diameter, 4 inches; outside height, 3 inches; inside diameter, 2½ inches; inside depth, 2 inches. Usually at the edge or partially under a grass tuft or clod. In short grass fields.

Eastern and central United States south to North Carolina, West Virginia, Missouri, and Kansas; also coast of Texas.

Horned Lark

11. Cup-shaped; of grasses; lined with rootlets, fine grass, and long hairs. Sometimes repairs and uses abandoned nests of other birds. Outside diameter, 4 inches; outside height, 1½ inches; inside diameter, 2½ inches; inside depth, 1⅛ inches. Generally sunk in a hollow in the ground and carefully concealed with tufts of grass or clover, or in the shelter of a clump of grass or other vegetation; occasionally in the fork of a low tree or bush up to 10 feet above the ground. See also Nests Above the Ground VI A a(2) 6 and VI B b(1) 6.

Fields and pastures and open knolls of Mississippi Valley south to Texas and Louisiana, and east to Ohio and northwestern West Virginia; also a colony in Michigan.

(Eastern) Lark Sparrow

a(6). *On flat ground, in slight depression*

1. No nesting material added. On gravel beaches, rocky knolls, or open barren fields unobstructed by tall shrubbery or trees, often on burned-over areas; also on flat, gravel roofs in towns and cities. May be no depression, or slight depression may be incidentally made by shoving aside of material by incubating bird. See also IV B 8 and Nests Above the Ground XI A a(1) 1.

Eastern and central United States south to Florida Keys and Gulf of Mexico (the Nighthawk breeding on the Keys is the Cuban Nighthawk).

Nighthawk

B. Arched Nest

b(1). *Along old fence rows or neglected brushy corner of field*

1. Well-hollowed; of dry grasses, straw, leaves, or weed stalks; lined with grass, straw, or bark strips; dead or growing grass or other vegetation usually woven into arch over nest, often completely concealing it and leaving a small opening in the side; if built among vines or briers, these are also woven into arch to make nest more durable; at times an arched passage up to a foot in length is constructed leading to it. Outside diameter, 5 to 7 inches; outside height, 2⅛ inches; inside diameter, 4½ inches; inside depth, 1¾ inches. Fields and farming country.

    Gulf of Mexico north through eastern and central United States except northern Minnesota and northern Maine.

    Bob-white

b(2). *Beneath a tuft of clover, sedge, or grass*

1. Of grasses and weeds, usually with a dome-shaped roof constructed of grass more or less interwoven with the attached and growing parts of the grasses and weeds against which it is built; lined with finer materials; sometimes with a covered grassy tunnel leading to it. On rare occasions the nest has two entrances. Well concealed. Outside diameter, 6½ inches; outside height, 7 inches; inside diameter, 4 inches; inside depth, 5 inches. Grassy fields, grasslands, and pastures.

    Eastern and central United States (from eastern Minnesota) south to Florida and Gulf of Mexico and west to Nebraska and Kansas.

    Eastern Meadowlark

b(3). *In or under a tussock of grass*

    1.   On ground beneath a tussock of grass or weeds; of grass and usually roughly arched with same material. Outside diameter, 7 inches; outside height, 5 inches; inside diameter, 3⅜ inches; inside depth, 2 inches.

        Prairies from Canadian border south to central Texas and east to Wisconsin and Illinois.

Western Meadowlark

    2.   See I A a(1) 5.

Grasshopper Sparrow

II

////////////////

In Woods, Thickets, and Wooded Hillsides

A. Open Nest

a(1). *At foot of tree, bush, stump, rock, or log; among roots of fallen tree or where earth has washed away from tree roots on bank*

1. See Nests Above the Ground VIII A a(3) 4.

    American Merganser

2. Generally a slight hollow in the ground; lined with twigs, leaves, moss, or grass. Usually placed under a low, protecting branch of a spruce, in deep moss, or in a tangle of bushes, and well concealed. Chiefly swampy coniferous woods.

    A northern species nesting along northern fringe of eastern and central United States.

    Spruce Grouse

3. Shallow depression in the ground; lined chiefly with dead leaves, sometimes entirely with pine needles. Inside diameter, 6½ inches; inside depth, 1 inch. Under dense cover in thick woods and wooded hills.

Eastern United States south to New Jersey and, in the Appalachians, to Georgia and Alabama, and central United States south in Mississippi Valley to Michigan, Wisconsin, northeastern Iowa, and locally to Ohio, Indiana, and Missouri.

Ruffed Grouse

4. A hollow in the ground; scantily lined with leaves, grass, and a few feathers. Usually partially concealed under a thick tuft of tall grass or under a bush. Prairie brushland and open forests.

Canadian border south to western Wisconsin, Minnesota, and central Nebraska.

Sharp-tailed Grouse

5. Large rough structure of leaves, weed stalks, bark strips, grass, moss, rootlets, and pine needles; lined with grasses, rootlets, feathers, and hair. Sometimes (in open situations) arched over or dome-shaped with a side entrance, only large enough to admit the bird. See also II B b(1) 2. In a hole in the ground or in a crevice in bank, in a hole in a tree or stump, fence post, fallen log, in a cavity in a stone wall, in tin cans, coffee pots, pails, small baskets, mail boxes, birdhouses, and in a great variety of nooks and crannies in or about or under buildings of various kinds and under bridges. Woodlands, orchards, thickets, brushy hollows, wooded swamps, along the banks of streams, and in the vicinity of human habitations. See also Nests Above the Ground VIII A a(3) 20 and IX A a(2) 2.

Southern Massachusetts, Rhode Island, lower Hudson River, Pennsylvania, Ohio, southern Iowa, and southwestern Nebraska south to Florida, Gulf Coast, and Texas.

Carolina Wren

6. Cup-shaped, compactly woven; of weed stems, grass stalks, fibrous strips of bark, twigs, and dried leaves;

lined with dried leaves, strips of soft bark, rootlets, pine needles, and horsehair. Outside diameter, 10 inches; outside height, 5 inches; inside diameter, 2 inches; inside depth, less than 2 inches. Sometimes on top of brush pile, in bushes, on a dead or sprouting stump, among rank ferns, or in a clump of briers, from 5 inches to 3 feet above the ground. Shady woods or wooded swamps. See also Nests Above the Ground VI A a(2) 4 and VIII A a(3) 22.

Eastern and central United States south to central Iowa, northern Indiana, northern Ohio, New Jersey, and, in mountains, to northern Georgia.

Veery

7. Rather bulky; of grasses, rootlets, bark strips, pine needles, leaves, and mosses; lined with finer grasses, rootlets, fern down, moss, hair, or similar soft material. Outside diameter, 3¾ inches; outside height, 2¼ inches; inside diameter, 1¾ inches; inside depth, 1½ inches. Usually in a depression scooped out by the bird, generally concealed among an accumulation of dead leaves that, arching over it, hides it from above. Leafy woodlands. See also II B b(1) 3.

Eastern and central United States south to northern parts of Gulf States.

Black and White Warbler

8. Variable in shape, often an inverted cone, sometimes a basket, usually very narrow and very deep, rather unusual and distinctive; built on a foundation of dry leaves, of bark strips, leaves, grass stems, and weeds; lined with bark shreds laid across instead of around the cup and often with a lining of fine grass stems laid over these. Woodland borders, swampy thickets, and swampy woods. See also II A a(3) 6.

Southeastern Minnesota, southern Michigan, and southern New England south to Kansas, Missouri, Delaware, and, in uplands, to Georgia.

Blue-winged Warbler

9. Slight depression in the ground; neat and compact; of strips of soft bark, dead grass, and plant fibers; thickly lined with fine dead grass, pine needles, and hair. Inside diameter, 2 inches; inside depth, 2 inches. Usually within a few feet (commonly within a few inches) of a jack pine; generally well concealed. Groves of jack pines with ground cover of blueberry, bearberry, or sweet fern.

North-central part of lower peninsula of Michigan.

Kirtland's Warbler

10. In a cavity in the ground or in a bed of moss, at the base of a stump or tree, or alongside a moss-covered log or on side of a bank; of moss, externally like that with which it is usually surrounded; lined with stems of some moss; sometimes bits of leaves, grass, rootlets, and twigs form part of it; carefully concealed. Swampy woods, along wooded watercourses, or low wooded shores of a pond. See also II A a(6) 3.

Northern Minnesota, northwestern Michigan, northeastern Ohio, New York, northern New England, and, in mountains, to West Virginia.

Northern Water Thrush

11. Bulky, well-made, cup-shaped; of mud-covered dry leaves, grass, rootlets, and moss; lined with dry grass, hair, and rootlets. Inside diameter, 2½ inches; inside depth, 2½ inches. Carefully concealed in a shallow cavity in a brook bank where earth has eroded from the tree roots or under upturned roots of fallen trees. Wooded valleys, rocky brooks, small streams, and wooded swamps.

Western New England, southeastern Minnesota, and eastern Nebraska south to central South Carolina, northern Georgia, northern Louisiana, and northeastern Texas.

Louisiana Water Thrush

12. Bulky, cup-shaped, rather loosely constructed; of dead leaves, grasses, and weed stalks; lined with rootlets or horsehair or both, sometimes with pine needles; well concealed by surrounding vegetation. On the ground at the foot of a bush or tree, under a fallen bough, or in a bunch of weeds a few inches above the ground. Woodlands, overgrown clearings, swampy thickets, and woodland borders. See also II A a(2) 4 and III A a(4) 7.

Gulf States north to southeastern Nebraska, southern Wisconsin, northern Ohio, and lower Hudson Valley (rare).

Kentucky Warbler

13. More or less bulky, somewhat formless, rather loosely made; of grass, dried leaves, moss, pine needles, and bark strips; lined with inner bark, fine rootlets, and hair, sometimes fern down. Outside diameter, 4½ inches; outside height, 2½ inches; inside diameter, 2¼ inches; inside depth, 1¾ inches. Usually well concealed; deciduous undergrowth in deep, damp forests or cool, damp, heavy woods of mixed growth. See also II A a(2) 6 and II A a(3) 8.

Canadian border south to Minnesota, Michigan, New York, northern New Jersey, and, in mountains, to northern Georgia.

Canada Warbler

14. See II A a(2) 7 and I A a(3) 1.

Rufous-sided Towhee

15. Cup-shaped, deep; of grasses, rootlets, moss, and bark shreds; lined with finer grasses and rootlets, sometimes

with cow or deer hair. Outside diameter, about 4⅛ inches; outside height, 1¾ inches; inside diameter, 2⅛ inches; inside depth, 1¼ inches. Well hidden among upturned roots or under the trunk of a fallen tree or under a steep overhanging bank. Coniferous forests and deciduous woodlands.

Northern Minnesota, northern Michigan, Maine, and, in higher Appalachians, to northern Georgia.

Slate-colored Junco

16. See I A a(4) 2 and Nests Above the Ground VI A a(1) 6.

(Eastern) Field Sparrow

17. Cup-shaped; of coarse grasses, rootlets, and leaves, and sometimes moss and bark strips; lined with fine grass or hair; like nest of Song Sparrow but larger. In a hollow in the ground at the foot of a sapling, under a fallen branch, often in a moss-covered hummock under overhanging shrubbery. Cutover areas with slash piles, and borders of clearings, openings in forest with growth of low shrubs and clumps of small trees. See also II A a(3) 9.

Canadian border south to central Minnesota, central Wisconsin, northern New England, and in mountains of Massachusetts, New York, and Pennsylvania.

White-throated Sparrow

a(2). *In or under tussocks of grass or weeds*

1. Of grass, weeds, and fibrous roots (seaweed if near the coast), and lined with gray down and white feathers from the female. Inside diameter, 7 inches or slightly more. Also in or beneath dense underbrush or shrubbery, beneath the overhanging branches of small conifers, or in a dense thicket of conifers, among the roots of a fallen tree, or in a pile of driftwood, and

well concealed, but sometimes placed in the open or in woods clear of dense undergrowth; generally within 25 yards of water. Woodlands bordering freshwater ponds, pools, rivers, and lakes; often in close proximity to the seacoast. See also II A a(3) 1 and II A a(4) 1.

Canadian border south to coast of Maine, southern New York, central Michigan, Wisconsin, and central Minnesota.

Red-breasted Merganser

2. Rather bulky, neatly cupped, but with an exterior presenting a disorderly, unkempt appearance; material loosely put together so that the nest resembles a rather coarse basketwork; of leaves, bark strips or shreds, fine grasses, and horsehair; lined with crisscross strips and shreds of inner bark and grasses, sometimes unlined and sometimes the webs of the tent caterpillar are used in the construction. Outside diameter, 4 inches; outside height, 4 inches; inside diameter, 2 inches; inside depth, 2 inches. Hidden deep in a clump of grass and usually supported by a base of dead leaves and weed stalks or small stems of some sprout or brier; as season advances leaves about the nest grow and frequently conceal it. Woodland borders, openings, and wooded swamps.

Minnesota, New York, and Massachusetts south to Iowa, northern Indiana, northern New Jersey, and, in mountains, to Georgia.

Golden-winged Warbler

3. See I A a(1) 2.

Nashville Warbler

4. See II A a(1) 12 and III A a(4) 7.

Kentucky Warbler

5. Rather bulky, cup-shaped, compact, well-built; of weed stalks, leaves, some bark strips, grass, and sometimes horsehair; lined with fine black rootlets or horsehair. Outside diameter, 5 inches; outside height, 3½ inches; inside diameter, 2 inches; inside depth, 2 inches. Also in tangles of raspberry, blackberry, or other briery shrubs. Old clearings and cutover land or slashings, edges of shady woods, and lowland thickets. See also II A a(3) 7.

Canadian border south to central Minnesota, Michigan, New York, and, in mountains, to West Virginia.

Mourning Warbler

6. See II A a(1) 13 and II A a(3) 8.

Canada Warbler

7. Of leaves, twigs, grass, and bark strips; lined with fine grass, pine needles, or hair; sometimes carelessly made, at other times firm and compact. Sometimes built in a shelter of a small bush, stump, or brush pile. Dense, brushy areas as abandoned fields, neglected pastureland, roadsides, and woodlands where canopy is not too dense to preclude desired cover. See also II A a(1) 14 and I A a(3) 1.

Eastern and central United States (except northern Maine) south to Florida and Gulf Coast.

Rufous-sided Towhee

8. See I A a(1) 7; also Nests Above the Ground VI A a(2) 7 and VI B b(1) 8.

Song Sparrow

a(3). *In or beneath dense underbrush or shrubbery*

1. See II A a(2) 1 and II A a(4) 1.

Red-breasted Merganser

2. A hollow in the ground; lined with a few leaves; very well concealed in or beneath dense underbrush or shrubbery. Woodlands.

    Southern woodlands north to Pennsylvania, eastern Kentucky, and southeastern Missouri.

    Turkey

3. Merely a depression in the leaves, with a lining of a few dead leaves and sometimes with a little dried grass. Abundance of fallen leaves appears an essential requirement. Generally 4 oval eggs (1.5 inches by 1.1 inches); buffy and sprinkled with small brown spots. Alder runs, swampy thickets, and along edges of woods.

    Northern Florida and southern Louisiana north through eastern and central United States.

    Woodcock

4. Cup-shaped, often bulky, but neat and compact; of coarse grass, moss, twigs, bark fibers, and strips of wood; ornamented on the outside by bits of green moss; lined with pine needles, delicate plant fibers, or fine rootlets. Outside diameter, 5 inches; outside height, 2 inches; inside diameter, 2½ to 2¾ inches; inside depth, 1½ to 2 inches. Woodlands, woodland borders, and woodland bogs.

    Canadian border south to central Minnesota, northern Michigan, Massachusetts, Long Island, New Jersey, and, in mountains, to Virginia.

    (Eastern) Hermit Thrush

5. Of leaves, or leaves and moss; lined with moss and sometimes grass and horsehair. In a hollow in the ground or simply on the ground and generally well concealed under a canopy of dead leaves drifted by the wind and piled up against shrubbery. Wooded hillsides covered with medium-sized deciduous trees

and with undergrowth of saplings and shrubbery, and deep, shady ravines.

Southwestern Massachusetts, Connecticut, northern Illinois, and southern Iowa south to northern Georgia and Missouri.

Worm-eating Warbler

6. See II A a(1) 8.

Blue-winged Warbler

7. See II A a(2) 5.

Mourning Warbler

8. See II A a(1) 13 and II A a(2) 6.

Canada Warbler

9. See II A a(1) 17.

White-throated Sparrow

a(4). *In woods clear of dense undergrowth*

1. See II A a(2) 1 and II A a(3) 1.

Red-breasted Merganser

2. No nest or nesting material, eggs simply being deposited on dry leaves or bare ground, sometimes at the foot of a tree; may be slight depression about eggs from presence of parent's body during incubation. Usually in deciduous woods but sometimes in rocky, bushy hillsides.

Florida north to southern Maryland, southern Ohio, southern Indiana, and southeastern Kansas.

Chuck-will's-widow

3. Adds no nesting material, simply placing eggs on leafy forest floor in mixed growth of oak, beech, and pine, either on open ground or under shadow of branches of small bush. May be slight depression about eggs from

presence of parent's body during incubation. Woodlands and woodland borders.

Eastern and central United States south to northern Georgia and northern Louisiana.

(Eastern) **Whip-poor-will**

4. Nest a symmetrical and well-proportioned structure of fine grasses; in northern part of range domed and cylindrical in shape. See II B b(2) 2.

Pine Woods Sparrow

a(5). *Among rocks or in hollow logs*

1. No nesting material, eggs being deposited on the ground, on ledge of rocks or among rocks, on the bottom chips of a hollow log, hollow stump or stub, hollow snag of an old tree and sometimes in a cave. Usually in a secluded place. See VI B 1 and Nests Above the Ground VIII A a(3) 5. Woodlands and precipitous cliffs.

Gulf of Mexico north to western Connecticut, western New York, and northern Minnesota.

Turkey Vulture

2. See III A a(4) 3 and III A a(6) 1.

Black Vulture

a(6). *In swampy woods*

1. A substantial structure; of dry grasses, plant fibers, leaves, and moss; lined with fine dry grass to which hair is sometimes added. Outside diameter, 3 to 4 inches; outside height, 2 to 3¼ inches; inside diameter, 1 to 2 inches; inside depth 1 to 1½ inches. In a hollow in moss on the ground; usually in a wet place, at the foot of a small bush, in the side of a small tussock, or in a clump or mound of sphagnum, and usually well concealed by overhanging grass. Boggy woods (spruce and tamarack swamps).

Northern fringe of eastern and central United States west to northern Minnesota.

Tennessee Warbler

2. Cup-shaped; of fine dead weed stalks, bark shreds, and dead grasses; lined with the finest of the same materials and hair and a few feathers worked in. Outside diameter, 3 to 3½ inches; outside height, 2½ inches; inside diameter, 2 inches; inside depth, 1 inch. Placed in moss or grass at the foot of a bush or tree or under low, thick bushes; sometimes in a bog in sphagnum moss at the base of a small spruce. Spruce and tamarack bogs. See also III A a(2) 11.

    Along Canadian border south to Maine and northern Minnesota.

Palm Warbler

3. See II A a(1) 10.

Northern Water Thrush

4. Rather deep, cup-shaped, compactly built; of bark shreds, leaves, leaf stems, and grass, sometimes entirely of dried grass; lined with fine grass, fine rootlets, and hair. Inside diameter, 2 inches; inside depth, 1½ inches. Sunk in a moss mound or in the ground at the base of a bush or in a bunch of dry grass. Tamarack and spruce swamps.

    Northern and central Minnesota and northern Michigan.

Connecticut Warbler

B. Arched Nest

b(1). *At foot of tree, bush, stump, rock, or log; among roots of fallen tree, etc.*

1. Bulky, ball-like, with a small circular opening in one side only, just large enough to admit the bird; of moss,

twigs, soft grasses, weed stems, and rootlets; lined with fine rootlets, feathers, fur, or hair. Outside diameter, 4 inches; outside height, 7 inches; inside diameter, 1¼ inches; inside depth, 2 inches; diameter of entrance hole, 1 inch. May be built in cavity of low stump or tree. See also Nests Above the Ground VIII A a(3) 18. Coniferous woodlands, wooded swamps, and streamsides.

Minnesota, New York, and, in mountains, to North Carolina.

Winter Wren

2. See II A a(1) 5 and Nests Above the Ground VIII A a(3) 20 and IX A a(2) 2.

Carolina Wren

3. See II A a(1) 7.

Black and White Warbler

b(2). *Among dead leaves of forest floor*

1. Bulky; of grasses and sedges, dry leaves, weed stems, rootlets, and bark strips (sometimes entirely of one material); lined with hair, fine grasses or pine needles, and tiny rootlets; usually sunk somewhat in the ground and roofed over with an arch of leaves, grass, or other materials, giving it the form of an old-fashioned brick oven; entrance on one side. Outside diameter, 6½ inches; outside height, 4½ to 5 inches; inside diameter, less than 3 inches; opening, 1½ inches high, 2½ inches wide. Usually in a slight depression in the ground among dead leaves of forest floor, generally in open situations, frequently along a woodland trail; usually well concealed by overhanging plants or the leaves of shrubs. Woodlands (preferably deciduous).

Eastern and central United States south to eastern North Carolina, northern Georgia, Arkansas, and Kansas.

Ovenbird

2. A symmetrical and well-proportioned structure; of fine grasses arranged in a neat manner; lined with fine grass tops; domed and cylindrical in shape; opening in side well hidden and usually facing west. Length, 7 to 8 inches; height, 3 inches; width, 4½ inches. In a depression in the ground in a clump of grass or palmetto or under a vine tangle or brushy growth. Dry open woods of pine or oak with a ground cover of grass or scrub palmetto. See also II A a(4) 4.

    Florida, Gulf Coast, and Texas north to Maryland, southwestern Pennsylvania, southern Ohio, central Illinois, and southeastern Iowa.

    Pine Woods Sparrow

III

↟↟↟↟↟↟↟↟↟↟↟↟↟↟

In Marshes and Wet Meadows

A. Open Nest

a(1). *In or among reeds, flags (cattails),* rushes, or sedges*

1. A floating, matted, loosely built, slightly hollowed, saucer-shaped structure with rim built up 2 or 3 inches above water; of dead reeds, flags, algae, and water mosses; lined with well-rotted flags. Outside diameter about 24 inches; inside diameter about 6 inches. Sometimes attached to surrounding vegetation. Sloughs, marshes, marshy ponds, and lakes.

   Western Minnesota and North Dakota.

   Holboell's Grebe

2. A mass of water-soaked, decaying vegetation, flags, water mosses, and algae floating among rushes. Outside diameter, about 14 inches; inside diameter, 4 to 7 inches; generally attached to its surroundings. Sloughs, marshy ponds, and lakes.

   Maine, Minnesota, and northern Nebraska.

   Horned Grebe

* Note: Henceforth the word "flag" refers to cattails.

3. A floating structure of reeds and sedges with a slight depression in the center; usually lightly fastened to the living reeds so that it will move up and down but not be carried away. Outside diameter, 18 to 25 inches; outside height, 3 to 5 inches; inside diameter, 7 to 9 inches. Sloughs and marshes.

Dakotas, Nebraska, and western Minnesota.

Western Grebe

4. Floating structure, somewhat wet and slimy, of partially decayed reeds or flags, bent or matted down, with (perhaps) some coarse sedge grass; most of nest material below surface of water; slightly hollowed and built up a few inches above the water; sometimes of water-soaked, decaying vegetation built up from bottom in shallow water. Occasionally attached to surrounding vegetation. Better concealed than those of other grebes. Sloughs, marshy ponds, and lakes.

Gulf States north through eastern and central United States.

Pied-billed Grebe

5. A practically flat platform of dead flags, a foot or more in diameter. In dense cattail marshes, raised above water or mud only a few inches; partially concealed by new flags growing among tall dead flags of previous season's growth. Paths, marked by a broken and trampled line of vegetation, frequently lead to and from nest. Occasionally flags are arched over nest. Sometimes in meadows over almost dry ground.

Gulf of Mexico north through eastern and central United States.

American Bittern

6. A flimsy platform of flags, reeds, and grasses, slightly hollowed, on foundation of flags bent down and interlaced, from a few inches to 4 or 5 feet above the water.

Tops of growing flags may also be interlaced over nest. Usual size: 4 or 5 inches deep by 6 or 7 inches across. See also Nests Above the Ground I A 1. Marshes.

Gulf of Mexico north through eastern and central United States to southern Maine and Minnesota.

(Eastern) **Least Bittern**

7. Well-made, bulky, and deep, of reeds or flags; lined with whitish down; frequently covered with a downy blanket and sometimes canopied with rushes. Outside diameter, 20 inches; outside height, 12 inches; inside diameter, 9 inches; inside depth, 4 inches. In or among cattails, on a mass of dead reeds or rushes built up out of shallow water, and in a tangled mass of broken-down flags. Cattail marshes and shallow marsh-bordered lakes. See also III B b(1) 1.

Canadian border south to central Nebraska, southern Wisconsin, and southeastern Michigan.

Redhead

8. Bulky, of dry grass, reeds, flags, and sedges; lined with gray down. Inside diameter, 8 inches; inside depth, 4 inches. In shallow water on a mass of dead reeds or in a clump of reeds or tall rushes. Sloughs and marshes.

Dakotas, Nebraska, Minnesota, and occasionally southern Wisconsin.

Canvas-back

9. A bulky, buoyant structure, often basket-like; of dry reeds, rushes, and grass; sparingly lined with down. Often the canopying rushes are bent over by the bird, and when nest is built above water a sloping pile of weeds is usually added as a stairway down which the duck can slide into the water on the approach of an enemy. Usually attached to reeds but sometimes floating and occasionally on the ground. Marshes and

shores of lakes and ponds. See also III B b(1) 2 and IV B 2.

Canadian border south to Nebraska, northern Illinois, and southeastern Michigan.

Ruddy Duck

10. Broadly cupped, well constructed basket; of dead flags and grasses. May have a canopy of flags and a runway leading to it. Outside diameter, 6 inches; inside diameter, 3 inches; inside depth, 2 inches. Usually well hidden in dense growth of cattails and held a few inches above water by surrounding flags; sometimes on the ground in an open situation and covered with a canopy of flags. Freshwater marshes.

Eastern and central United States south to Maryland, southern Ohio, northern Missouri, and Kansas.

Sora

11. A slightly hollowed heap of reeds, grass, or flags; lined with grass; with (usually) a sloping pathway or runway of flags leading from nest to water. Outside diameter, 15 to 20 inches; inside diameter, 7 inches; inside depth, 2 to 2½ inches. Usually among clumps of tall water plants and generally on a buoyant platform of broken-down flags, a few inches above water but sometimes on the ground in an isolated tussock. Freshwater marshes.

Gulf of Mexico north to Vermont, New York, Minnesota, and Nebraska.

Florida Gallinule

12. A floating basket-shaped structure; of dead reeds, grasses, flags, and bits of decaying vegetation firmly woven together; neatly lined with pieces of dry flags and other smooth material. Outside diameter, 14 to 20 inches; inside diameter, about 7 inches. Generally firmly attached to growing reeds or flags to prevent

drifting and partially or well concealed but sometimes in open sight in an isolated clump. Often in colonies. Borders of sloughs and marshy ponds.

Northern edge of central and eastern United States south to Arkansas, Tennessee, and New Jersey; casually to Florida.

Coot

13. See IV A 3.

Black-necked Stilt

14. Generally a large floating mass of dead reeds but sometimes well-built-up among standing reeds and well secured; cavity slightly hollowed. Outside diameter from 12 to 30 inches; inside diameter about 5 inches. Marshes bordering lakes and rivers. Nesting in colonies.

North and South Dakota and southeastern Minnesota.

Franklin's Gull

15. Generally a large and elaborate structure, remarkably well-built; of dead sedges and grasses, deeply hollowed with a well-rounded and compactly woven rim; neatly lined with split reeds and grasses; sometimes a mere hollow in a pile of reeds or a hollow in sand or mud and, perhaps, lined with grasses. Outside diameter, 7 to 8 inches; inside diameter, 4 to 5 inches; inside depth, 1½ inches. In or among reeds and flags and buoyed up by them in several feet of water. Nesting in colonies. Salt marshes and western prairie marshes. See also IV A 8.

Along coast from Maryland to Texas, and in western prairie marshes east to Minnesota and northeastern Illinois.

Forster's Tern

16. Usually a careless structure of a few dead sedges, reeds, and grass; sometimes well-built, at times a mere hollow in a pile of floating rubbish or in prostrate and closely matted vegetation or on a bit of driftwood or on an old muskrat house. Nesting in colonies. Sloughs, marshes, and wet meadows.

   Canadian border south to Missouri and Tennessee and east to western Pennsylvania, central New York, and northern Vermont.

   Black Tern

a(2). *In weeds or grass*

1. Beautifully built of grass and lined with fine grass and little down; in a hummock about 6 inches above the ground and in an opening about 4 to 5 feet square. Marshes and rice fields.

   Texas and Louisiana.

   Fulvous Tree Duck

2. Of reeds, flags, grasses, and leaves; warmly lined with down from female's breast; down is dark gray or sepia with conspicuous white centers and faintly indicated whitish or light brown tips. Breast or flank feathers with central brown streaks or broadly banded with dusky and tipped with brown generally found in nest together with more or less rubbish. Usually near water and commonly hidden by reeds, flags, leaves, and low branches, or in a tussock of grass in fields or on dry cultivated ground. See also I A a(1) 1. Marshes, fields, and pastures.

   Canadian border south to southern Texas, southern Kansas, southern Missouri, southeastern Illinois, southwestern Indiana, and southern Ohio.

   Mallard

3. Large, rather cup-shaped, neatly constructed of weeds, grass, flags, and leaves; lined with duck down (olive-

brown with whitish centers) and breast or flank feathers (dusky with central buffy streak or buffy edgings), which often, as in the case of other ducks, is added to as incubation advances. Outside diameter, 18 inches; inside diameter, 8 inches; inside depth, 2 inches. Generally in dry ground but usually not very far from water. Marshes.

Eastern states, Maine south to North Carolina, and west to northern Illinois, Wisconsin, and Minnesota.

Black Duck

4. A slightly concave saucer of grasses and leaves rimmed with down and feathers. Inside diameter, about 6 inches. Usually on dry ground. Marshes and along the banks of rivers.

    Florida and coastal belt of Louisiana and Texas.

Mottled Duck

5. Rather bulky; of grass and leaves; lined with dark-gray down, sometimes thickly lined. Breast feathers are sometimes mixed with the down. Inside diameter, about 6 inches; inside depth, 3 inches. On the ground in marsh grass or rushes. Wet meadows and marshy borders of shallow lakes.

    Canadian border south to northern Nebraska and northern Iowa and locally east to western Pennsylvania and Maine.

Ringed-neck Duck

6. Usually a slight affair and little hollowed (an inch or two thick) on dry ground, but bulky, high, and deeply hollowed if on wet ground, when it may be raised on a platform of sticks to a height of 15 to 18 inches; of dry grass, stubble, and weed stalks; lined with finer material of the same character. Outside diameter, 20 to 30 inches; inside diameter, 8 to 9 inches; inside

depth, 2 inches. Bogs, bushy marshes, and sproutlands near a swamp or meadow.

Gulf of Mexico north to northeastern United States.

Marsh Hawk

7. Of grasses, weeds, and roots, usually on a slight knoll or grassy flat, often on a platform of dead vegetation in shallow water; sometimes bulky, measuring 3 to 5 feet in diameter. Frequently a mere depression in the ground and lined with dry grass and weed stems. See also III A a(3) 7. Marshes and wet prairies.

Minnesota, Michigan, Wisconsin, and Dakotas; also in Florida and southern Georgia.

Sandhill Crane

8. Broadly cupped, deeply hollowed; of weeds and grasses; lined with grasses; well concealed by interlacing of surrounding grass. About 8 inches in diameter and sometimes from 6 inches to a foot above water. Freshwater marshes.

Gulf of Mexico north to (and possibly including) Massachusetts, New York, and southern Minnesota, and west to Kansas.

King Rail

9. Broadly cupped, slightly hollowed, and rather compactly constructed; of weeds, coarse grasses, and dead stalks; lined with chips of cattail blades; well concealed. Outside diameter, about 8 inches; inside diameter, about 4½ inches. Sometimes built on mud or on a pile of broken-down reeds or drift. Usually in drier location than Sora. Freshwater marshes.

Eastern and central United States south to Nebraska, Missouri, Kentucky, and eastern North Carolina.

Virginia Rail

10. Not as broadly cupped as those of other rails; of finest grasses; sometimes with a slight canopy; 1 inch thick; outside diameter, 4 to 5 inches; inside diameter, 3½ inches; inside depth, 2 inches. Well concealed. (An erratic "mystery" bird, inhabiting a locality for one season, then perhaps not appearing the following season or for several years.) Marshes and grassy meadows.

     Locally in northern parts of eastern and central United States.

     Yellow Rail

11. See II A a(6) 2.

     Palm Warbler

12. See III A a(4) 8 and III B b(1) 6.

     Yellowthroat

13. Loosely woven, coarsely built, cup-shaped; of dried grass or seaweed; lined with fine grass or similar material. Sometimes placed among driftwood or dry seaweed just above high water mark of summer tides. Outside diameter, 3½ to 4½ inches; outside height, 3½ to 4 inches; inside diameter, 2 to 2½ inches; inside depth, 1½ to 2 inches. Salt hay meadows of upper salt marshes along coast; also along borders of inland prairie marshes.

     Virginia north; also Minnesota and the Dakotas.

     Sharp-tailed Sparrow

14. Of dried grasses; lined with fine grass; in areas of fine grass in salt marshes, over water and carefully concealed, or in drift above high water mark. Outside diameter, 3 to 4½ inches; outside height, 2 to 3½ inches; inside diameter, 2 to 2½ inches; inside depth, 1 to 1½ inches.

Along coast from southern Massachusetts to Florida and along Gulf to Texas.

Seaside Sparrow

15. Of dry salt-marsh grass and lined with very fine grass; attached to some upright marsh grass.

Coastal prairie near Cape Sable, Florida (an area about 6 miles in length and not more than ½ mile in width).

Cape Sable Seaside Sparrow

16. Cup-shaped; of grass and a few leaves; lined with similar materials; sometimes arched over with grasses or sedges with entrance on side. In a dense tussock or mat of marsh vegetation and well hidden. See also III B b(1) 7. Outside diameter, 4 inches; inside diameter, 2½ inches; inside depth, 1½ inches. Open freshwater marshes filled with rank vegetation, borders of ponds and streams fringed with marsh plants, and alder thickets.

Eastern and central United States south to New Jersey, West Virginia, northern Missouri, and northern Nebraska.

Swamp Sparrow

a(3). *In the ground*

1. See IV B 1.

Common Loon

2. A slight hollow scooped in dry ground, padded with grasses and weed stems; lined with down; down dark "hair brown" with whitish centers and grayish tips. Breast feathers (small, light colored, with variable patterns of dusky markings in the center but with light tips) frequently mixed with the down. Among grass, tall reeds, or patches of coarse weeds; well concealed. Usually near water but frequently some distance from it. See also I A a(5) 1.

Canadian border south to Kansas, northern Iowa, and southern Wisconsin, and locally east to western Pennsylvania and coastal Delaware and North Carolina.

Gadwall

3. Generally well-made; of grasses, sedges, weeds, feathers, and much down, sometimes with a few fine twigs and leaves; down very small and very dark-colored, dark "hair brown" or "clove-brown" with large conspicuous white centers. Inside diameter, 5 to 6 inches; inside depth, about 3½ inches. In a hollow in the ground in a dense growth of grass or beneath a bush, on dry ground and usually fairly well concealed. See also III A a(4) 1. Vicinity of marshes.

    Dakotas, northern Nebraska, southern Minnesota, and northern Michigan.

Green-winged Teal

4. Well-built of fine grass mixed with down and lined with down and breast feathers; down light brown to drab with large whitish centers. More down added as incubation advances. In a hollow in the ground in long, thick grass near water but on dry ground. Borders of sloughs and small pond holes.

    Canadian border south to Kansas, Missouri, Illinois, Ohio, and New Jersey.

Blue-winged Teal

5. A slight hollow lined with grasses and weeds and an abundance of gray down; down with whitish centers and conspicuous whitish tips. Breast feathers frequently found in nest, pure white or with pale brownish or grayish centers. A well-built structure for a duck. Usually in dry ground and though sometimes in the open generally concealed among grasses or in clumps of herbaceous plants; at times rather distant from water. Marshes about ponds and bays.

North Dakota, Minnesota, Wisconsin, Michigan south to northern Nebraska and northern Indiana.

Baldpate

6. A hollow in the ground lined with grasses and rimmed with down; down varies from dark to light brown with large grayish-white centers. Breast feathers, sometimes mixed with down, with large rounded gray centers and with broad buff and white tips and margins. Usually hidden in grass or under bushes. Marshes, wet meadows, and fields. See also III A a(4) 2 and I A a(5) 3.

Canadian border south to Nebraska and western Iowa and locally east to western Pennsylvania.

Shoveller

7. See III A a(2) 7.

Sandhill Crane

8. A depression or shallow hollow in grass or moss on dry ground; lined with a little grass or leaves, sometimes a very slight affair of straw and leaves is made and raised above the surrounding surface. Outside diameter, 6 inches; inside diameter, 3 inches. Marshes and low ground.

Eastern and central United States south to northwestern Pennsylvania, northern Illinois, and South Dakota.

Wilson's Snipe

9. A mere depression in the ground, lined with grass, reeds, sedges, or small sticks, but sometimes a deep hollow 6 or 7 inches in diameter, and occasionally a carelessly built structure of small reeds and grass. Depression or hollow usually well concealed in the grass; the built structure in a tussock or grass or weeds; in either case close to water. Coastal marshes and inland prairies. See also III A a(4) 5.

Mainly along Atlantic Coast from Delaware Bay to Texas and in prairies south to Iowa and Nebraska.

Willet

10. Cup-shaped; of moss, dead leaves, fine weed stalks, and grasses; lined with fine dead grass and a few hairs. Outside diameter, 3½ inches; outside height, 3½ inches; inside diameter, 1¾ inches; inside depth, 1⅕ inches. On the ground or sunk in it, often in moss, at the base of alders or small shrubs, or among such bushes, and well concealed by swamp grass. Moist sphagnum bogs.

Northern Maine, New Hampshire, Vermont, Michigan, and Minnesota.

Wilson's Warbler

a(4). *Beneath bushes or grass clumps*

1. See III A a(3) 3.

Green-winged Teal

2. See III A a(3) 6 and I A a(5) 3.

Shoveller

3. No nest or nesting material. Eggs deposited on the ground under logs and bushes, in grass clumps, in cavities in rocks, under boulders, in the shade of a rock or partly fallen tree or in a hollow log. Woodlands and dry spots in wooded swamps or marshes. See also II A a(5) 2 and III A a(6) 1.

Gulf States north to Maryland, West Virginia, southern Ohio, southern Indiana, and Missouri.

Black Vulture

4. A somewhat bulky platform, loosely constructed; of grass, leaves, dead vines, moss, and other old vegetation. Inside diameter, 2 inches or more. On the ground in grass clumps and securely attached to upright grow-

ing stems of tall grass, near water; sometimes a short distance above ground in a maze of vines or thick bushes. See also Nests Above the Ground VI A a(2) 1. Wooded swamps and marshes.

Florida and southern Georgia.

Limpkin

5. See III A a(3) 9.

Willet

6. A slight depression or hollow in the ground; of matted vegetation; lined with scanty vegetation, grasses, weed stalks, and some owl feathers; sometimes the nest seems to consist only of the flattened or dead vegetation of the spot selected. Usually partly hidden by a clump of grasses or weeds, but also at the foot of a bush. Marshy and open country.

Eastern and central United States south to New Jersey, northern Ohio, and southern Kansas.

Short-eared Owl

7. See II A a(1) 12 and II A a(2) 4.

Kentucky Warbler

8. Rather large and bulky, loosely put together, deep and cup-shaped; of coarse grass, weed stems, dried leaves, and bark strips; lined with finer grasses, tendrils, rootlets, and sometimes hair. Outside diameter, 3¼ inches; outside height, 3½ inches; inside diameter, 1¾ inches; inside depth, 1½ inches. On the ground or a few inches above the ground beneath bushes or briers; also in tussocks of grass; well concealed. Wet situations such as borders of large marshes and small islands in marshes, near springs, and small brooks. See also III A a(2) 12 and III B b(1) 6.

Eastern and central United States south to Florida and Gulf Coast.

Yellow-throat

9. Cup-shaped and deep, of fine grass; lined with hair. Carefully concealed in the center of a thick tuft of grass or in a tangle of rank old growth. Outside diameter, 3½ to 4½ inches; inside diameter, 2½ inches; inside depth, 1¼ inches. Boggy meadows and prairie marshes.

   North Dakota, Minnesota, and northwestern Michigan.

   Leconte's Sparrow

10. Of grasses; lined with fine blades of the same material. Outside diameter, 3½ inches; outside height, 1¾ inches; inside diameter, 2 inches; inside depth, 1 inch. Borders of wet meadows and woodland (tamarack) bogs.

    Northern fringe of eastern and central United States.

    Lincoln's Sparrow

a(5). *In moss or under a stump or upturned root*

1. Cup-shaped; of sphagnum or other moss; lined with fine black rootlets, a few pine needles, and grass stems. Inside diameter, about 3 inches; inside depth, 1½ inches. Usually imbedded and well concealed in sphagnum moss or other low vegetation on the sides of hummocks or mounds or under a stump or upturned root. Secluded mossy coniferous swamps.

   Along northern fringe of United States (northern Michigan, southern Minnesota, Maine) and in southern New Hampshire and rarely to Pennsylvania.

   Yellow-bellied Flycatcher

a(6). *Among rocks and in hollow logs*

1. See II A a(5) 2 and III A a(4) 3.

   Black Vulture

B. Arched Nest

b(1). *Beneath bushes or in clumps of grass*

   1. See III A a(1) 7.

                            Redhead

   2. See III A a(1) 9 and IV B 2.

                          Ruddy Duck

   3. Usually well-cupped; of dry sedges, reeds, and grass; lined with finer and shorter pieces of the same material. Frequently nests are provided with a canopy formed by an interlacing of surrounding grass and sometimes have well-defined runways leading to them. Inside diameter, 5 to 6 inches. In clumps of marsh grass, from 8 to 12 inches above water, or on the ground beneath drift trash; well concealed. Salt marshes.

     Along Atlantic Coast and Gulf Coast from Connecticut to Texas.

                          Clapper Rail

   4. Loosely put together; of fine grasses; with a covering of standing grasses woven over it and a passage and entrance at one side. Resembles nest of Meadowlark. Outside diameter, 3½ inches; outside height, 4½ inches; inside diameter, 3 inches; inside depth, 2½ inches. In grass that may be 8 to 10 inches high. Marshes and wet meadows.

     Along coast from Florida to Massachusetts and locally inland to Iowa and Kansas.

                          Black Rail

   5. A mere hollow in the ground or sometimes a collection of grasses or sedges; lined with a little grass; surrounding grass or other vegetation usually drawn together by bird to form a canopy over nest. Outside

diameter, 3 to 4 inches. In clump of grass and usually well concealed. Wet or moist meadows, sloughs, grassy marshes, and marshy islands.

Canadian border south to Nebraska, Iowa, and north-western Indiana.

Wilson's Phalarope

6. See III A a(2) 12 and III A a(4) 8.

Yellow-throat

7. See III A a(2) 16.

Swamp Sparrow

IV

↗↗↗↗↗↗↗↗↗↗↗↗↗↗

On or Near Seashore and Lake Beaches

A. Nesting in Colonies

1. Ground nest varies in size and structure from a slightly built one to a large and well constructed affair; of sticks, reeds, straws, and grasses. Arbored nest, in bushes, a substantial platform of similar materials. Outside diameter, from 18 to 24 inches; outside height, from 4 to 5 inches, sometimes 10 inches. See also Nests Above the Ground VII B b(3) 1. Islands in lakes or lagoons, frequently in mangrove growth.

   Along the Atlantic and Gulf Coasts from North Carolina to Texas.

   (Eastern) Brown Pelican

2. Of mosses, seaweed, sticks, or grass; lined with gray down from breast of bird, the lining being added gradually during the month of incubation; usually sheltered by rocks, trees, undergrowth, or grasses. Rocky shores and island beaches.

   Principally on islands along Maine coast.

   Common Eider

3. Sometimes a mere hollow in the sand and lined with pieces of dry sticks, twigs, weed stems, small bits of shell, fish bones, and grasses; at other times a fairly well-built floating platform of sticks, grass, and small stems and lined with small sticks. Outside height, 4 to 7 inches. Hollow nest in dry ground; floating nest among grasses, sedges, and rushes in shallow water. See also III A a(1) 13. Wet meadows and beaches.

Florida, coastal South Carolina, and coast of Louisiana and Texas.

Black-necked Stilt

4. Large and bulky, well-cupped; of dry grasses, mosses, twigs, and rubbish; sometimes nest is a mere depression in the turf 9 to 10 inches in diameter. Small islands.

Along coast, Maine to Long Island (rarely).

Great Black-backed Gull

5. Usually a rough-looking structure, shape and size varying with location; of eelgrass or other seaweeds but often of marsh grass, weeds, sticks, chips of wood, and sometimes a few feathers, shells, and mosses (*Climacium spp.*); occasionally lined with grasses or feathers. Outside diameter, 13 to 24 inches; outside height, 5 inches; inside diameter, 8 to 10 inches; inside depth, 3 inches. Either in a hollow or in plain view, along a sandy, gravelly, or rocky shore; often among rocks along the shore. Also in grassy dunes and sometimes under bushes. Usually on islands. Sometimes on rocks or cliffs. See also VI A 2.

Along the coast, Maine to Long Island; also about larger lakes of Canadian border.

Herring Gull

6. Rather bulky and well-built; of grasses, seaweed, and sticks, firmly interwoven; neatly lined with grass;

sometimes a mere hollow in the sand and lined with
dry grasses, bits of sticks, and rubbish. Among thick,
low vegetation such as beach grass, and well concealed,
but sometimes in plain view; when built in thick grass
a well-trodden path over-arched with grass leads up
to it on one side and away from it on the other. Occasionally nest is placed under a bush or in a clump of
bushes. Hollow nest in sand without concealment.
Grassy islands and salt marshes.

Along coast from Maine to Texas.

Laughing Gull

7. Usually a mere depression in the sand and lined with
    a few small pieces of shells and straw but sometimes
    a large pile of dead sedge stems or grasses and the
    shells of oysters, clams, and scallops; lined with smaller
    shells. Outside diameter, 18 inches; inside diameter,
    4 inches. On high, dry sand flats back of beaches
    above ordinary tides; nests of sedge stems and grasses
    usually among grasses. Occasionally found in colonies
    of other terns. See also IV B 7. Ocean beaches.

    Locally along coast from Maryland to Texas.

    Gull-billed Tern

8. A mere hollow on muddy shore. See also III A a(1)
    15.

    Forster's Tern

9. Usually a mere depression in the beach sand or peb-
    bles; lined with a few bits of shell or small stones;
    sometimes a well-built hollow mound of grasses, bits
    of twigs, and seaweed, and occasionally of fish bones;
    at other times a hollow in stranded eelgrass. Three eggs
    (1.6 inches by 1.2 inches); pale brown with dark

spots (colors variable). Sandy beaches and small islands.

Locally from Canadian border south to Gulf of Mexico.

Common Tern

10. Similar to that of Common Tern but usually with less nesting material; merely a hollow in sand, gravel, or rocks with occasionally a thin lining of grass. Two eggs (1.6 inches by 1.2 inches); brownish or greenish, irregularly marked with brown. Sandy or rocky sea islands.

Maine and Massachusetts.

Arctic Tern

11. A mere hollow in the bare sand and often lined with grass and seaweed. Two eggs (1.7 inches by 1.2 inches); pale buff to olive-buff with reddish-brown spots. Usually on the open beach but sometimes well concealed among beach grass and other vegetation when the nest is often arched over with the tall grass and has a pathway leading to it. Sandy and rocky sea islands.

Scattered localities along Atlantic and Gulf Coasts from Maine to Texas; most common near eastern Long Island and southern New England. A small colony on Dry Tortugas, Florida.

Roseate Tern

12. A shallow, oval depression scooped out in the sand; sometimes leaves are placed around the rim of the depression. On the open beach of ocean islands.

On Dry Tortugas, Florida.

Sooty Tern

13. A slight hollow in the sand. Two or three eggs (1.2 inches by 0.98 inch); buff to olive-buff with reddish-

brown spots. Broad, flat, open sand beaches devoid of vegetation along the coast and low sandy islands of the interior.

Massachusetts to Texas; also in Mississippi and Missouri River systems north to Ohio, Iowa, southwestern Kansas, and Nebraska.

Least Tern

14. A slight hollow in the sand. Two or three eggs (2.6 inches by 1.7 inches); grayish buff, with small and large markings of brown, gray, and black. On the open beach of sandy sea islands.

Along coast from Virginia to Texas.

Royal Tern

15. A mere hollow in the sand; sometimes not even a hollow is excavated, the eggs being simply deposited on the sand. Often nests in company with Royal Terns. Two or three eggs, cream or buff, irregularly spotted and scrawled with dark brown, chestnut, black, and lavender. On the open beach of low sandy sea islands.

Locally along coast from North Carolina to Texas.

Cabot's Tern

16. A slight depression or sometimes a large deep hollow scooped in sand or gravel; lined with sticks, coarse straws, bits of shell, and other rubbish; rim of nest usually built up and nest generally decorated with shells and sometimes feathers. Two or three eggs (2.6 inches by 1.7 inches); gray to greenish buff, marked with brown and lilac. On the open beach of sea and lake islands.

Along Gulf of Mexico and locally on Great Lakes.

Caspian Tern

17. A slight hollow scooped out in the sand, pebbles, or shells of the beach. Four eggs (1.8 inches by 1.3

inches); varying from pale bluish to buff, heavily marked with brown. On open beach of low, flat, sandy islands or on higher salt flats and shell ridges.

Along coast from Texas to Long Island and occasionally Massachusetts.

Black Skimmer

18. A loose mass of dead grass, sometimes with a few feathers. At the end of a burrow in the soil or in fissures of rocks. Burrow generally about 30 inches long, often curved and descending at (right) angle to a few inches or a foot below the surface. Sea islands. See also V A 2 and VI A 4.

Along coast of Maine.

Atlantic Puffin

B. Nesting Singly

1. Usually a mere hollow in the ground, within a few feet of water, and generally without nesting material, but sometimes with a rim of dry grass, bits of sticks, and rubbish; also a large circular mass of wet, soggy, decayed reeds and other vegetable matter; sometimes only slightly hollowed, at other times fairly deep. Outside diameter, about 24 inches; inside diameter, about 18 inches; inside depth, 3 inches or less. On the shore among small scattered underbrush or on edge of marsh; occasionally the top of an old muskrat house is utilized. Shores and marshes of inland lakes. See also III A a(3) 1.

Northern edge of eastern and central United States.

Common Loon

2. See III A a(1) 9 and III B b(1) 2.

Ruddy Duck

3.   A hollow or slight depression in the sand, often decorated with a few bits of shells. Two or three eggs (2.2 inches by 1.5 inches); buffy or brownish buff, irregularly spotted with blackish brown with subdued markings of lavender. In the sand or on little mounds or elevations of sand. Ocean beaches.

Locally along coast from Virginia to Texas.

American Oyster Catcher

4.   A slight hollow in the sand; sometimes lined with pebbles and bits of shell and driftwood. Four eggs (1.2 inches by 0.95 inch); pale buff, dotted lightly and evenly with black. On open beach or in a clump of beach grass, or at the base of a low sand dune, well above the high-water mark. Sandy beaches.

Along coast, Maine south to North Carolina and locally inland to Pennsylvania, northern Ohio, northeastern Illinois, and Nebraska.

Piping Plover

5.   A slight depression in the sand, sometimes lined with broken shells or fish bones. Egg (1.2 inches by 0.9 inch); pale clay, marked with small scratch dots of black. Open beaches.

Along Gulf Coast from Florida to Texas.

(Cuban) Snowy Plover

6.   A slight depression in the sand, sometimes containing a few straws and often encircled with broken bits of shells. Four eggs (1.4 inches by 1.05 inches); olive gray, spotted and scratched with blackish brown, with some fainter markings of gray. Sometimes in the open sand, but usually near some object such as pieces of driftwood or other rubbish or partially sheltered by a few blades of grass. Sandy reefs or flats and ocean beaches.

Coastal islands from Virginia to Texas.

Wilson's Plover

7. See IV A 7.

Gull-billed Tern

8. See I A a(6) 1 and Nests Above the Ground IX A a(1) 1.

Nighthawk

V

In Burrows in the Ground

A. Nesting in Colonies

1. A slight collection of pebbles, short grasses, weeds, rootlets, and perhaps a few feathers; usually at the end of a burrow. The burrow, only a few inches in diameter and from 1 to 3 feet long, extends downward, then runs along nearly horizontally not many inches below the surface and into a roundish chamber at the end, slightly enlarged; or the burrow may be a short one under a rock. Sea islands.

   Maine and Massachusetts.

   Leach's Petrel

2. See IV A 18 and VI A 4.

   Atlantic Puffin

3. Flimsy; of straw, weed stalks, rootlets, and pine needles; lined with feathers. In a chamber at the end of a tunnel excavated in a nearly vertical bank of a lake or stream or in a bank made by excavations of railway, gravel and sand pits, or road cuts. Length of tunnel from 15 inches to 8 feet or more; external opening about 1 inch by 2 inches; nesting chamber about 5 inches in diameter. Vicinity of water and rural areas.

58

Eastern and central United States south to Virginia, northern Alabama, Louisiana, and Texas.

Bank Swallow

B. Nesting Singly

1. A collection of weed stalks, dried broken bits of horse or cow dung, bits of skin, or any convenient material, placed in an enlarged chamber from 5 to 10 feet from entrance of abandoned prairie-dog, skunk, fox, or badger burrow. Sometimes digs own burrow if ready-made one is not available and if soil is not too hard. Treeless plains and prairies.

    Minnesota, western Iowa, and Louisiana; also prairies of central and southern Florida.

    Burrowing Owl

2. Nest an enlarged chamber at the end of a burrow a little to one side and slightly above level of tunnel. Chamber varies in shape and size but roughly circular or dome-shaped and about 10 to 12 inches in diameter and 6 to 7 inches in height; frequently lined with bits of clean, white fish bones, fish scales, or fragments of shells of crustaceans, probably the remains of ejected pellets, sometimes with leaves, sticks, and grasses. At the end of a burrow, about 4 inches in diameter, excavated in a sandy, clayey, or gravelly bank, preferably near water, but sometimes a distance from water if a suitable site is not available near the bird's favorite fishing grounds. The burrow may be at any height from the base of the bank, though usually not more than 2 or 3 feet from the top. The burrow slants upward slightly and continues more or less in a straight line but at times curves or turns near the inner end; from 3 to 15 feet (usually about 4 to 5 feet) in length. Vicinity of water.

Eastern and central United States south to Gulf of Mexico.

(Eastern) Belted Kingfisher

3. Large, bulky, loosely constructed; of sticks, roots, straw, weed stalks, grass, and leaves; lined with grasses, rootlets, bits of dead leaves, pine needles, and sometimes feathers. In a burrow usually in precipitous banks of clay, sand, or gravel, near water. Length of burrow from 9 inches to 6 feet. Also in holes in masonry, sides of wooden buildings, quarries and caves, crannies and ledges under bridges, culverts, and wharf and bridge supports. See also IX A a(7) 1. Vicinity of water.

Gulf of Mexico north to Massachusetts, New York, Minnesota, and North Dakota.

Rough-winged Swallow

VI

✓✓✓✓✓✓✓✓✓✓✓✓✓✓✓

On Rocks or Rocky Ledges

A. On Ledges of Rocks on Islands off Coast

1. A platform rather loosely put together, but sometimes
    well-built; of sticks, weed stalks, seaweed, grasses,
    feathers, and bark; lined with grasses or seaweed;
    occasionally decorated with sprigs of evergreen, feath-
    ers, and birch bark. Outside diameter, 22 inches; out-
    side height, 4 to 9 inches; inside diameter, 9 inches.
    On ledges of rocks, but at times in the crotch or on
    the horizontal limbs of trees 60 feet or more above the
    ground, or in mangrove trees or bushes from 6 to 10
    feet above the water in southern part of range. See also
    Nests Above the Ground VII B b(3) 2. Coastal is-
    lands, small islands and rocky reefs of inland lakes,
    and wooded swamps in the interior.

    Locally throughout eastern and central United States
    south to Florida and Gulf of Mexico.

    Double-crested Cormorant

2. See IV A 5.

    Herring Gull

3. Eggs merely laid in a crevice, rift, or fissure in a cliff
    or sea ledge or under some rock or among loose rocks;

    61

sometimes eggs are laid so far back under or among rocks as to be inaccessible; often deposited on bare ground or rock but more frequently on rough beds of pebbles, broken stones, or shells. Two or three eggs (2.4 inches by 1.6 inches); pale bluish or greenish white with markings of various shades of brown and black. Islands and shore cliffs.

Along coast of Maine.

Black Guillemot

4. A burrow in the fissures of rocks. See IV A 18 and V A 2.

Atlantic Puffin

B. On Rocky Ledge of Cliff

1. See II A a(5) 1 and Nests Above the Ground VIII A a(3) 5.

Turkey Vulture

2. See Nests Above the Ground VII B b(1) 6.

Swainson's Hawk

3. A large bulky structure of sticks; lined with hay, twigs, or green grass; if used for many years becomes moist and in part decayed. Outside diameter, from 30 to 60 inches. Usually on inaccessible cliffs, on a shelf of rock or earth, or high bank of lake or stream but sometimes in a tall tree on a mountainside and occasionally relatively low in a tree in rather open country. See also Nests Above the Ground VII A 4. Mountainous regions, vicinity of lakes and streams, and open country.

Locally in Appalachians from Canadian border to southern states.

Golden Eagle

4. A slight hollow scraped in accumulated soil and rubbish; sometimes lined with grass and surrounded by flakes of rock, a few twigs, bones of birds, and pellets. Inside diameter 12 inches; inside depth, 1½ inches. Mountain regions and river valleys.

   Locally throughout eastern and central United States south to northern Georgia and Louisiana.

   Duck Hawk

5. See Nests Above the Ground VII B b(1) 8 and VIII A a(3) 6.

   (Eastern) Pigeon Hawk

6. See Nests Above the Ground VII A 8.

   Raven

*Nests of Birds East of the
One-Hundredth Meridian*

✔✔✔✔✔✔✔✔✔✔✔✔✔✔✔

Nests Above the Ground

I

Hanging or Semihanging

A. Attached to Reeds or Bushes in Marshes or Wooded Swamps

1. See Nests On or In the Ground III A a(1) 6.

   (Eastern) Least Bittern

2. Cup-shaped and well built; of dead reeds and plant stems. Size varies since nest is enlarged as eggs are laid. In low bushes. Nesting in colonies. Wooded swamps and marshes.

   Locally in peninsular Florida.

   Eastern Glossy Ibis

3. Cup-shaped, compactly built of dead reeds; lined with finer pieces of reeds and grasses. Nesting in colonies. Wooded swamps and marshes.

   Southern Texas and southern Louisiana; occasionally in Florida.

   White-faced Glossy Ibis

4. A platform or shallow basket; of dried leaves and stems of rushes, cattails, and pickerel weed. Outside diameter, 8 to 10 inches; inside depth, 3 inches. Suspended among and woven into vegetation and rarely

less than 2 feet above water. Lowlands, wooded swamps, and marshes.

Florida and Texas north to South Carolina and Tennessee.

Purple Gallinule

5. Coconut-shaped or spherical, sometimes egg-shaped with entrance on side, usually near top, and occasionally plastered with mud; of grasses, cottony leaves, and weed stalks; lined with finer grasses, cattail down, and feathers. Vertical outside diameter, 3 inches; horizontal outside diameter, 5 inches. Usually in cattail marshes, from 1 to 3 feet above the ground, but also in the banks of tidal rivers and sluggish inland streams, and the marshy shores of ponds.

Massachusetts, northern Vermont, Great Lakes, North Dakota south to Florida and Gulf Coast.

Long-billed Marsh Wren

6. Globular or spherical; a ball of dry and green grasses with a well concealed opening on the side; usually the growing grasses are woven into the ball rendering it inconspicuous; frequently the growing grasses are arched over it, further concealing it; lined with plant down. Vertical outside diameter, 6 inches; horizontal outside diameter, 5 inches; inside diameter, 3 inches. Well hidden in sedges or grasses or other low herbage close to the ground, mud, or very shallow water, not more than a foot or two above it. Drier marshes or wet meadows or the intermediate area bordering meadows and dry wooded swamps.

Eastern and central United States (except northern Maine) south to northern Delaware, Indiana, Missouri, and eastern Kansas.

Short-billed Marsh Wren

7. Bulky, loosely constructed, and inartistic; of water-soaked leaves (sweet gum, water oak, pepperidge, holly, cane); lined with fine pine needles, moss, leaves, rootlets, grass stems, and sometimes horsehair. Outside diameter, 5 inches; outside height, 6 inches; inside diameter, 1½ inches; inside depth, 1¼ inches. In bushes, canes, masses of vines and briers, from 2 to 10 feet, usually 3 feet, above the ground; generally in swampy locations but occasionally in high land some distance from water. Wooded swamps.

   Maryland, southern Virginia, southern Indiana, Oklahoma south to northern Florida and Louisiana.

   Swainson's Warbler

8. Cup-shaped; generally compactly built with a well-woven rim; of bark strips, leaves, weeds, plant down, and canes; lined with dry weeds, rootlets, mosses, grasses, pine needles, and horsehair or, in southern swamps, with the dead inner fibers of tillandsia. Outside diameter, 3½ inches; outside height, 3 inches; inside diameter, 2 inches; inside depth, 2⅛ inches. Attached to reeds or suspended in bush or sapling, from 1 to 5 feet above the ground; at the northern limit of range laurel is frequently selected; at southern limit canes. Bushy borders of upland woods, hillside thickets, dry or swampy woodlands, and ravines. See also I C c(1) d(1) 11.

   Rhode Island, central New York, southern Michigan, northern Iowa, northeastern Nebraska south to northern Florida and Gulf of Mexico.

   Hooded Warbler

9. Bulky, rather compact, basket-shaped, thick-edged, and finely woven; of blades of grass and sedge; lined with finer blades. Inside diameter, 3 inches; inside depth, 2½ inches. Attached to cattails, reeds, and

wild rice, from 1 to 3 feet above water that is preferably 2 to 4 feet deep. Marshes.

Canadian border south and east locally to Nebraska, Iowa, southern Wisconsin, and northern Indiana.

Yellow-headed Blackbird

10. Bowl-shaped, deeply hollowed, rather bulky; of grasses, sedges, and weed stalks; interstices filled with rotton wood, rootlets, and similar materials; lined with finer grass and rootlets. Attached to cattails, rushes, sedges, tussocks of marsh grass, and such water-loving bushes as buttonbush, alder, and willow. Marshes, sloughs, and shores of ponds, lakes, and sluggish streams.

Eastern and central United States south to Florida and Gulf of Mexico.

Red-winged Blackbird

11. Cup-shaped; of fine grass stems woven around the supporting stems of the grass or rush clump in which it is concealed. Attached to reeds from 4 to 16 inches above the ground, not arched but usually hidden from view by wisps of grass carelessly arranged as if for protection against the sun. Outside diameter 5 inches; outside height, 4 inches; inside diameter, 3 inches; depth, 2½ inches. Salt marshes.

Merritt Island in vicinity of Titusville, Florida.

Dusky Seaside Sparrow

B. Attached to Bushes in Wet Meadows or Swampy Thickets

1. Carelessly and loosely made of twigs and leaves of the mangrove (usually) but also of reed stalks and weeds. Size varies since nest is enlarged as eggs are laid; from 6 inches to as much as 24 inches in diameter. Placed

at low elevation in reeds, tangles, bushes, and trees. Nesting in colonies. Mangrove thickets and low country. See also VII B b(3) 12.

South Carolina to Texas.

White Ibis

2. Cup-shaped, compact, somewhat loosely finished, even ragged appearance outside and below; of bark, grasses, vegetable fibers, and weed stalks; lined with finer grasses, hair, or plant down. Outside diameter, 3½ to 4 inches; outside height, 2 inches; inside diameter, about 3 inches; inside depth, about 1½ inches. Placed loosely in upright crotch or fork, or between independent twigs that furnish a similar support, of a small bush, most often a wild rose, from 2 to 4 feet above the ground. Damp thickets, along the banks of a small stream, around the shores of a pond, on the borders of a marsh or bog, sometimes some distance from the water.

Eastern and central United States south to central Arkansas, Kentucky, northern New Jersey, and Connecticut, and, in mountains, to West Virginia.

Alder Flycatcher
(Traill's Flycatcher)

3. Cup-shaped, neatly made, walls firmly interwoven; of dried grass, bark shreds, cotton, lichens, and spiders' webs; lined with soft cotton-like fibers or rootlets; sometimes entirely of seaweed. Suspended between two twigs or in the fork of trees and bushes, from 10 to 20 feet above the ground. Mangrove swamps.

Southern Florida (Keys, southern tip, and southern coast to Tampa Bay).

Black-whiskered Vireo

4. Somewhat compressed and compact; of fine grasses and leaves; lined with black rootlets. Outside diameter,

4 inches; outside height, 3½ inches; inside diameter, 2 inches; inside depth, 1½ inches. In vines, bushes, or canes from 1 to 3 feet above the ground. Cypress swamps and river bottoms.

Southeastern Missouri, northeastern Arkansas, western Kentucky, northern Alabama, and South Carolina.

Bachman's Warbler

C. Attached to Upland Trees and Bushes

c(1). *Fully suspended*

d(1). Less than 2 inches deep inside

1. Cup-shaped, walls unusually thick, bulging sides arch over mouth of nest giving it a somewhat spherical shape; a perfectly woven structure of bark strips, leaves, coarse grasses, skeleton leaves, spiders' webs, and caterpillar silk; lined with fine grasses. Outside diameter, 3 inches; outside height, 2¼ inches; inside diameter, 1½ inches; inside depth, 1½ inches. Suspended from the horizontal forked twig of (usually) stunted elms and small oaks, generally about 4 feet above the ground. Woodland thickets, oak woods, and ravines in bluffy prairie lands.

   Central Texas, Oklahoma, and southern Kansas.

   Black-capped Vireo

2. A beautiful structure shaped like an inverted cone, more or less long and narrow and quite pointed at the bottom; of bark strips, grasses, rootlets, plant fibers, small pieces of wood and plant down, bound together with spiders' silk; lined with fine grasses; decorated externally with green mosses, bark strips, lichens, bits of paper, cotton, wool, and pieces of wasps' nests. Outside diameter, 3 inches; inside diameter, 2 inches; inside depth, 2 inches. Suspended from a forked twig

of small tree or bush from 1 to 8 feet above the ground. Briery thickets, upland pastures, and old fields.

Florida and Gulf of Mexico north to Massachusetts, New York, Ohio, and southern Wisconsin.

White-eyed Vireo

3. Neat, cup-shaped structure, compact and smooth; of plant strips and shreds, fibers, spiders' webs and co-coons, leaf fragments, and small pieces of bark; lined with fine grass stems, rootlets, hair, and down. Outside diameter, 3 inches; outside height, 3 inches; inside diameter, 1¾ inches; inside depth, 1½ inches. Sus-pended in a forked twig of a bush or small tree (wil-low) from 2 to 5 feet above the ground. Low, dense thickets, preferably along the banks of a river or small stream.

Texas north to northwestern Indiana, northern Illinois, and southern South Dakota.

Bell's Vireo

4. Cup-shaped and well-made; of bark strips and plant fibers; lined with finer grasses, beautifully adorned with lichens and cocoons held in place with caterpil-lars' silk and spiders' webs. Outside diameter, 3 inches; outside height, 2½ inches; inside diameter, 2 inches; inside depth, 1½ inches. Suspended in a middle fork and firmly attached to supporting twigs of a variety of deciduous trees (rarely in conifers) from 3 to 60 feet above the ground. Woodland borders, orchards, groves, and open stands of oak, maples, and other hardwood trees.

Eastern and central United States (except northern Maine) south to northern Florida and Gulf Coast.

Yellow-throated Vireo

5. Basket-like or cup-shaped; of bark strips, soft plant fibers, fine rootlets, pieces of thread, and fine grasses, mixed with lichens, bits of mosses, hair, paper, string, spiders' webs, cotton, and soft feathers; lined with fine rootlets, thin, dry grasses, hair, feathers, fur, and pine needles; usually decorated externally with birch bark strips, oak catkins, or with leaves, lichens, and plant down. Outside diameter, 3 inches; outside height, 2¼ inches; inside diameter, 2 inches; inside depth, 1½ inches. Suspended in terminal forks of evergreens (usually) between the prongs of a forked twig, or between two twigs projecting side by side from the upright stem of a sapling or deciduous tree, from 4 to 30 feet above the ground; sometimes in bushes. Stands of conifers or mixed woods.

   Canadian border south to Minnesota, Michigan, northern New Jersey, and, in Appalachians, to northern Georgia.

   Blue-headed (Solitary) Vireo

6. Cup-shaped, dainty, durable, a beautiful example of avian workmanship; of fine grasses, rootlets, bark strips, bits of dead wood, paper from wasps' nests, and plant down; lined with fine strips of bark, vine tendrils, and sometimes pine needles; ornamented with cocoons and bits of wasps' and spiders' webs. Outside diameter, 3 inches; outside height, 2½ inches; inside diameter, 2 inches; inside depth, 1½ inches. Suspended in a forking, horizontal branch of a shrub or low branch of a tree, usually from 5 to 10 feet above the ground. Woodlands.

   Eastern and central United States south to central Florida and Gulf Coast.

   Red-eyed Vireo

7. Cup-shaped; of shreds of bark and weed stalks; beautifully decorated on the exterior with thin strips of

birch bark, seed tufts of willow, held together with shreds of Usnea; lined with pine needles and fine grass, arranged circularly in deep layers around the sides and bottom of the cup. Outside diameter, 3 inches; outside height, 2½ inches; inside diameter, 2 inches; inside depth, 1 inch. Suspended in forks of tall shrubs or trees (willows, poplars, and alders) from 8 to 40 feet above the ground. Usually found in second growth woods along the edges of farmlands but also along roadsides, woodland borders, bottom lands, and streams.

Along the northern fringe of eastern and central United States.

Philadelphia Vireo

8. Deeply cup-shaped or basket-like with a somewhat contracted brim, elaborately woven, and more carefully, neatly, and closely built than that of other vireos; of grasses, bark shreds, plant fibers; lined with finer grasses and hair. Lacks exterior ornamentation of other vireos' nests. Outside diameter, 3 inches; outside height, 2 inches; inside diameter, 1¾ inches; inside depth, 1½ inches. Suspended in end forks in the upper part of large deciduous trees, from 25 to 50 feet above the ground. Orchards, open country, roadsides.

Eastern and central United States south to North Carolina, southern Louisiana, and northwestern Texas.

(Eastern) Warbling Vireo

9. Gourd-shaped, hollowed out of Usnea where available, with entrance hole in one side, sometimes opening is at top; lined with grass, hair, or pine needles; otherwise built of fine dry grasses, bark shreds, bits of down, Spanish moss when available, and various other materials. Outside diameter, 3¼ inches; outside height, 2½ inches; inside diameter, 1¾ inches; inside depth,

1¾ inches. In bunches of Usnea (where found) suspended from horizontal or sloping branches of (preferably) coniferous but also of deciduous trees, from 5 to 40 feet above the ground; rarely, built on a branch among twigs and covered with Usnea brought for the purpose; where Usnea is scarce nest often built in hanging cluster of twigs of hemlock and spruce. Usually humid woodlands and old orchards where Usnea or Spanish moss is found but also in areas where neither is available.

Eastern and central United States south to Florida, Gulf Coast, and Texas.

Parula Warbler

10. Cup-shaped, rather shallow; of weed stems, fine grasses, bark strips, and plant fibers, securely bound together with spiders' webs and decorated with bits of lichens; lined with hair, dead grass, bark strips, and moss. Outside diameter, 2¾ inches; outside height, 1¾ to 2 inches; inside diameter, 1¾ inches; inside depth, 1 inch. In forks of small branches or saddled on horizontal or drooping branches of deciduous trees, from 30 to 90 feet above the ground. See also II B 2. Mixed woods or open forests in the lowlands and often along streams.

Central New York, Ohio, southern Michigan, southeastern Minnesota, and southeastern Nebraska south to northern parts of Gulf States, chiefly west of the Appalachians.

Cerulean Warbler

11. See I A 8.

Hooded Warbler

d(2). Over 2 inches deep inside

1. Gourd-shaped, bulging at the bottom, and normally gray-colored; of plant fibers, string, yarn, grasses, hair,

and bark; at the bottom sometimes a lining of hair, wool, or fine grass. Outside height 5 inches or more; entrance oval in shape, 3¼ inches by 2 inches; cup 4½ inches deep by 2½ inches wide. Suspended at extreme ends of drooping branches in such trees as large elms or near the trunk in smaller maples or other trees. Orchards, roadsides, and farmlands.

Eastern and central United States south to northern Georgia, Louisiana, and southern Texas (absent in southeastern coastal plain).

Baltimore Oriole

c(2). *Partly suspended*

d(1). Less than 2 inches deep inside

1. A frail shallow basket or saucer-shaped structure; of rootlets, grasses, mosses, weed stems, or similar materials, usually decorated with catkins and sometimes with the blossoms from some tree, so loosely woven that the eggs may be seen from below but deceptive in appearance since it can withstand the severest storms. Not as neat, deep, or well-built as those of other flycatchers; with a little lining and thin bottom; often resembles a bunch of "drift" left in crotch of a low branch by the high water of the stream which it overhangs. Outside diameter, about 3½ inches; outside height, 2 inches; inside diameter, about 2 inches; inside depth, 1 inch. Partly suspended on a low, rather horizontal or drooping branch, usually in a fork toward the leaf-bearing tip of a tree, or in the fork of a sapling, from 5 to 20 feet above the ground. Well-watered woodlands and thickets.

Florida and Gulf of Mexico north to Nebraska, Iowa, southern Michigan, Lake Erie, western New York, and southern New England.

Acadian Flycatcher

2. Globular, with small opening at top; rim slightly contracted or arched over hollow; of green moss, Usnea, and other lichens, soft bark strips, bits of leaves, and rootlets; lined with feathers. Outside diameter, 3 to 4 inches; outside height, 2½ to 3½ inches; inside diameter, 2 inches; inside depth, 1½ inches. Partly suspended from a horizontal evergreen bough, such as hemlock, spruce, or fir, from 6 to 50 feet above the ground and usually well concealed by foliage. Coniferous forests.

Minnesota, Michigan, New York, and, in mountains, to North Carolina.

(Eastern) **Golden-crowned Kinglet**

d(2). Over 2 inches deep inside

1. Beautifully and compactly woven, basket-shaped; of grass. Inside diameter, 3 inches; inside depth, 2½ to 3 inches. Partly suspended on small branches of (usually) fruit but sometimes shade trees. When new, difficult to detect in the foliage. Orchards, roadsides, and farmlands.

Gulf of Mexico north to Massachusetts, central New York, Ohio, Michigan, northwestern Minnesota, and North Dakota.

Orchard Oriole

II

✓✓✓✓✓✓✓✓✓✓✓✓✓✓✓

Covered on Outside with
Lichens and Saddled on Branch

A. Less than 2 Inches, Outside Diameter

1. Cup-shaped, very small; of bud scales and plant down; fastened to limbs and branches with spiders' silk and covered so perfectly with lichens as to appear a protuberance on the limb. Outside diameter, 1½ inches; outside height, 1¼ inches. Usually saddled on a small, down-sloping branch of various trees, from 6 to 50 feet above the ground. Woodlands and orchards.

    Eastern and central United States south to Gulf of Mexico.

    Ruby-throated Hummingbird

2. Cup-shaped, gracefully contracted at brim; of soft silky plant down, withered blossoms or other dainty material, pinned together with fine grasses, old leaf stems, and horsehair; exterior decorated with lichens held in place with spiders' silk; lined with fibrous materials such as fine strips of bark, fine grasses, tendrils, feathers, and horsehair. Outside diameter, 2 inches; outside height, 2½ inches; inside diameter, 1¼ inches; inside depth, 1⅜ inches. Usually saddled on

79

a horizontal limb but often in a fork formed by an upright branch and a horizontal or slanting one of trees, rarely in saplings, from 10 to 75 feet above the ground. If saddled on a limb resembles a knot. Also looks much like a large hummingbird's nest. Woodlands, forested areas, wooded swamps, pine lands, and along water courses.

Southern New Jersey, southwestern Pennsylvania, southern Michigan, and Iowa south to Florida and the Gulf of Mexico.

Blue-gray Gnatcatcher

B. Over 2 Inches, Outside Diameter

1. Saucer-shaped, dainty, somewhat flat, compact, with fairly thick felted low sides and thin bottom; of fine grass, plant fibers, and bark shreds; lined with finer materials, sometimes with a little plant down, a few horsehairs, and bits of thread. Often the branch forms a portion of the bottom of the nest. Like that of the hummingbird, it is frequently indistinguishable at a distance from a knot on the limb. Outside diameter, 2¾ inches; outside height, 1¾ inches; inside diameter, 1¾ inches; inside depth, 1¼ inches. Generally saddled on a small limb, often dead, or in or near a level fork well out from the trunk of the tree at a height of about 20 feet. Open mixed woods, orchards, borders of fields, rural areas, clearings, and in the vicinity of human habitations.

Northern Florida and Gulf of Mexico throughout eastern and central United States.

Wood Pewee

2. See I C c(1) d(1) 10.

Cerulean Warbler

III

✓✓✓✓✓✓✓✓✓✓✓✓✓✓✓

Felted Nests of
Cottony Materials

A. In Forks of Bushes or Saplings

1. Cup-shaped, compact, well-made, the materials being
firmly and smoothly interwoven, thick-walled; of sil-
ver-gray plant fibers, fine grasses, bark shreds, and
plant down; lined with plant down, fine grasses, and
sometimes long hair. Often an especially deep nest
will be found resulting from the building of two or
more floors to cover over and leave unhatched a cowbird's eggs deposited with the previous warbler's eggs.
Outside diameter, 2¼ to 3 inches; outside height, 2 to
5 inches; inside diameter, 1¾ inches; inside depth,
1¼ to 1½ inches. In upright forks or crotches of
bushes or saplings, rarely 6 to 8 feet above the ground
or less than 3 feet, sometimes at higher levels in apple
trees or in small trees about houses but, rarely, as high
as 30 or 40 feet. Along small streams and brooks,
borders of wooded swamps, ponds, and lakes; among
willows, alders, and blueberries in open brushy
marshes; in shrubbery along brush-grown fences; in
rural areas and roadside thickets.

Eastern and central United States south to northern
Georgia, southern Missouri, and Oklahoma. Also in mangroves in Florida Keys.

Yellow Warbler

2. Cup-shaped, thin-walled but firm and compact; of bark
    strips, leaf stalks, small rootlets, plant fibers, and plant
    down; lined with fine rootlets, grass, hair, and some-
    times a few feathers; outside walls covered with plant
    fibers and ornamented with small lichens, bits of birch
    bark, bud scales, seed pods, and plant down bound in
    with spiders' silk. Outside diameter, 2⅞ inches; out-
    side height, 3 inches; inside diameter, 1½ inches; in-
    side depth, 1½ inches. Usually in an upright 3- or
    4-pronged crotch of a dead or live hardwood sapling,
    from 4 to 20 feet above the ground (average height
    about 7 feet) but also in a small bush or shrub a few
    inches to 2 or 3 feet above the ground, either in a
    crotch or saddled on a horizontal limb; occasionally
    in grapevine tangles. Woodlands, roadsides, and alder
    and willow thickets bordering streams and ponds.

    Eastern and central United States south to North Caro-
    lina, northern Georgia, southern Alabama, Louisiana, and
    Oklahoma.

    American Redstart

3. Cup-shaped, compact, artistic; of fine grasses, bark
    strips, and moss; lined characteristically with thistle-
    down. Outside diameter, 3 inches; outside height, 1½
    inches; inside diameter, 2 inches; inside depth, ¾ inch.
    In upright fork of a bush or small tree from a few feet
    to 20 feet or more above the ground. Open country
    with neglected fields and scattered woody growth.

    Eastern and central United States south to northern
    Georgia, northern Alabama, central Arkansas, and south-
    ern Oklahoma.

    American Goldfinch

B. On Horizontal Branch or in Upright Crotch of Small Tree

1. Cup-shaped, carelessly built; of twigs, plant stems, rootlets, weeds, thistledown, cotton, or wool; felted and lined with rootlets, horsehair, and cotton; sometimes built entirely of cotton. Outside diameter, 4½ to 6½ inches; outside height, 2¾ to 3 inches; inside diameter, 2¾ to 3 inches; inside depth, 1¾ to 2¼ inches. Generally on a horizontal limb or fork, less commonly in a fork of (usually) an isolated tree, from 5 to 40 feet above the ground. Also in bushes and various other places such as the crossbars of telegraph poles. Country roadsides, pastures, edges of scattered woodlands, and in the vicinity of farm houses.

   Texas, Oklahoma, Kansas, and southern Nebraska, occasionally east to western Louisiana and southwestern Missouri.

   Scissor-tailed Flycatcher

2. Cup-shaped, walls rather thin, upper rim often somewhat incurved, neat, compact; of bark shreds, plant fibers, fine weed stems and grasses, dried blossoms of weeds and grasses, thistledown, cotton, bits of string and paper, spiders' webs, insect cocoons, various vegetable fibers, and rubbish; smoothly lined with the finest grasses, cowhair, or horsehair, down of various plants such as thistle, milkweed, dandelion, and a few feathers. Outside diameter, 2½ to 3 inches; outside height, 1¾ to 2½ inches; inside diameter, 1¾ to 2 inches; inside depth, 1¼ to 1½ inches. On ends of horizontal branches, usually partially supported by upright twigs, in upright fork of small branch or on horizontal branches near the trunk of trees (preferably apple trees in some parts of range), from 7 to 15 feet above

the ground (sometimes as high as 60 feet), or in bushes from 2 to 6 feet above the ground. Orchards, country roads, borders of streams and ponds, woodland borders, coniferous woods, and dense thickets.

Eastern and central United States south to Oklahoma, Missouri, Indiana, northern New Jersey, and, in mountains, to North Carolina.

Least Flycatcher

IV

✔✔✔✔✔✔✔✔✔✔✔✔✔✔

Containing a Layer of Mud

A. Built in Trees

a(1). *Under 4 inches, inside diameter*

1. Cup-shaped, thick-walled, bulky, sometimes rough appearing and unkempt; of coarse grasses, twigs, rootlets, paper, cloth, and string, with an inner wall of mud; lined usually with fine grass. Outside diameter, about 6½ inches; outside height, about 3 inches; inside diameter, 4 inches; inside depth, 2½ inches. On horizontal branches of trees (fruit or shade) or in crotches between the branches, from 5 to 30 feet above the ground. Also on fence rails, fence posts, on projections on buildings, or on open shelves erected by man for the purpose. Woodlands, orchards, and in the vicinity of human habitations. See also IV B b(3) 1 and IX A a(2) 3.

   Eastern and central United States south to western South Carolina, northern Georgia, northern Louisiana, and northern Mississippi.

   Robin

2. Cup-shaped, firm, compact; of grasses, weed stalks, leaves, rootlets, and fine twigs, with a foundation of leaves and an inner wall of mud or leaf mold; lined

85

with fine rootlets; frequently contains rags, paper, and cellophane; similar to nest of Robin but somewhat more hollowed; can also be distinguished from Robin's nest by the presence of dead leaves and sometimes moss and by the further fact that the thrush nest is lined with brown rootlets whereas the Robin's nest is lined with dried grass. Inside diameter, 3½ inches; inside depth, 2 inches. Usually built in a fork of saplings or undergrowth but sometimes saddled on horizontal branches of a tree and cemented to the branch with mud, from 5 to 50 feet above the ground. Low, cool, damp forests, often near streams; sometimes in the vicinity of human habitations.

Southern South Dakota, central Minnesota, central Wisconsin, New York, and central New Hampshire south almost to Gulf of Mexico.

Wood Thrush

3. Rather bulky, well-built; of twigs, grass, lichens, and "duff" which, when dried, appears as mud; lined with fine grasses. Inside diameter, 3½ inches; inside depth, 2½ inches. In evergreen or deciduous trees such as alders and willows; often within a foot or two of water and usually less than 10 feet above water. Swampy woodlands.

Northern New York and northern New England.

Rusty Blackbird

4. Large and bulky; composed externally of a rough frame of twigs, stalks, bark, and rootlets, mixed and held together with a layer of mud; lined with fine rootlets, grasses, and horse and cow hairs. Outside diameter, 6 inches; outside height, 4½ inches; inside diameter, 3½ inches; inside depth, 3 inches. Usually low in trees and bushes, but sometimes in trees as high as 30 feet above the ground. Often in large colonies.

Brushy grasslands, meadows, and margins of lakes and streams.

Western prairie country east to Minnesota, Wisconsin, northern Illinois, and Kansas.

Brewer's Blackbird

a(2). *Over 4 inches, inside diameter*

1. A large, bulky, basket-shaped, rough structure; of sticks, grass, bark strips, saw grass, seaweed, and roots, generally coated inside with mud. Among reeds and in saplings and small trees or bushes; in fully grown trees as high as 40 feet above the ground. Vicinity of salt water (preferably marshes) and, in Florida, in marshes and about shallow island ponds. See also IV C 1.

    Along coast from Delaware and Chesapeake Bay south to Florida Keys and west to Texas; also inland throughout Florida.

    Boat-tailed Grackle

2. A loose, bulky structure; of twigs, grass, weed stalks, frequently reinforced with mud; lined with similar finer materials. Inside diameter, 4 inches; inside depth, 3 inches. On a bough but often in a fork formed by topmost whorl of branches, preferably in a conifer but sometimes in a deciduous tree; also in a tree cavity, a hollow stub, or birdhouse. See also VIII A a(3) 27. Coniferous groves, open and swampy woods, reedy marshes, and farmlands.

    Southern New England, southern New York south to Florida between the Appalachians and the coast, and southern Louisiana.

    Purple Grackle

3. Substantially built, cup-shaped, bulky, coarse; of sticks, grass, weeds, roots, leaves, and similar materials held in place with mud; lined with fine grasses and

rootlets, sometimes hair and feathers are added. Similar to Robin's nest but larger. Inside diameter, 4 inches; inside depth, 3½ inches. Preferably in a conifer but also in a deciduous tree or in low shrubs and bushes, sometimes in buildings, barns, etc. Wooded swamps and farmlands. See also IV B b(3) 2.

Canadian border south to Massachusetts and west of Appalachians (throughout Mississippi Valley and plains) to Louisiana and Texas.

Bronzed Grackle

B. Built on or in Buildings, on Bridges, or Against Rocks

b(1). *Outer layer of mud with strengthening of grass or straw*

1. Cup-shaped if built on a flat surface, cone-shaped if on a vertical surface, the upper tip being more than half a circle and the lower end pointed; if built in corners smaller and made to fit the spaces; of mud mixed with grass and straw; profusely lined with poultry feathers. Nests in narrow crannies or holes with supporting floor and sides built without mud. Outside diameter of circular tip, 5 inches; inner diameter of circular tip, 3 inches. Usually built on a rafter inside barns or other buildings but also under eaves of dwelling houses, on wharves, and under bridges and culverts. See also IX B b(1) 1. Rural areas.

   Eastern and central United States south to North Carolina, northern Alabama, Tennessee, and Arkansas; also locally on Gulf Coast.

Barn Swallow

2. Gourd-shaped or shaped like a flask, retort, or bottle, with a narrow entrance on side leading into an enlarged chamber; of mud strengthened with straw and horsehair; scantily lined with a few dried grass stems

and feathers. Built beneath the eaves of buildings. See also IX A a(3) 1. Rural areas, cities, and towns.

Eastern and central United States south locally to western Virginia, northern Alabama, and Texas.

(Northern) **Cliff Swallow**

b(2). *Outer layer of mosses*

1. Cup-shaped if built on a beam or rafter, semicircular if attached to wall or side of overhanging rock; of mud, dry grass, and plant fibers; lined with finer fibers and hair, and covered with moss. Outside diameter, 4½ inches; outside height, 4 inches; inside diameter, 2½ inches; inside depth, 1¾ inches. Against rocks in rocky ravines, in or on bridges, barns, sheds, abandoned farmhouses, and in similar places. See also IX A a(4) 1. Woodlands, rural areas, and in the vicinity of human habitations.

Eastern and central United States south to northern Mississippi, Texas, and mountains of Georgia.

Eastern Phoebe

b(3). *Outer layer of grasses*

1. See IV A a(1) 1 and IX A a(2) 3.

Robin

2. See IV a(2) 3.

Bronzed Grackle

C. Among Reeds in Swamps

1. See IV A a(2) 1.

Boat-tailed Grackle

V

/////////////////

Made Chiefly of Bark, Fibers, Twigs, and Rootlets

A. Less than 2 Inches, Inside Diameter

a(1). *Usually in conifers*

1. With basket-like frame but otherwise cup-shaped, carelessly built, flimsy, fairly shallow, somewhat variable in construction; of fine twigs, stiff dead grass, weeds, pine needles, spiders' webs, and cocoons; lined with fine black roots or hair, plant down, and stems of haircap moss. Outside diameter, 2¾ to 4 inches; inside diameter, 1¾ to 2 inches; inside depth, 1 inch or less. Usually rather low on horizontal branches away from trunk of (generally) conifers but also at higher levels, from 12 inches to 35 feet above the ground. Low hemlock thickets, dense thickets, or old clearings of small spruce or fir, and edges of coniferous woods.

   Minnesota, northern Wisconsin to northern Massachusetts, and, in Appalachians, to Virginia.

   Magnolia Warbler

2. Rather bulky, cup-shaped; of twigs, vine stems, grasses, moss, with spiders' webs, interwoven with fine

fibers and knotted into numerous little balls which are found on the surface; lined with rootlets, hair, feathers, and fur; exterior roughly made but more compact than that of the Magnolia Warbler, which it resembles; lining laid with precision and fashioned into a neat cup with the brim accurately turned into an almost perfect circle. Outside diameter, 4 inches; outside height, 2¼ inches; inside diameter, 1¾ inches; inside depth, 1 inch. On a horizontal branch, generally near the trunk, of a conifer (spruce), from 30 to 60 feet above the ground. Open stands of fir and spruce.

Northern Maine and New Hampshire.

Cape May Warbler

3. Cup-shaped, rather bulky; sometimes loosely made; of fine bark strips, twigs, dried grass, rootlets, weed stalks, bound with spiders' webs; lined with hair and feathers or plant down. Outside diameter, 3 to 5 inches; outside height, 2 inches; inside diameter, 2 inches; inside depth, 1¾ inches. Usually in a conifer but also in other trees, from 5 to 50 feet above the ground. Thickets of evergreens along roadsides, along the banks of streams, about the shores of ponds or lakes, and in pastures and orchards.

Northern Minnesota, northern Michigan, New Hampshire, Maine, and in mountains of New York and Massachusetts.

Myrtle Warbler

4. Cup-shaped, beautiful, compact, deeply hollowed; of conifer twigs, grasses, seaweed, strips of inner bark, and mosses; bound together with caterpillars' or spiders' webs; frequently lined with fine grasses, pine needles, bark strips, hair, and feathers. Outside diameter, 3 to 4 inches; outside height, 2 inches; inside diameter, 2 inches; inside depth, 1½ inches. Usually

placed on horizontal branches but often on slanting (upward or downward) limbs, sometimes between two horizontal limbs, from 3 to 70 feet above the ground. Pine woods, mixed woods where conifers predominate, old neglected pastures or hillsides containing scattered growths of cedars, and pasture-bordering copses.

Eastern and central United States south to southern Minnesota, northern Ohio, New Jersey, Long Island, and, in mountains, to northern Georgia.

Black-throated Green Warbler

5. Cup-shaped, elegant, compact, but somewhat variable in size and materials; sometimes thick and heavily built, sometimes light and airy; commonly of coniferous twigs, but sometimes including bark strips, pine needles, and lichens; lined with fine rootlets and hair, occasionally also fine grass and feathers. Usually placed toward end of limb or near top of tree, from 5 to 80 feet above the ground. Deep evergreen woods, where spruces, firs, and hemlocks predominate, and swampy coniferous woods.

Canadian border south to central Minnesota, Wisconsin, central Michigan, southern New England, and, in Appalachians, to northern Georgia.

Blackburnian Warbler

6. Cup-shaped; of twiglets, strips of bark, leaf stems, and fine grasses, sometimes found with Spanish moss, caterpillar silk, or plant down; lined with soft vegetable down, hair, or feathers; compact and somewhat like a Pine Warbler's nest but without the black grapevine bark. Outside diameter, 2½ to 3 inches; outside height, 2 inches; inside diameter, 1½ to 2½ inches; inside depth, 1¾ to 2½ inches. In northern part of range in a (usually) sycamore, but in southern part

of range usually on the horizontal branch of a pine but sometimes in a live oak, fastened to the limb with silky fibers, from 10 to 120 feet above the ground, usually concealed in Spanish moss or fine foliage. Pine foods and cypress swamps.

Along Atlantic coastal plain from Florida north to Maryland and southern New Jersey (probably). Also Mississippi Valley from Gulf States north to southern Michigan and southern Wisconsin.

Yellow-throated Warbler

7. Somewhat bulky, cup-shaped; of twigs, mosses, pieces of bark, grasses, rootlets, wool, plant fibers, and lichens; lined with fine mosses, lichens, and feathers, the latter a characteristic. Outside diameter, 4½ inches; outside height, 3 inches; inside diameter, 2 inches; inside depth, 1½ inches. Usually on a horizontal branch low in a spruce tree, from 1 to 7 feet above the ground. Principally spruce forests.

    Northern Michigan, northern Maine, and mountains of New York, New Hampshire, Vermont, and Massachusetts.

Black-poll Warbler

8. Cup-shaped, well-made, compact; of grapevine bark strips, weed stems, pine needles, twigs, and caterpillars' or spiders' webs; lined with pine needles, fern down, hair, bristles, or feathers. On horizontal branches of pines (usually), from 10 to 35 feet above the ground, generally well concealed among pine needles. Open pine woods.

    Eastern and central United States south to southern Florida and Gulf States.

Pine Warbler

9. Cup-shaped, frail, loosely constructed, rather shallow; of bark fibers, rootlets, weed stalks, and grasses; lined

with hair. From 5 to 60 feet above the ground. Openings in forests made by swamps, streams, and ponds, and man-made clearings.

North Dakota, central Minnesota, northern Illinois, and New England, south in mountains to Maryland.

(Eastern) **Purple Finch**

10.   Saucer-shaped, rather flat, and somewhat large for size of bird; of grass or twigs, pine needles, rootlets, moss, lichens, and bark strips; lined with rootlets, plant down, fur, hair, feathers, or moss. Outside diameter, 3⅓ inches; outside height, 2 inches; inside diameter, 2 inches; inside depth, 1 inch. Usually saddled on a branch well out near the end, from 8 to 30 feet above the ground; generally well concealed among thick foliage. Evergreen forests.

Northern Minnesota, northern New England, and in mountains of North Carolina.

Pine Siskin

a(2).   *In bushes or saplings*

1.   Cup-shaped, neat, thick-walled, and rather bulky outside; of bark strips, rootlets, grasses, vines, twigs, and spiders' webs; neatly lined with fine black rootlets or horsehair; always decorated exteriorly with corky bits of wood and woolly parts of cocoons; often bits of dead wood in bottom. Outside diameter, 3½ inches; outside height, 2½ inches; inside diameter, 2 inches; inside depth, 1⅛ inches. Placed low in bushes, preferably broadleaf evergreens (laurels and rhododendrons), small saplings of conifers (spruce, fir, and hemlock) and deciduous trees, from 7 inches to 2 feet above the ground. Heavy deciduous woods or wet thick undergrowth of broadleaf evergreens and low growth of conifers.

Northern fringe of eastern and central United States

west to northern Minnesota and south to Massachusetts and, in mountains, to Georgia.

Black-throated Blue Warbler

2. Cup-shaped, usually rather loosely woven and flimsy but sometimes compactly woven, walls thin, not very neat; of bark strips, plant fibers, fine grasses, bunches of spiders' webs, and plant down; lined with rootlets, fine grasses, and horsehair. Outside diameter, 2½ inches; outside height, 2 inches; inside diameter, 1¾ inches; inside depth, 1¾ inches. In bushes (preferably hazel) or small saplings, from a few inches to a few feet above the ground, usually at a height of 2 to 3 feet. Shrubby deciduous slashings, bushy pastures, sproutlands, country roads, and woodland borders.

Eastern and central United States south to Nebraska, Illinois, northern Ohio, northern New Jersey, and, in uplands, to Tennessee and western South Carolina.

Chestnut-sided Warbler

3. Cup-shaped, well-made, compact; of soft strips of inner bark, plant stems, and other fibrous material, dry leaves, and cottony fibers, firmly bound together with spiders' silk; lined with plant down, hair, feathers, or golden-colored moss stems. Outside diameter, 3 inches; outside height, 2¼ inches; inside diameter, 2 inches; inside depth, 2 inches. Usually in a fork in the leafy top of a low shrub or sapling, commonly less than 3 or 4 feet above the ground but sometimes as high as 10 to 25 feet and generally artfully concealed in the foliage. Shrubby pastures, dry sproutlands, dry, bushy slashings, burns, and scrubby pine and oak barrens. In Florida, mangroves are preferred.

Florida and Gulf States locally north to southern New Hampshire, southern New York, southern Ohio, southern Michigan, and eastern Nebraska.

Prairie Warbler

B. Over 2 Inches, Inside Diameter

b(1). *Usually in conifers*

1. Saucer-shaped, shallow; of twigs, rootlets, bark, weed stalks, and Usnea; lined with grass, moss, rootlets, and pine needles. Inside diameter, about 2 inches; inside depth, about 1 inch. Usually on a horizontal limb and among a mass of fine twigs projecting from the limb of a conifer from 10 to 50 feet above the ground. Coniferous forests.

   Northern Minnesota, northern Michigan, New York, Massachusetts, and, in mountains, to North Carolina.

   Olive-sided Flycatcher

2. Cup-shaped, compact; of fine twigs, fine grasses, moss and pine needles; neatly and smoothly lined with fine black rootlets and horsehair. Outside diameter, about 4 inches; outside height, 2 to 2¾ inches; inside diameter, 2 to 2½ inches; inside depth, 1¼ to 1½ inches. On a horizontal branch toward end or near trunk, from 3 to 50 feet above the ground. Coniferous forests and heavy dense woods.

   Northern Maine, the mountains of New Hampshire and Vermont, and the Adirondacks in New York.

   Bay-breasted Warbler

b(2). *In bushes or moderately low trees*

1. Cup-shaped, rather bulky, somewhat ragged and loose exteriorly, but well cupped and brimmed; of dried weed stems, grasses, small twigs, and mosses, and often containing bits of cloth, feathers, wool, and pieces of string; lined with fine dry grass, plant down, rootlets, and hair. Outside diameter, 5½ inches; outside height, 3¼ inches; inside diameter, 3 inches; inside depth, 1¾ inches. Generally placed at the extremity of a

branch, often in a bush or low tree on a river bank, but also on a stump, fence post, fence rail, and in an eaves trough. Rural areas, orchards, and banks of streams.

Eastern and central United States south to Gulf of Mexico.

Eastern Kingbird

2. Generally a compactly built structure; cup-shaped; of twigs, leaves, weed bark, rootlets, wool, cocoons, hair, string, down, rags, and paper; thickly and warmly lined with finer materials of the same kind. Outside diameter, 6 inches; outside height, 3 inches; inside diameter, 3 inches; inside depth, 1¾ inches. Preferably in a tree, in a crotch or on a horizontal branch, against the trunk, from 8 to 40 feet above the ground; or in bushes as low as 5 feet from the ground; also in fence posts, in corners of houses, or in any convenient spot. See also IX A a(5) 2. Open country.

Eastern limit is western Minnesota, western Iowa, Kansas, and Oklahoma.

Arkansas Kingbird

3. Cup-shaped, bulky, rather deep; rough externally and somewhat loosely put together; of twigs, dry grass, weed stalks, plant down, plant fibers, moss, leaves, rootlets, rags, paper, bark strips, and twine; lined with finer bits of these materials and sometimes with horsehair or wool. Outside diameter, 4½ to 5 inches; outside height, 4 to 4½ inches; inside diameter, 3 to 3¼ inches; inside depth, 3 to 3¾ inches. Usually placed on nearly horizontal branch, but sometimes in a fork between upright branches of a tree, 4 to 40 feet above the ground but sometimes in a bush. Orchards and woodland thickets.

Eastern and central United States south to North Carolina, northern Georgia, and Kansas.

Cedar Waxwing

4. Cup-shaped, somewhat bulky, usually well-made, but sometimes a carelessly constructed affair; of thick twigs, rootlets, weed stems, coarse grass, corn stalks, paper, wool, and feathers; thickly lined with rootlets, feathers, hair, and wool. Outside diameter, 5 inches; outside height, 4½ inches; inside diameter, 3 inches; inside depth, 2¼ inches. In thorny trees (hawthorns), hedges, and thickets, usually within 10 feet of the ground. Rural areas.

    Eastern and central United States locally to Florida and Gulf Coast.

Loggerhead Shrike

5. Rather small, cup-shaped, and somewhat flat, loosely constructed and so thin that the eggs usually may be seen from below; of fine bark strips, weed stems, grasses, and twigs; lined with fine rootlets. Inside diameter, 2½ inches; inside depth, 1½ inches. Usually near the end of a horizontal tree branch, from 10 to 30 feet above the ground. Woodlands, groves (preferably oak), and old orchards.

    Eastern and central United States south to western South Carolina, northern Georgia, northern Alabama, and Kansas.

Scarlet Tanager

6. Cup-shaped; of bark strips, rootlets, a few leaves, and grass. A firm structure, but so thin and shallow that the eggs may be seen from below, but in southern states sometimes more compactly built with the addition of moss and down. Outside diameter, 4 inches; outside height, 2 inches; inside depth, ½ inch. Usually near end of horizontal limb of deciduous tree, from

5 to 30 feet above the ground. Woodlands, groves, and old orchards.

Florida and Gulf of Mexico north to Delaware, central Ohio, southern Wisconsin, southern Iowa, and southeastern Nebraska.

Summer Tanager

7. Carelessly constructed, loosely put together, cup-shaped; of small twigs, strips of bark, weed stems, grasses, leaves, and rootlets; lined with fine grass, rootlets, or hair. In tree, vine, or bush, from 3 to 30 feet above the ground but usually quite low; sometimes on top of bush-covered fence, vine-covered stump, or in brush heap. Dense thickets and tangles near open areas, borders of fields and woodlands, stream banks, open marshes, and the vicinity of human habitations.

Eastern and central United States east of plains and north to southern New York, Massachusetts, Lake Erie, southern Minnesota, and southeastern South Dakota.

Cardinal

8. Saucer-shaped, loosely made; of plant fibers, grass, and twigs; lined with finer materials, rootlets, or pine needles. Insecurely placed in fork of trees or in high bushes, from 5 to 20 feet above the ground; usually not far from water. Woodlands, farming country with patches of woodland and shrubbery areas, and the vicinity of human habitations.

Eastern and central United States south to Kansas, southern Missouri, central Ohio, central New Jersey, and, in mountains, to northern Georgia.

Rose-breasted Grosbeak

9. Saucer-shaped, loosely woven, shallow; of small twigs, grass, rootlets, bark strips; lined with fine rootlets or horsehair. Outside diameter, 4½ inches; outside height, 3 inches; inside diameter, 3 inches; inside

depth, 1 inch. Usually in top of a conifer (but sometimes in other trees) amid a dense leaf cluster and near end of branch, from 20 to 60 feet above the ground. Coniferous forests.

Northern Michigan and New England.

(Eastern) **Evening Grosbeak**

VI

↗↗↗↗↗↗↗↗↗↗↗↗↗↗↗↗

Made Chiefly of Grasses,
Rootlets, Leaves, and Straw

A. In Bushes, Weeds, or Ferns

a(1). *Under 2 inches, inside diameter*

1. Compactly woven but inartistic, cup-shaped; of grass stems, bark strips, weeds, and dead leaves; lined with fine grass and sometimes with hair or feathers. In a crotch in a dense patch of cover formed by low woody growth, coarse weeds, or vines, generally only a few feet from the ground. Outside diameter, 3¼ to 3¾ inches; outside height, 2½ to 4 inches; inside diameter, 2½ inches; inside depth, 2 inches. Open brushy places, old pastures, abandoned farms, woodland clearings and old burns, and forest edges adjacent to fields, streams, and lakes.

   Eastern and central United States south to central parts of Gulf States, and northwestern Florida.

   Indigo Bunting

2. A deep, compact, thin-walled, cup-shaped structure; of leaves, grass, rootlets, bark strips, and twigs; lined with fine grasses, rootlets, and horsehair (sometimes). Resembles nest of Indigo Bunting but more neatly

   101

made. In a crotch or fork of a bush or low tree, normally about 3 feet from the ground but occasionally higher. See also VI B b(1) 4. Brushy and weedy tangles in rural areas and along woodland borders and stream banks. Well planted areas in southern towns.

Gulf States north to southeastern North Carolina, northern Mississippi, central Arkansas, and southern Kansas.

(Eastern) **Painted Bunting**

3. See Nests On or In the Ground I A a(1) 3 and Nests Above the Ground VI B b(1) 5.

Dickcissel

4. Cup-shaped, cleverly interwoven; of fine grass and rootlets; lined with hair of horse, cow, or deer; sometimes constructed entirely of horsehair. Outside diameter, 4 inches; outside height, 2½ inches; inside diameter, 2 inches; inside depth, 1 inch. Usually in dense shrubbery, bush, vine, or very young evergreens, from 3 to 5 feet above the ground. See also VI B b(1) 7. Open grassy woodlands and openings in dense woodlands, especially where grass is short and rather sparse, open orchards, and the vicinity of human habitations.

Eastern and central United States south to northern parts of Gulf States.

(Eastern) **Chipping Sparrow**

5. See Nests On or In the Ground I A a(4) 1.

Clay-colored Sparrow

6. See Nests On or In the Ground I A a(4) 2 and II A a(1) 16.

(Eastern) **Field Sparrow**

a(2). *Over 2 inches, inside diameter*

1. See Nests On or In the Ground III A a(4) 4.

Limpkin

2. Cup-shaped, usually bulky, well-made; of moss, fine sedges, leaves, vegetable fibers, twigs, rootlets, grasses, strips of bark, and strips of weed stems; lined with dead leaves, lichens, and rootlets. Outside diameter, about 4 inches; outside height, 2 to 3 inches; inside diameter, 2 to 3 inches; inside depth, 1½ inches. Sometimes in bushes but usually on two or more horizontal branches and close to the trunk of a small fir or spruce tree, from 2 to 20 feet above the ground. See also VI B b(1) 1. Spruce and fir forests, preferably in lower and damper sections, or near woodland streams, but also dry, upland coniferous woods.

   Northern Michigan, northern New York, northern New England, and, in mountains, to West Virginia.

   Olive-backed Thrush
   (Swainson's Thrush)

3. Cup-shaped, rather compact; of fine sedges, leaves, dry grasses, rootlets, strips of fine bark, and moss; lined with grasses and rootlets. Outside diameter, about 4 inches; outside height, 2¾ inches; inside diameter, 2½ inches; inside depth, 2 inches. Usually in spruce and fir scrub, 2 to 4 feet above the ground. Spruce forests on mountain tops. See VI B b(1) 2.

   Northern New England and New York south to Catskills and higher Berkshires in Massachusetts.

   Gray-cheeked Thrush

4. See Nests On or In the Ground II A a(1) 6 and Nests Above the Ground VIII A a(3) 22.

   Veery

5. Cup-shaped, rather large, compact; of grasses, leaves, vine and weed stems, and bark strips, well interwoven; lined with fine grasses and fine plant stems. Outside diameter, 5 inches; outside height, 3 inches; inside di-

ameter, 3 inches; inside depth, 2 inches. In tangles of grapevine, smilax, and briers, or in dense clumps of bushes 1 to 5 feet above the ground and well concealed. Brier thickets and bushy clearings on low damp ground, along small streams, about the borders of ponds or wooded swamps, and tangled shrubbery on high dry ground, in old neglected pastures, and along the edges of woodlands.

Massachusetts (local), central New York, Michigan, and southern Minnesota south to northern Florida and Gulf of Mexico.

Yellow-breasted Chat

6. See Nests On or In the Ground I A a(5) 11 and Nests Above the Ground VI B b(1) 6.

(Eastern) Lark Sparrow

7. See Nests On or In the Ground I A a(1) 7, II A a(2) 8, and Nests Above the Ground VI B b(1) 8.

Song Sparrow

B. In Trees

b(1). *Cup-shaped*

1. See VI A a(2) 2.

Olive-backed Thrush

2. See VI A a(2) 3.

Gray-cheeked Thrush

3. A compact, well-built structure; of dried grass, plant fibers, leaves, and rootlets; lined with fine brown rootlets and sometimes with horsehair; usually a cast snakeskin is incorporated into the nest. Generally on a low branch of a tree but sometimes in low brambles, from 3 to 12 feet above the ground. Inside diameter,

2⅜ to 3 inches; inside depth, 2 inches. Woodland borders, roadsides, low moist areas, and willow thickets.

Gulf States north to Maryland, southern Illinois, and Nebraska.

(Eastern) Blue Grosbeak

4. See VI A a(1) 2.

(Eastern) Painted Bunting

5. See Nests On or In the Ground I A a(1) 3 and Nests Above the Ground VI A a(1) 3.

Dickcissel

6. See Nests On or In the Ground I A a(5) 11 and Nests Above the Ground VI A a(2) 6.

(Eastern) Lark Sparrow

7. See VI A a(1) 4.

(Eastern) Chipping Sparrow

8. See Nests On or In the Ground I A a(1) 7, II A a(2) 8 and Nests Above the Ground VI A a(2) 7.

Song Sparrow

b(2). *Spherical*

1. Bulky, domed, loosely constructed, with entrance on side when built in the open; of grass and straw; warmly lined with feathers. When built in trees, birdhouses, electric-light hoods, cornices, water-spouts, and similar places about buildings, the nests vary in size, the cavity used being filled with the nesting materials. See also VIII A a(3) 26 and IX A a(5) 4. Cities, towns, villages, and farms.

Throughout eastern and central United States.

House Sparrow

VII

↗↗↗↗↗↗↗↗↗↗↗↗↗↗↗↗

Containing Twigs or Sticks

A. Very Large, 30 to 60 Inches, Outside Diameter

1. A simple, well-built platform of large sticks, firmly interwoven; smoothly lined with small twigs and dry (mangrove) leaves. Usually in low bushes, 5 to 10 feet above the ground but also in tall trees. Nesting in colonies. Dense mangrove growth.

   Extreme southern Florida and the Florida Keys.

   Great White Heron

2. A flat platform of sticks and twigs, ¼ to ½ inch in diameter; smoothly lined with finer twigs and grass; new nests often so frail that the eggs can be seen through them from below but older nests which have been added to each year much thicker and firmer, the accumulated filth helping to cement the materials together. Usually built high in trees and near extremity of branches but sometimes in low trees and bushes. Nesting in colonies. Several nests may be built in the same tree. Wooded swamps.

   Florida Keys and Gulf Coast north throughout eastern and central United States.

   Great Blue Heron

3. Saucer-shaped or flattened, very bulky; of sticks; lined with hemlock or pine twigs, sometimes a little grass or weed stalks, birch or coniferous bark. Often an old nest of some other large hawk is appropriated and repaired. Outside diameter 36 to 48 inches; outside height 35 inches. In the crotch of a small birch or maple not over 30 feet above the ground or on the horizontal branch and against the trunk of a pine, sometimes well out in the fork of a large limb, as high as 55 feet above the ground; preferably in deciduous trees. Mixed woods.

   Northern Michigan, northern New York, and northern New England, and sparingly in mountains to Pennsylvania.

   (Eastern) Goshawk

4. See Nests On or In the Ground VI B 3.

   Golden Eagle

5. Rather flat-topped, with egg cavity 4 to 6 inches deep and 20 inches across; of sticks, sedges, grasses, and rubbish; lined with grass or pine needles; often decorated with white down feathers. May be repaired and used year after year until it becomes overly large in size; from 5 to 8 feet across and 8 feet or more high. Usually in or near top of high trees. Chiefly near oceans, rivers, and lakes.

   Gulf of Mexico north throughout eastern and central United States.

   Bald Eagle

6. Cup-shaped; of twigs, driftwood, and stalks of weeds; often lined with grass or seaweed and a few feathers; sometimes contains such materials as old shoes, bones, pieces of cow dung, and a vast number of other materials. Nests vary greatly in size, those on artificial supports usually very flat, from a few inches to a foot

high; old nests in trees frequently repaired, for the Osprey is accustomed to utilizing the same nesting site year after year and as a result of building on the old nest and repairing it, the nest in time becomes almost as large as that of an eagle. Usually in a treetop, from 10 to 60 feet from the ground, and near water but also on buildings, telephone poles, chimneys, poles near houses, fences, and old stumps. Shores of wilderness lakes, timbered or open islands along coast, valleys of inland streams, open farming country, or in the vicinity of human habitations. See also IX A a(6) 1.

Gulf of Mexico north throughout eastern and central United States.

Osprey

7. A large, bulky platform with only a slight depression, rather loosely made; of twigs, sticks, and branches; lined with small sticks, roots, and grasses, frequently without a lining. In trees and bushes, from 8 to 50 feet above the ground; sometimes in cliffs (Texas). Brushy prairie regions.

Central peninsular Florida and southern Texas.

Audubon's Caracara

8. Cup-shaped; of large sticks and twigs, well interlaced; lined with coarse grass, bark strips, hair, wool, and, in maritime sites, seaweed. Outside diameter, 2 to 4 feet; inside diameter, 1 foot; inside depth, 6 inches. Near top of tall, thick-topped coniferous tree or on shelf of high cliff, usually well sheltered by projecting rock above. Coniferous forests and high cliffs. See also Nests On or In the Ground VI B 6.

Maine, Michigan, Minnesota, and locally in Appalachians to Georgia; occasionally along coast from New Jersey to North Carolina.

Raven

B. Smaller, 15 to 30 Inches, Outside Diameter

b(1). *Saucer-shaped or flattened*

1. Usually a broad, rather flat or saucer-shaped platform; of small sticks; lined chiefly with twigs, sometimes with bark, rarely with grass, moss, or leaves. On horizontal branches against trunk of white pine (preferably) but also in other conifers and rarely in a deciduous tree, from 20 to 90 feet above the ground. Coniferous and mixed woods.

   Northern Florida and Gulf Coast north throughout eastern and central United States.

   Sharp-shinned Hawk

2. A clean substantial structure, generally saucer-shaped; varying in size and shape according to location; rather broad and flat in a white pine but not as broad in a deciduous tree; of sticks and twigs; lined with chips of outer bark of pine or oak. Sometimes old nest is repaired and sometimes a nest is built on an old squirrel's or crow's nest. Nest in pine: outside diameter, 24 to 28 inches; outside height, 7 to 8 inches. Nest in deciduous tree: outside diameter, about 18 inches; outside height, about 30 inches. Either nest: inside diameter, about 7 inches; inside depth, 2 to 4 inches. On horizontal branches and against trunk of a white pine; on upright crotches of deciduous trees. Coniferous, deciduous, and mixed woods.

   Eastern and central United States south to Gulf of Mexico.

   Cooper's Hawk

3. Quite flat and shallow, saucer-shaped, well-made; of large twigs or sticks; lined with strips of inner bark, grasses, weeds, dead leaves, cornhusks, moss, and a

few sprigs of pine, cedar, or hemlock. Outside diameter, 28 to 30 inches; inside diameter, 14 to 15 inches; inside depth, 4 to 5 inches. On a horizontal branch against the trunk or in an upright crotch of a tree, from 15 to 90 feet above the ground; often nearly at top of tall trees, preferably oak or white pine. Built higher than a Red-shouldered Hawk's nest. Edges of dry woodlands, small patches of heavy tall timber, and isolated trees in open country.

Eastern and central United States south to Gulf of Mexico and northern Florida.

Red-tailed Hawk

4. Well-built, substantial, saucer-shaped, rather flat on top, somewhat smaller than a Red-tailed Hawk's nest; of sticks and twigs, well-decorated with bits of white down and mixed with strips of inner bark, dry leaves, and lichens; lined with finer shreds of inner bark, soft mosses, or lichens, and sprigs of pine, cedar, or hemlock; often decorated with leaves of deciduous trees when they become available. Outside diameter, 18 to 24 inches; outside height, 8 to 12 inches; inside diameter, about 8 inches; inside depth, 2 to 3 inches. Usually on branches next to trunk or in crotch of tree. Dry woodlands, dry parts of woods, near swamps or streams, and in small patches of large trees near open fields and meadows in rural areas.

Eastern and central United States south to Florida and Gulf of Mexico and west to Great Plains.

Red-shouldered Hawk

5. Usually small and sometimes crudely built, at other times well-built with handsome, well-hollowed, and lined interior and with an encircling fringe; of twigs, sticks, leaves, and sometimes mosses; lined with chips of outer bark of oak or pine, sometimes with sprigs of

pine and green oak leaves. Outside diameter, from 12
to 21 inches; outside height, from 5 to 12 inches; inside diameter, from 6 to 7 inches; inside depth, from
1 to 3 inches. In the main crotch of a deciduous tree
or on the horizontal branch and near the trunk of a
pine, from 24 to 40 feet above the ground. Dry forests,
wooded hills, and occasionally maple swamps or narrow strips of mixed woods along a stream.

Gulf of Mexico north throughout eastern and central
United States.

Broad-winged Hawk

6. Saucer-shaped; of large sticks, twigs, weeds, and
    grasses; lined with weeds, wool, inner bark, and
    leaves; often decorated with flower clusters of willows
    and other trees, lichens, and down or feathers. Some-
    times old nests are rehabilitated. Outside diameter, 21
    to 23 inches; inside diameter, 8 to 9 inches; inside
    depth, 2 to 5 inches. In the crotch or on the horizontal
    branch of a tree from 7 to 40 feet above the ground;
    sometimes in bushes and hedges or on the rocky ledge
    of a cliff. Usually in a commanding situation and so
    located that the incubating bird can have a good out-
    look. See also Nests On or In the Ground VI B 2.
    Woods, groves, isolated trees in open country, and
    rocky cliffs.

    Plains of Minnesota, Nebraska, Kansas.

Swainson's Hawk

7. Saucer-shaped, rather flat without much of a hollow;
    of cypress twigs and Spanish moss; lined with finer
    cypress sticks and dry magnolia leaves. Outside diam-
    eter, about 24 inches; outside height, about 12 inches.
    In tall trees, frequently cypress, up to 95 feet above
    the ground. Forested swamps.

    Local in southern Florida and the Keys.

Short-tailed Hawk

8. Saucer-shaped; of sticks; lined with grasses, rootlets, pieces of bark, leaves, moss, and feathers; sometimes merely a hollow in the ground and lined with bits of twigs, bark, and feathers. Outside diameter, 15 to 20 inches; outside height, 5 inches; inside diameter, 8 to 9 inches; inside depth, 2 inches. On horizontal branch near top of tall tree, sometimes in a hollow tree, and occasionally on a ledge. See also VIII A a(3) 6 and Nests On or In the Ground VI B 5. Coniferous forests.

Northern fringe of eastern and central United States.

(Eastern) **Pigeon Hawk**

b(2). *Cup-shaped*

1. Of sticks and twigs, thickly covered with Spanish moss; lined with a little moss. Frequently nest is built on foundation of old one. Outside diameter, from 15 to 20 inches; outside height, about 12 inches; inside diameter, 6 inches; inside depth, 4 inches. Generally placed among topmost branches of tall trees (pines and various deciduous trees), from 60 to 150 feet above the ground (occasionally far out on a horizontal limb), and concealed in the thick foliage. Chiefly wooded river swamps.

Florida, South Carolina, and Louisiana.

Swallow-tailed Kite

2. Rarely builds own nest, preferring to use the deserted nest of a Red-tailed or Red-shouldered Hawk or Crow or an old squirrel's nest; of sticks and twigs; lined with twigs, bark, or with down from the mother's breast and containing, as a rule, bones, fur, feathers, and refuse of food; sometimes impregnated with the odor of skunk. Outside diameter, from 18 to 32 inches; outside height, 8 inches; inside diameter, 12 inches;

inside depth, from 2 to 8 inches. On branches of trees. Heavily forested regions and scattered woodlands.

Eastern and central United States south to Florida and Texas.

Great Horned Owl

3. Commonly uses the deserted nest of a bird such as a crow, heron, or hawk; cup-shaped; of sticks, strips of inner bark, pine needles, and twigs; lined with bark and feathers. Outside diameter, 20 to 24 inches; inside diameter, 6 to 12 inches; inside depth, 2 inches. Usually in a conifer, from 20 to 40 feet above the ground. Dense groves of coniferous trees and deciduous timber belts around lakes and along streams.

Eastern and central United States south to Virginia and northern Texas.

Long-eared Owl

b(3). *Like platform*

1. See Nests On or In the Ground IV A 1.

(Eastern) Brown Pelican

2. See Nests On or In the Ground VI A 1.

Double-crested Cormorant

3. A loosely built platform, often quite bulky, irregular in shape; of twigs, coarse sticks, grass, roots, moss, and dead leaves; lined with leaves, moss, and rootlets. Outside diameter, 15 inches or more. In small trees or bushes, but sometimes attached to the upper branches of a high tree, and always over water. Wooded swamps and marshy lakes.

Gulf Coast and Florida north locally to North Carolina, northeastern Tennessee, southern Illinois, and Arkansas.

Water-Turkey

4. A flat, bulky platform of sticks, loosely put together; often little or no attempt at nest lining but sometimes nest is lined with fine twigs, vines, or weed stems. Outside diameter, 15 inches or more. Usually in a tall tree (40 feet above the ground), sometimes in bush or other growth (4 to 10 feet above the ground). Nesting in colonies. Marshes and wooded swamps.

    Gulf Coast and Florida north to Tennessee and New Jersey.

    American Egret

5. A flimsy platform of sticks; lined with finer twigs and rootlets. Outside diameter, 15 inches or more. Usually in low trees or bushes. Nesting in colonies. Wooded swamps and in southern mangrove swamps.

    Along coast from North Carolina to Louisiana and Texas. Recently found nesting on Martha's Vineyard.

    Snowy Egret

6. A platform of sticks and twigs; smoothly lined with finer twigs, rootlets, straw, and grasses; well-built for a heron. Outside diameter, 15 inches or more. In low bushes, 2 to 3 feet above ground or water. Nesting in mixed colonies. Marshy places.

    Gulf Coast of Texas; rare in southern Florida but increasing in the Keys.

    Reddish Egret

7. A frail platform of small sticks; smoothly lined with fine twigs. Outside diameter, 15 inches or more. In small trees and bushes 2 to 12 feet above the ground; often several nests in the same tree. Nesting in colonies or in mixed colonies of other herons. Mangrove and willow swamps.

    Coastal North Carolina to Texas.

    Louisiana Heron

8. A frail, loose platform of sticks and twigs, slightly hollowed; lined with finer twigs. Outside diameter, 15 inches or more. Usually over water and 3 to 10 feet high in bushes or small trees. Nesting in colonies or in company with other herons. Edges of ponds or wet wooded areas.

    Gulf Coast and Florida north to New Jersey and Massachusetts (casually).

    Little Blue Heron

9. Varies greatly in size and construction; from a small, crudely built platform of sticks, lined with twigs, to a large, well-built structure of sticks, lined with twigs, roots, grass, and pine needles. Outside diameter, 15 inches or more. In bushes and trees from a few feet above the ground to 30 or more feet high; usually built toward the tips of branches. Nesting in colonies. Wooded swamps but sometimes dry hillside thickets.

    Florida and Gulf of Mexico north throughout eastern and central United States.

    Black-crowned Night Heron

10. A substantially built platform of good-sized sticks; perhaps well-hollowed; lined with twigs, fibrous roots, or weeds. Outside diameter, 18 to 20 inches. In bushes and trees from 2 to 25 feet or more above water. Nesting in colonies, often nesting with other species. Chiefly wooded swamps.

    Gulf of Mexico north to Missouri, Tennessee, Maryland, New Jersey, and casually Long Island and Massachusetts.

    Yellow-crowned Night Heron

11. A platform of sticks, slightly depressed; lined with moss and leaves. The same sites are occupied each year and the nests become very bulky from the addition of material each season. Outside diameter, 15

inches or more. In trees (cypress), sometimes very high, as much as 100 feet above the ground. Nesting in colonies. Wooded swamp regions.

Chiefly near coast, from South Carolina to Texas.

Wood Ibis

12. See I B 1.

White Ibis

13. A platform of sticks; lined with strips of inner bark, water moss, finer twigs, or dead leaves of mangrove. Inside diameter, about 7 inches; inside depth, about 2 inches. Usually in cypress trees or mangrove bushes, 8 to 20 feet above the mud or water. Dense tropical marshes.

Locally in southern Florida, on Texas coast, and locally in Louisiana.

Roseate Spoonbill

14. Quite variable in structure but usually platform-shaped and very hollow; loosely put together; of sticks, leaves, seaweed, and grasses; sometimes lined with sea shells and coral. Frequently nests remaining from year to year are used, some old nests being of enormous size due to the addition of new materials at each successive season. Outside diameter, 15 inches or more. In low bushes, at varying heights up to 12 feet. Nesting in colonies. Ocean Islands.

Dry Tortugas, Florida.

Noddy

C. Small, Under 15 Inches, Outside Diameter

c(1). *Usually in evergreens*

1. Bulky, high-walled, neatly built structure; of twigs, bark strips, grasses; with warm, soft lining of lichens

or mosses and feathers or down, the whole being fastened together with small bunches of spiders' webs
and cocoons. Outside diameter, 7 to 8 inches; outside
height, 3 to 5 inches; inside diameter, 3 to 3½ inches;
inside depth, 2 to 2½ inches. Usually placed on horizontal branches against the trunk or in an upright
crotch of an evergreen, from 6 to 8 feet above the
ground. Dense coniferous forests.

Northern fringe of eastern and central United States.

Canada Jay

2. Cup-shaped, rather bulky, compactly built but usually
with a ragged rim; of sticks, twigs, bark, moss, lichens,
paper, rags, string, wool, leaves, dry grasses, in fact
anything that may capture the bird's fancy; usually
lined exclusively with fine rootlets but also with bark
strips. Outside diameter, 7 to 8 inches; outside height,
4 to 4½ inches; inside diameter, 3½ to 4 inches; inside depth, 2½ inches. In a crotch or close to the main
trunk or on the extremity of a horizontal limb among
the outer branches of (usually) an evergreen but also
in deciduous trees or bushes, from 5 to 50 feet (but
generally below 20 feet) above the ground. Mixed
woods and dense coniferous thickets.

Eastern and central United States south to Florida and
Gulf of Mexico.

Blue Jay

3. Substantial, well-built, cup-shaped, crude in external
appearance; of sticks and twigs; warmly lined with
strips of bark, grasses, moss, and fine roots. Sometimes
the interior has a warm yellowish color. Occasionally
the nest will contain such materials as seaweed, corn-
stalks, pieces of rope and twine, feathers, dried cow
dung, and horse manure. Outside diameter, 12 inches;
outside height, 9 inches; inside diameter, 7 inches;

inside depth, 4½ inches. Usually in a conifer and close to the trunk but also in other trees, averaging 30 feet above the ground. Woodlands and coniferous forests.

Eastern and central United States south to Florida and Texas.

Crow

4. A platform of sticks with sides of bark, twigs, and grasses; lined with grapevine or other bark, grass, and a few leaves, usually with some pine needles. Outside diameter, 14 inches; inside diameter, 7 inches; inside depth, 5½ inches. Commonly in pine or other conifer (usually in a crotch), from 15 to 50 feet above the ground and sometimes higher, frequently near top. Coastal regions or near some body of water.

Southern New England south to Florida and along coast to eastern Texas; also in Florida and in river valleys such as the Hudson and Delaware.

Fish Crow

5. Rather flat; of twigs, rootlets, and moss, with a well-woven inner nest of twigs, grass, bark strips, and fine rootlets. On lower branch of a conifer or in a shrub, from 6 to 30 feet above the ground. Spruce forests and mountains.

Northern New England.

(Canadian) Pine Grosbeak

6. A shallow cup, loosely constructed; of evergreen twigs, shreds of bark, and rootlets; lined with moss, leaves, grass, hair, or fur, well-felted together, and generally some bits of hemlock or cedar tips. Usually rather low (within 20 feet above the ground) in thick foliage of a conifer but sometimes quite high and in a bare deciduous tree, from 5 to 80 feet above the ground. Outside diameter, 5¼ to 5½ inches; outside height,

3 to 3½ inches; inside diameter, 2 to 2½ inches; inside depth, 1 to 1½ inches. Forests and mountain tops.

Locally in Appalachians from New England to Tennessee.

Red Crossbill

7. Saucer-shaped; of twigs and strips of birch bark; covered exteriorly with Usnea; lined with soft moss and hair. In fork of an evergreen tree, height above ground variable but frequently quite low. Outside diameter, 4 inches; outside height, 2½ inches; inside diameter, 1¾ to 2 inches; inside depth, 1½ inches. Coniferous forests.

Northern edge of eastern and central United States.

White-winged Crossbill

c(2). *In chimney, inside barn wall or similar structure, and at times in a primitive site—a hollow tree*

1. A semicircular basket or hammock of twigs, glued together and to the chimney or similar structure with the glutinous saliva of the Swift. Usually in chimneys about 10 feet from the top but also in vacant buildings. See also IX B b(2) 1. Towns and villages and about human habitations.

Eastern and central United States south to Gulf of Mexico.

Chimney Swift

c(3). *Inside the loose bark of trees*

1. A loosely hung hammock shaped like a new moon with the horns built high at the sides of the nest, the latter seemingly suspended between them; of slim twigs, bark strips, moss, and dead wood; lined sometimes with a few spiders' cocoons, feathers, and hair. Outside diameter, 3½ inches; outside height, 6 inches; inside diameter, 1 to 2½ inches; inside depth, 1½ inches. Behind or inside the loose bark of trees, from 5 to

15 feet above the ground; occasionally found in a knot-hole or a deserted cavity of a woodpecker. See also VIII A a(3) 16. Woodlands and wooded swamps.

Canadian border south to eastern Nebraska, northern Indiana, New York, Massachusetts, and, in mountains, to North Carolina.

Brown Creeper

c(4). *In trees or bushes, vines or tangles*

1. Compact, well-built; of sticks; lined with leaves or Spanish moss. Sometimes old nest of some other species is used and remodeled. Outside diameter, about 10 inches; outside height, about 8 inches. Usually in a crotch or fork and occasionally on a horizontal branch of a tree but sometimes in bushes, vines or tangles, from 12 to 120 feet above the ground. Woodlands and neglected pastures.

Gulf States north to Kansas, southern Missouri, and southwestern Tennessee; also east to northeastern Florida and South Carolina.

Mississippi Kite

2. A rather flat, carelessly put together structure of sticks and twigs, grasses, and old leaves; lined with a few dried heads of saw grass. Outside diameter, about 12 inches; inside depth, 3 inches. In a bush from 4 to 7 feet above the ground. Freshwater marshes.

Locally in Florida.

Everglade Kite

3. A crude platform of sticks; sometimes scantily lined with grasses; on the whole a bulky structure for a pigeon. Outside diameter, less than 15 inches. In low bushes and trees. Nesting in colonies. Mangrove swamps.

Southern tip of Florida and Florida Keys.

White-crowned Pigeon

4. A hollowed platform, frail, and so loosely constructed that the eggs appear to be in danger of falling through the interstices; of sticks and small twigs with a few straws and weed stalks and sometimes leaves and a little moss. Outside diameter, about 6 inches; outside height, 2 inches; inside diameter, 4 inches; inside depth, 1 inch. In trees or bushes, vines or tangles, but often in the lower branches of a pine. Open country.

    Eastern and central United States (except northern Maine) south to Gulf Coast.

    Mourning Dove

5. A frail, shallow structure; of twigs, sometimes with the addition of pine needles and frequently with an interior of grasses. Outside diameter, 2½ to 3 inches. Usually in vines, bushes, and small trees from 1 to 10 feet above the ground but sometimes on the ground in weed patches or tall grass. See also Nests On or In the Ground I A a(2) 1. Near ocean beaches and sea islands in Georgia and South Carolina.

    Coastal plain and low country from South Carolina to Texas. Occasional in North Carolina.

    (Eastern) Ground Dove

6. A loosely made structure of a few dry sticks. In low branches of trees and in bushes. Mangrove swamps.

    Southwestern coast of Florida and Keys.

    Mangrove Cuckoo

7. A shallow platform or saucer-shaped structure, rather ragged; of small twigs rarely over 4 or 5 inches long, rootlets, leaves, mosses, and bark strips; lined with catkins, dry blossoms of horse chestnut and other flowering plants, tufts of grass, pine needles, and mosses. Outside diameter, about 6 inches; outside height, 4

inches. Usually on a horizontal limb of tree or in thick bushes overrun with vines, from 2 to 8 feet above the ground, rarely 20 feet; generally well concealed by overhanging and surrounding foliage. Woodland thickets, shady roadsides, dense thickets along small streams, and orchards.

Eastern and central United States south to Florida Keys and Gulf of Mexico.

Yellow-billed Cuckoo

8. A platform or saucer-shaped affair similar to that of the Yellow-billed Cuckoo, sometimes flimsy but usually more firmly constructed; of sticks, grass, fern stalks, and twigs; lined with catkins, dried leaves, fine rootlets, and similar materials. Outside diameter, about 8 inches; inside diameter, about 3 inches; inside depth, 1 inch. Usually at low elevations from 2 to 4 feet above the ground but sometimes as high as 15 feet, in various small trees or bushes; generally on horizontal branches against the trunks of trees; fairly well concealed. Woodlands, brushy thickets along a brook, wooded hillsides, and neglected pastures.

Eastern and central United States south to Arkansas and North Carolina and, in mountains, to Georgia.

Black-billed Cuckoo

9. A frail, loosely built structure; of twigs; lined with small plant stems, grass, and moss. In tree or bush, usually in low mangroves or live oaks, from 3 to 12 feet above the ground or, in some instances, above water; occasionally high in trees. Mangrove swamps or in or near woodlands.

Locally along east and west coasts of Florida and rarely to South Carolina. Most common in Florida Keys.

Gray Kingbird

10.   A substantial, thick-walled, cup-shaped structure; of
       small dry sticks, leaves, and plant stems; lined with
       moss, fibrous plant stems, and often with wool and
       feathers. In scrub oak, from 4 to 12 feet above the
       ground. Low scrub regions.

       Florida Peninsula.

                                                    Florida Jay

11.   Cup-shaped, bulky; of twigs, leaves, moss, bark strips,
       weeds, grass, rags, cotton string, rootlets, feathers,
       hair, down, and tree blossoms; lined with fine rootlets,
       horsehair, dried grass. On branch, in fork among twigs
       of trees, shrubs, vines, or dense tangles, from 3 to 20
       feet above the ground. Occasionally in a hollow stump
       or cavity of decayed tree trunk. See also VIII A a(3)
       21. Open woodland edges, pastures, wood lots, and in
       the vicinity of human habitations.

       Massachusetts, Ohio, Illinois, southern Iowa, Nebraska
       south to Gulf of Mexico.

                                        (Eastern) Mockingbird

12.   Usually deeply cup-shaped, rather rough, straggly, and
       bulky outwardly, loosely built; of coarse sticks, twigs,
       grasses, leaves, weed stems, bark strips, and paper;
       neatly lined with skeleton leaves, pine needles, fine
       shreds of pine, and dark fibrous rootlets, sometimes
       with horsehair, cotton, tow, string, and rags. Outside
       diameter, 6 inches; outside height, 3 inches; inside di-
       ameter, 3 inches; inside depth, 1½ inches. In bushes,
       low trees or tangles of vines from 2 to 10 feet above
       the ground; well concealed. Dense thickets, roadsides,
       woodland borders, orchards, vegetation bordering
       marshes and streams, and in the vicinity of human
       habitations.

       Eastern and central United States south to northern
       Florida, Louisiana, and southeastern Texas.

                                                      Catbird

13. Cup-shaped, bulky, loosely built; of sticks, twigs, leaves, bark strips, and weed stalks; lined with rootlets. Outside diameter, 6 inches or more; outside height, 3¾ inches; inside diameter, 3¾ inches; inside depth, 1 inch. In brush pile, bush, vine tangles, brier patches, or low tree, from 2 to 15 feet above the ground. Thickets, bushy pastures, sproutlands, brushy hillsides, and edges of woodlands.

   Eastern and central United States south to central Florida and Gulf of Mexico.

   (Eastern) **Brown Thrasher**

c(5). *In bushes and small trees over water*

1. A simple, frail platform of sticks, so loosely put together and so thin that not only may the eggs be seen from below but they appear in danger of being dislodged when the tree branches wave in the wind; unlined. Outside diameter, 10 to 12 inches. Usually over water and 3 to 10 feet high in bushes or small trees, but occasionally in the tops of tall trees and sometimes some distance from water. Unlike nests of many other herons it is commonly built alone rather than in a colony. Wet woodlands and wooded areas along a pond or stream; occasionally dry woods and orchards.

   Gulf of Mexico north throughout eastern and central United States.

   (Eastern) **Green Heron**

VIII

✓✓✓✓✓✓✓✓✓✓✓✓✓✓✓

In Holes in Trees or Stumps, in Birdhouses or Similar Places

A. Nesting Singly

a(1). *Drilling nesting cavity but building no nest in bottom; using chips of wood only*

1. Opening with diameter of from 2 to 4 inches; depth of cavity, from 10 to 36 inches; diameter of cavity near bottom, from 4½ to 10 inches. In various trees, dead or alive, telephone poles, and fence posts, from 2 to 100 feet above the ground. Often uses natural cavities and sometimes strange places—such as barns and icehouses—drilling through wall to haymow or insulating material. Frequently uses birdhouses. Open country, lightly wooded regions, deciduous woodlands, and orchards. See also IX A a(5) 1.

    Eastern and central United States south to Florida and Gulf of Mexico.

    Flicker

2. Opening, though sometimes quite circular, tends to be triangular in outline, broader at base, angular at top, about 3½ inches across; depth of cavity, from 10 to 26 inches; diameter of cavity at top, 7 to 8 inches;

diameter of cavity at bottom, 6 inches or more. Cavity ordinarily conical in form, tapering slightly from a low, domed roof downward to a bowl-like bottom. Usually in dead, sound, but sometimes live deciduous trees, from 15 to 85 feet above the ground. Deep woods or edges of heavy woodland.

Eastern and central United States south to Florida and Gulf of Mexico.

Pileated Woodpecker

3. Opening with diameter of about 1¾ inches; depth of cavity, about 12 inches. Usually in softer deciduous trees but also in pines and stumps, from 5 to 70 feet above the ground. Deciduous or mixed forests to coniferous in northern parts of range; flat, low pine woods, groves, heavily timbered bottom lands, and swampy woods in southern parts of range.

Florida and Gulf of Mexico north to Delaware, Lake Erie, southeastern Minnesota, and southeastern South Dakota.

Red-bellied Woodpecker

4. Opening slightly elliptical, about 1¾ inches by 2 inches; depth of cavity 8 to 24 inches, about 3½ by 2 inches across at bottom; cavity gourd-shaped. In telephone poles, dead trees, stubs, or stumps, from 5 to 80 feet above the ground. Open country, open groves, slashings, old barns, and tracts of half-dead forest with scattered live trees and abundant dead stubs.

Gulf of Mexico north to southern New England, western New York, southern Michigan, and Minnesota.

Red-headed Woodpecker

5. Opening about 1½ inches in diameter, circular; depth of cavity, about 14 inches; diameter of cavity at bottom, 5 inches; cavity gourd-shaped. In large dead trees, usually birches, from 8 to 40 feet above the

ground and often near water. Wooded areas along the banks of rivers and lakes, occasionally the interior of woodlands.

Eastern and central United States south to western Massachusetts, northern Ohio, Indiana, Missouri, and, in mountains, to North Carolina.

Yellow-bellied Sapsucker

6. Opening slightly elliptical, 1⅞ inches high and 1½ inches wide; depth of cavity 10 to 12 inches or more; cavity gourd-shaped; diameter of cavity at bottom, 4½ inches. Usually in living trees in dry upland deciduous woodlands, from 5 to 60 feet or more above the ground, though sometimes in maple swamps and apple orchards.

    Gulf of Mexico north throughout eastern and central United States.

    Hairy Woodpecker

7. Opening about 1¼ inches in diameter, circular; depth of cavity, 8 to 12 inches; cavity gourd-shaped. Generally in dead or dying trees from 8 feet (rarely less) to 50 feet (rarely more) above the ground. Open woodlands and orchards.

    Gulf of Mexico north throughout eastern and central United States.

    Downy Woodpecker

8. Cavity gourd-shaped with generally a glazed patch of gum around opening; depth of cavity 8 to 12 inches. Usually in a living pine but sometimes in a deciduous tree, from 25 to 80 feet above the ground. Pine woodlands.

    Gulf States north to southeastern Virginia, western Kentucky, and southern Missouri.

    Red-cockaded Woodpecker

9. Opening 1⅝ inches to 1¾ inches in diameter, opening beveled on lower edge; depth of cavity, 9 to 18 inches; cavity gourd-shaped. In a living or dead (usually) conifer, from 2 to 27 feet above the ground but usually at no great height. Open woodlands and burned-over clearings of coniferous forests.

Occasionally in northern parts of eastern and central United States.

Arctic Three-toed Woodpecker

10. Opening about 1½ inches in diameter, opening beveled on lower edge; depth of cavity 10 to 12 inches; cavity gourd-shaped. In a spruce, larch, balsam, or cedar tree, and usually in tree killed by insects, fire, or water, from 5 to 40 feet above the ground. Coniferous woodlands.

Occasionally in northern parts of eastern and central United States.

American Three-toed Woodpecker

a(2). *Using hole excavated by woodpecker, natural cavity, or birdbox; adding little or no nesting material, placing eggs on chips left by woodpecker or litter left by some previous occupant, such as a mouse or squirrel*

1. Woodlands and open country.

Florida and Gulf of Mexico north throughout eastern and central United States.

Sparrow Hawk

2. Open country, towns, and villages. Also frequently makes use of old buildings or church steeples, where it scrapes a nest in rubbish on a shelf. See also IX A a(2) 1.

Massachusetts (occasional), Ohio, southern Wisconsin, and Nebraska south to Florida and Gulf of Mexico.

Barn Owl

3. Orchards, woodland borders, mixed woods, and in the vicinity of human habitations.

   Eastern and central United States south to Florida and Texas.

   Screech Owl

4. Deep, dark woods, heavily wooded swamps, hemlock forests, or thick growths of tall dense pines. In southern part of range marshes, sloughs, streams, and ponds. If a natural cavity or other suitable site is not available, an old nest of a hawk or squirrel is used. If a hawk's nest is used it may be relined with Usnea or fresh, green sprays of white pine, and occasionally the rim is built up somewhat with fresh sticks; if that of a squirrel is appropriated the owl removes the top structure and hollows out the center so that little more than the shell remains. In southern part of range (Florida) low hummocks of cabbage palmetto and live oaks are used as nesting sites.

   Eastern and central United States south to Florida and Texas.

   Barred Owl

5. Deep woods and wooded swamps.

   Eastern and central United States south to northern Indiana, northern Illinois, and mountains of Pennsylvania, Maryland, and West Virginia.

   Saw-whet Owl

a(3). *Using woodpecker hole, natural cavity (or sometimes excavating cavity), or birdbox and building nest at bottom of cavity*

1. Nest of down from breast of females on punky wood of hole or cavity, sometimes on leaves and other soft rubbish which squirrel may previously have carried into cavity. Down grayish-white or pale mouse-gray with nearly pure white centers. From 3 or 4 feet to

40 or 50 feet above the ground. Wooded swamps, river timber, apple orchards, and shade trees about farm buildings.

Gulf of Mexico north throughout eastern and central United States.

Wood Duck

2. Nest of rotten chips and white down, or of grass, leaves, and moss and lined with white down; down light-gray, each feather with a paler center. From 6 to 8 feet to 50 or 60 feet above the ground, usually over or near water. Nest may be on a level with and scarcely back from hole or at the bottom of hollow, 6, 10, 15, or more feet below entrance, which may vary from 15 inches to a diameter so small as scarcely to admit bird. Forested country, generally about lakes or rivers.

Along northern edge of eastern and central United States.

American Goldeneye

3. Nest of grasses and weeds, occasionally some moss; lined with down from breast of female. In almost any kind of hole or hollow tree provided hole is large enough to admit the bird and of the proper shape to hold the eggs; sometimes placed in open hollowed top of a stump or fallen log; often high above ground or water. Forests near water, woodland pools, and wooded swamps.

Eastern and central United States south locally or rarely to southern states.

Hooded Merganser

4. Nest of grasses, twigs, leaves, and lichens; lined with grayish-white down. Inside diameter, 7 to 8 inches; inside depth, 4 inches. Usually in hollow tree or in top of broken stub, but sometimes on the ground in dense tangles of bushes and beneath piles of rocks; usually

near water. See also Nests On or In the Ground II A a(1) 1. Woodlands and along rivers.

Along northern edge of eastern and central United States.

American Merganser

5. See Nests On or In the Ground II A a(5) 1 and VI B 1.

Turkey Vulture

6. See VII B b(1) 8 and Nests On or In the Ground VI B 5.

(Eastern) Pigeon Hawk

7. Bulky, filling bottom of cavity; of grass, leaves, small twigs, rootlets, bark, hair, and pine needles; lined with finer materials. Often contains cast snakeskins, strips of cellophane, or onion skins, feathers, fur, seedpods, cloth, paper, paraffined or oiled paper, bits of egg-shells, and pieces of horse manure. Inside diameter, 2¾ to 3½ inches; inside depth, 1½ to 2 inches. Preferably in a natural cavity but also in abandoned holes of larger woodpeckers, from 3 feet in low stumps up to 70 feet above the ground in large trees, but usually below 15 to 20 feet; also in hollow logs attached to buildings, hollow posts, gutter pipes, old tin cans, in almost any cavity of suitable size and location. Open country, old orchards, edges of clearings, woodland glades, and in the vicinity of human habitations.

Eastern and central United States south to Florida and Gulf Coast.

Crested Flycatcher

8. Cup-shaped; of grasses and straw; profusely lined with (preferably) white feathers, and sometimes pine needles. Outside diameter, 5¼ inches; outside height,

2¾ inches; inside diameter, 2½ inches; inside depth, 1½ inches. In a hole in a tree and in birdhouses. Open wooded swamps, old apple orchards, farmlands, and in the vicinity of human habitations.

Eastern and central United States south to Virginia, northeastern Arkansas, and Kansas.

Tree Swallow

9. Cup-shaped; of cottony plant fibers, hairs, wool, moss, and leaves; lined with hair, plant down, wool, or feathers. Outside diameter, about 4 inches; outside height, 2 inches; inside diameter, 1½ inches; inside depth, 1 inch. In a natural cavity of an apple or other deciduous tree but frequently in a hole excavated by the birds themselves in a decaying stump or stub of a gray or white birch, from 4 to 8 feet above the ground. Orchards and woodlands.

Eastern and central United States south to Kansas, Missouri, Illinois, Ohio, Pennsylvania, northern New Jersey, and, in mountains, to North Carolina.

Black-capped Chickadee

10. Cup-shaped; of dry grasses, shreds of fibrous bark; with a warm lining of feathers, cattle hair, and fur of small animals.* In a natural cavity or woodpecker hole or in a hole excavated by the birds themselves, preferably in a fence post or a decayed stub of a small sapling, about 5 or 6 feet above the ground. Wooded areas.

New Jersey, Ohio, Missouri, and Oklahoma south to Florida and Gulf of Mexico.

Carolina Chickadee

11. Of dry or green mosses, bits of lichens, fine strips of the inner bark of cedars, and fern down; lined with feathers and fur.* In a natural cavity in a stump or

* Measurements of nest similar to those of Black-capped Chickadee.

stub usually of spruce or in one excavated by the birds themselves, from 1 to 10 feet above the ground. Spruce forests.

Mountains of northern edge of eastern and central United States.

Brown-capped Chickadee

12. Of moss, leaves, grass, bark, hair, feathers, and cast snakeskins; lined with hair or fur of whatever kind is available. In an abandoned woodpecker or squirrel hole or knothole, usually in a tree but also in a stub or fence post, from 3 to 90 feet above the ground, usually rather low. Woods, orchards, groves, rural areas, towns and villages.

Florida and Gulf of Mexico north to northern New Jersey, Lake Erie, Illinois, Iowa, and Nebraska.

Tufted Titmouse

13. Substantial matted bed of soft shreds of inner bark and fur (usually rabbit), sometimes with small twigs, grasses, rootlets, leaves, hair, and feathers. In a natural cavity, woodpecker hole, or knothole, usually high in a tall tree, from 15 to 50 feet above the ground. Woodlands and orchards. May excavate hole in decaying stump or stub, as chickadee.

Eastern and central United States south to central Florida and Gulf Coast.

White-breasted Nuthatch

14. Of fine short grasses, roots, bark shreds; and lined with feathers; but sometimes of no material except the chips of the excavation. In a natural cavity or old woodpecker hole, or in a cavity excavated by the birds in a rotten stub or branch of a dead tree, with an entrance 1 inch in diameter, but usually in a conifer, in which case pitch is generally smeared on the bark

about the entrance hole. Forested (coniferous) regions.

Northern Minnesota, Michigan, northern New England, and, in Appalachians, to North Carolina.

Red-breasted Nuthatch

15.   Of small bits of grass, weed stems, strips of inner bark, chips of wood, wool, pine needles, and feathers. In a cavity in a tree or stump, usually partially or wholly excavated by the birds, preferably in pine or pine stubs, often fire-blackened but also in deciduous trees, either dead or living, from 2 to 50 feet above the ground but usually at less than 10 feet. Depth of cavity, from 8 to 12 inches. Pine woods, clearings, and burnt-over areas in mixed forests, and in the southern part of range small cypress swamps in such forests.

Florida and Gulf of Mexico north to coastal Delaware and southern Missouri.

Brown-headed Nuthatch

16.   See VII C c(3) 1.

Brown Creeper

17.   Bulky; of coarse sticks and twigs, grass, feathers, wool, leaves, weed stalks, rootlets, and bark; lined with grass, hair, feathers, rootlets, strips of bark, spiders' egg cases, and catkins; generally filling hole selected as nesting site. Outside diameter, 4½ inches; outside height, 2 inches; inside diameter, 2 inches; inside depth, 1½ inches. In a tree or stump, birdhouse, or any one of innumerable places which have been recorded, such as old tin cans, watering pots, paper nests of hornets and wasps, teapots, flowerpots, old boots and shoes, hats, pockets of scarecrows, weathervanes, pipe railings, holes in a brick wall, and even in the rear axle of an automobile used daily, the wren accompany-

ing the automobile wherever it is driven. Woodland borders, towns, and villages, and in the vicinity of human habitations. See also IX A a(3) 2 and IX A a(5) 3.

Eastern and central United States south to Virginia, Kentucky, southern Missouri, and central western Texas.

House Wren

18. See Nests On or In the Ground II B b(1) 1.

Winter Wren

19. Generally bulky but size determined by that of cavity in which it is built; of sticks, straw, twigs, leaves, coarse feathers, chips, rootlets, moss, cotton, hair, wool matted together with spiders' webs; warmly lined with soft materials such as fur, hair, and feathers. Outside diameter, 5 inches; outside height, 2 inches; inside diameter, 2 to 3 inches; inside depth, 1½ to 1¾ inches. In any suitable cavity such as a knothole, woodpecker hole, tin can, empty barrel, basket, watering pot, birdhouse, dense brush heap, crevice in stone or brick wall, and natural cavity in trees, stumps, and fence posts. Open woodlands, upland thickets and hills, orchards, rural areas, and the vicinity of human habitations.

Mississippi Valley and southern Appalachian Plateau from central Pennsylvania, southern Michigan, northern Illinois, and southern Nebraska south to central Georgia, Alabama, Mississippi, and Arkansas.

Bewick's Wren

20. See Nests On or In the Ground II A a(1) 5, II B b(1) 2 and Nests Above the Ground IX A a(2) 2.

Carolina Wren

21. See VII C c(4) 11.

Mockingbird

22. See Nests On or In the Ground II A a(1) 6 and Nests Above the Ground VI A a(2) 4.

Veery

23. Poorly and loosely built; often entirely of dried grasses and weed stems carelessly arranged but may contain a few fine twigs; lined with finer grasses, a little hair or feathers. In a natural cavity, a woodpecker's hole, in open hollows in trees, in the rotten tops of posts and stumps, and in birdhouses. Open country, apple orchards, country roadsides, open groves, in burnt-over or cutover woodlands, and the vicinity of human habitations.

     Eastern and central United States south to Florida and Gulf of Mexico.

Eastern Bluebird

24. Rather bulky and loosely made, cavity generally loosely filled with material to fill space up to within a few inches of the opening; of coarse and fine grasses and straws, rootlets, small twigs, cornhusks, leaves, and occasionally bits of cloth, paper, string, or other trash; lined with finer pieces of grass or sparingly with poultry feathers; nest slovenly and often filthy with large amounts of excrement; size of nest determined by size of cavity but the inner cup usually about 3 inches in diameter. In any hole or cavity, but preferably in a natural cavity or hole of large woodpecker, in trees from 2 to 60 feet above the ground; also in holes in telephone poles, fence posts, and in bird-houses. Rural and farming districts, cities, and towns.

     Eastern and central United States south to Gulf of Mexico.

Starling

25. Often entirely of moss but sometimes with grass, lichens, bark strips, rootlets, bits of decaying wood,

and other plant substances; carefully lined with moss, fine rootlets, rarely with hair and feathers; amount of material varies with size of cavity; cup for eggs neatly rounded. Inside diameter, 2 inches; inside depth, 1½ inches. In a natural cavity or woodpecker hole in a tree or stump, from 3 to 30 feet above the ground, generally between 5 and 10 feet. Also in birdhouses, coffee cans, tin pails, and similar locations. Woody swamp-lands and river swamps, and vicinity of human habitations.

Southeastern Minnesota, southern Michigan, western New York (local), and southern New Jersey (rarely) south to central Florida and Gulf Coast.

Prothonotary Warbler

26. See VI B b(2) 1 and IX A a(5) 4.

House Sparrow

27. See IV A a(2) 2.

Purple Grackle

B. Nesting in Colonies, Usually in Martin-houses

1. Of leaves, twigs, straw, feathers, bits of string, rags and paper, sometimes with a little mud as foundation. Open country, wide river valleys, and the vicinity of human habitations.

Gulf of Mexico north throughout eastern and central United States.

Purple Martin

IX

✓✓✓✓✓✓✓✓✓✓✓✓✓✓✓

In or On Buildings

A. Outside

a(1). *On flat roofs*

   1.   See Nests On or In the Ground I A a(6) 1 and IV B 8.

Nighthawk

a(2). *On shelf or projection*

   1.   See VIII A a(2) 2.

Barn Owl

   2.   See Nests On or In the Ground II A a(1) 5, II B b(1) 2, and Nests Above the Ground VIII A a(3) 20.

Carolina Wren

   3.   See IV A a(1) 1 and IV B b(3) 1.

Robin

a(3). *Beneath eaves*

   1.   See IV B b(1) 2.

(Northern) Cliff Swallow

   2.   See VIII A a(3) 17 and IX A a(5) 4.

House Wren

138

a(4). *On wall*
1. See IV B b(2) 1.

Eastern Phoebe

a(5). *In a corner or cornice*
1. See VIII A a(1) 1.

Flicker

2. See V B b(2) 2.

Arkansas Kingbird

3. See VIII A a(3) 17 and IX A a(3) 2.

House Wren

4. See VI B b(2) 1 and VIII A a(3) 26.

House Sparrow

a(6). *On chimney*
1. See VII A 6.

Osprey

a(7). *In the side*
1. See Nests On or In the Ground V B 3.

Rough-winged Swallow

B. Inside

b(1). *On a rafter*
1. See IV B b(1) 1.

Barn Swallow

b(2). *In a chimney*
1. See VII C c(2) 1.

Chimney Swift

PART TWO

✓✓✓✓✓✓✓✓✓✓✓✓✓✓✓

NESTS OF BIRDS
WEST OF THE
ONE-HUNDREDTH
MERIDIAN

✓✓✓✓✓✓✓✓✓✓✓✓✓✓✓

Nests On or In the Ground

I

↗↗↗↗↗↗↗↗↗↗↗↗↗↗↗

In Fields, Pastures, or Prairies

A. Open Nest

a(1). *In or under a tussock of grass*

1. See III A a(2) 3.

   Mallard

2. See I A a(2) 3, also I A a(3) 3 and I A a(5) 20.

   Bobolink

3. For description of nest see Part One, page 9. See also Nests Above the Ground VI A a(1) 6 and VI B b(1) 12.

   Eastern Wyoming and eastern Colorado.

   Dickcissel

4. For description of nest see Part One, page 10. See also I A a(5) 21. Prairie country.

   Montana, Wyoming, Colorado, eastern New Mexico, and northwestern Texas, chiefly on Great Plains but also sparingly west of Continental Divide.

   Lark Bunting

5. For description of nest see Part One, page 10. See also I B b(3) 2.

Eastern Washington and Montana south to southern California (west of Sierras), Colorado, and southern Texas.

(Western) Grasshopper Sparrow

6. Of small twigs, grasses, and rootlets; lined with fine grass, bark strips, and hair. Outside diameter, 6 to 9 inches; outside height, 6 inches; inside diameter, 2½ inches; inside depth, 2 inches. Commonly placed on the ground but sometimes in low bushes. See also Nests Above the Ground VI A a(2) 6. Dry high mountain meadows or clearings.

Western United States from Canadian border south in Rocky Mountains to northern New Mexico and in Sierras to central California.

White-crowned Sparrow
(Gambel's Sparrow)
(Puget Sound Sparrow)
(Nuttall's Sparrow)

7. For description of nest see Part One, page 11. See also II A a(2) 5, and Nests Above the Ground VI A a(2) 8 and VI B b(1) 17.

Western United States south to southern California, southwestern Arizona, and northern New Mexico.

Song Sparrow

a(2). *In tall grasses*

1. Compactly woven; of grass; lined with feathers and down; usually near water. Sometimes a deep depression in the ground lined sparsely with bits of grass and copiously with down; at other times an inch or two above water and firmly fastened to marsh grass of which it is made. See also I A a(5) 3 and III A a(2) 4. Inside diameter, about 5 inches; inside depth, about 5 inches. Pastures and grainfields.

Washington and Montana south to northern California, Nevada, Utah, and New Mexico.

Cinnamon Teal

2. See Nests Above the Ground VII C c(4) 6.

Mexican Ground Dove

3. For description of nest see Part One, page 11. See also I A a(1) 2, I A a(3) 3, and I A a(5) 20.

Eastern United States and diagonally northwest through Colorado, Wyoming, Montana, and northern Utah to northwestern Nevada, northeastern California, eastern Oregon, and eastern Washington.

Bobolink

4. For description of nest see Part One, page 11. Open country.

Canadian border south to central California, Nevada, Colorado, and northern New Mexico.

Savannah Sparrow
(Bryant's Sparrow)

5. A slight affair; of grasses and weed stalks; about 4 inches in outside diameter. Inside diameter, 2½ inches; inside depth, 1½ inches. Dry upland prairies.

Canadian border south to central Montana (rarely).

Baird's Sparrow

6. Of dried grasses; lined with hair and feathers.

Great Plains west to eastern Montana, eastern Wyoming, and northeastern Colorado.

McCown's Longspur

7. For description of nest see Part One, page 12.

Great Plains west to Montana and eastern Wyoming.

Chestnut-collared Longspur

a(3). *Under a thistle, small bush, or weed stalk*

1. See II A a(4) 2.

    Stephens's Whip-poor-will

2. Of grass, leaves, bark strips, pine needles, and moss; lined with fine rootlets or pine needles and grass. Outside diameter, 4 inches; outside height, 2 inches; inside diameter, 1¾ inches; inside depth, 1¼ inches. Usually where pastures are overgrown with scrub.

    Pacific States from Canadian border south to central Sierras in California; also east to Idaho.

    Calaveras Warbler

3. See I A a(2) 3, I A a(1) 2, and I A a(5) 20.

    Bobolink

4. For description of nest see Part One, page 12.

    Canadian border south to Oregon, northeastern California (east of Sierras), northern Arizona, northern New Mexico, and Texas.

    Vesper Sparrow

5. Of coarse grass and weed stalks; lined somewhat scantily with horsehair, very loosely put together. Outside diameter, 4 inches; outside height, about 2 inches; inside diameter, 2 inches; inside depth, 1¼ inches. Sometimes in a slight hollow under a bush. See also I A a(5) 23. Dry hillsides covered with low bushes and grass.

    Western Texas, western Oklahoma, southern New Mexico, Arizona, and southern and central California.

    Rufous-crowned Sparrow
    (Santa Cruz Sparrow)
    (Ashy Sparrow)
    (Rock Sparrow)
    (Scott's Sparrow)

6. Frail; of dried grasses; lined with finer ones and a few hairs. Outside diameter, 4 inches; outside height, 3½ inches; inside diameter, 2½ inches; inside depth, 2 inches. Open chaparral and thick bushes.

Southeastern Nevada, southeastern Colorado, Arizona, New Mexico, western Oklahoma, and western and southern Texas.

Cassin's Sparrow

a(4). *Under low, thick bushes or growth of sprouts and briers*

1. See II A a(3) 4.

Poor-will

2. For description of nest see Part One, page 13. See also Nests Above the Ground VI A a(1) 13.

Prairies of north-central United States west to eastern Montana, eastern Wyoming, and eastern Colorado.

Clay-colored Sparrow

a(5). *In a depression of the ground*

1. See III A a(3) 2.

Gadwall

2. For description of nest see Part One, page 13.

Canadian border south to north-central California, western Nevada, northern Utah, and northern Colorado.

Pintail

3. See I A a(2) 1 and III A a(2) 4.

Cinnamon Teal

4. See III A a(3) 6 and III A a(4) 2.

Shoveller

5. For description of nest see Part One, page 14. Prairie Chicken.

   Open prairie country.

   Great Plains west to southeastern Colorado and eastern New Mexico.

   Greater Prairie Chicken

6. Nest similar to that of Greater Prairie Chicken. See above.

   Southern Great Plains west to southeastern Colorado and eastern New Mexico.

   Lesser Prairie Chicken

7. A slight depression in the ground, scratched out by the bird, usually under sage bushes; poorly lined. Six to 12 eggs (2.15 inches by 1.5 inches); greenish drab color, spotted with brown.

   Sagebrush plains east of Cascades and Sierras from southeastern Washington and Montana south to eastern California, Nevada, Utah, and northern Colorado.

   Sage Hen

8. For description of nest see Part One, page 14.

   Locally in various western states.

   European Partridge

9. A slight hollow scooped out of the sand beneath a clump of weeds or grass or under a bush; lined with a few leaves or coarse grass. Arid country.

   Central and southern Arizona, southern Colorado, New Mexico, and western, central, and southern Texas.

   Scaled Quail

10. A slight hollow lined with grass; found under brush heaps, rocks, bushes, old fences, and other shelters, often in curious places; sometimes in gardens. Inside

diameter, 4 to 6 inches; inside height, ½ to 2 inches. Grassy plains, hillsides, and cultivated fields.

Southern Oregon and California (except deserts of California).

California Quail
(Valley Quail)
(Catalina Quail)

11. For description of nest see Part One, page 14.

Locally in many sections of western United States.

Ring-necked Pheasant

12. A depression in the ground; lined with leaves and grass. Eggs brownish gray, spotted and blotched with blackish brown. Prairies, open fields, and alkali flats.

High plains east of Continental Divide from Montana south to New Mexico and western Texas.

Mountain Plover

13. For description of nest see Part One, page 14.

Western United States south to Mexico.

Killdeer

14. A slight hollow lined with a few grasses. Three or four eggs buff or greenish-buff, spotted with brownish black. Open prairies and alkaline flats.

Great Basin and Great Plains regions (eastern Washington, eastern Oregon, northeastern California, southern Idaho, Utah, Nevada, Montana, Wyoming, Colorado, and northern New Mexico).

Long-billed Curlew

15. For description of nest see Part One, page 15.

Sparingly in plains country from Canadian border south to eastern Oregon (rare), northeastern Utah, Colorado, and New Mexico.

Upland Plover

16. For description of nest see Part One, page 15.

    Western United States south to southern California, northern Arizona, and New Mexico.

    Spotted Sandpiper

17. For description of nest see Part One, page 15.

    Western United States south to Mexico.

    Horned Lark

18. Bulky, compact; of dried grass and moss; lined with feathers and hair.

    Near timberline from Canadian border south to Oregon and northern New Mexico.

    American Pipit

19. Of fine grasses interwoven in a circular form and without lining; sometimes the surrounding grasses are formed into an arch. Inside diameter, 3 inches; inside depth, 1½ inches. See also I B b(4) 1.

    Prairies of Montana east of the mountains.

    Sprague's Pipit

20. See I A a(2) 3, also I A a(1) 2 and I a(3) 3.

    Bobolink

21. See I A a(1) 4.

    Lark Bunting

22. For description of nest see Part One, page 16. (Eastern) Lark Sparrow.

    See also Nests Above the Ground VI A a(2) 5 and VI B b(1) 14.

    Western United States, except in humid northwest coast belt, south to Mexico.

    (Western) Lark Sparrow

23. See I A a(3) 5.

Rufous-crowned Sparrow

a(6). *On flat ground, in slight depression*

1. For description of nest see Part One, page 16. See also IV B 6 and Nests Above the Ground IX A a(1) 1.

   Western United States south to Texas, New Mexico, Arizona, mountains of southern California, and coast of northern California.

   Nighthawk

2. No nesting material, the eggs usually deposited in exposed situations among sparse chaparral on ground baked almost as hard as a brick by the intense heat of the sun.

   Southwestern United States, north to north-central California, southern Nevada, southern Utah, and central Texas.

   Texas, or Lesser, Nighthawk

B. Arched Nest

b(1). *Along old fence rows or neglected brushy corner of field*

1. For description of nest see Part One, page 17.

   Locally in various western states.

   Bob-white

b(2). *Beneath a tuft of clover, sedge, or grass*

1. Of grasses and weeds; lined with finer materials; sometimes with a grass-covered tunnel leading to it. Upon rare occasions the nest has two entrances. Well concealed.

   Southeastern Arizona, southern New Mexico, and southern Texas.

   Rio Grande Meadowlark

b(3). *In or under a tussock of grass*

    1.   For description of nest see Part One, page 17. Eastern Meadowlark.

        Western United States south to Mexico.

                                    Western Meadowlark

    2.   See I A a(1) 5.

                          (Western) Grasshopper Sparrow

b(4). *In a depression*

    1.   See I A a(5) 19.

                                      Sprague's Pipit

II

↑↑↑↑↑↑↑↑↑↑↑↑↑↑↑↑↑

In Woods, Thickets, and Wooded Hillsides

A. Open Nest

a(1). *At foot of tree, bush, stump, rock, or log; among roots of fallen tree or where earth has washed away from tree roots on bank*

1. See Nests Above the Ground VIII A a(3) 7.

    American Merganser

2. In a depression in the ground. A well-built rim of green mosses and ferns; lined with dry leaves, grass, ferns, bits of rubbish, and plenty of grouse feathers. Inside diameter, 7 inches; inside depth, 1½ inches.

    Evergreen forests in high mountains of Pacific States from Washington to southern California, except in section east of Cascades in Washington and Oregon.

    Sooty Grouse
    (Sierra Grouse)
    (Mount Pinos Grouse)

3. Of dry leaves and grass; often at foot of decayed stump or by the side of fallen timber in dense moun-

    153

tain woods. Inside diameter, 6 inches; inside depth, 2 inches.

Mountain regions east of Cascades from Canadian border south to northeastern Oregon, central Idaho, and western Montana.

Franklin's Grouse

4. For description of nest see Part One, page 19.

Coastal belt from western Washington south to northwestern California and east of Cascades from Canadian border south to northern Utah and eastern Oregon.

Ruffed Grouse

5. For description of nest see Part One, page 20.

Great Plains west to foothills in Montana, Wyoming, and central Colorado; also eastern Washington, eastern Oregon, Idaho, Nevada, western Montana, southwestern Colorado, and northern New Mexico.

Sharp-tailed Grouse

6. See II A a(2) 3.

Mountain Quail

7. Of weed stems, dry grasses, plant fibers, down, fine rootlets, dead leaves, and bits of moss; lined with finer materials of the same kind, fine shreds of inner bark, and occasionally with hair and a few feathers. Sometimes the nest is coated with moss and at other times it is made entirely of this material. Outside diameter, 4 inches; outside height, 2 inches; inside diameter, 2 inches; inside depth, 1 inch. Built in a variety of places, but generally near water, such as among the roots of an upturned tree, in the crotch or against the trunk of a very small tree, in a cavity in a tree, or on a beam in an unoccupied building. See also Nests Above the Ground VI B b(1) 2, VIII A a(3) 18, and IX B b(1) 1. In deciduous woods.

Western United States south to Mexico.

Western Flycatcher

8. Of twigs, grasses, weeds, dead leaves, and sometimes bark strips; lined with fine grasses, rootlets, pine needles, or horsehair. Outside diameter, 4 inches; outside height, 3⅕ inches; inside diameter, 2¼ inches; inside depth, 1⅕ inches. Sometimes raised a bit on sprouts or stems, on a dead or sprouting stump, among rank ferns, or in a hollow tree. See also Nests Above the Ground VI A a(2) 1 and VIII A a(3) 36. Woodlands along stream bottoms.

East of Cascades from eastern Washington and Montana south to northeastern Oregon, Nevada, Utah, and Colorado.

Willow Thrush

9. In a cavity in the ground or in a bed of moss, at the base of a stump or tree or alongside a moss-covered log or on side of a bank; of moss, externally like that with which it is usually surrounded; lined with stems of some moss; sometimes bits of leaves, grass, rootlets, and twigs form part of it; carefully concealed. Along wooded watercourses or low, wooded shores of a pond.

Canadian border south locally to western Montana.

Grinnell's Water-Thrush

10. Of grass; lined with grass and hair. Usually near canyon bottoms. Outside diameter, about 4 inches; outside height, 1⅝ inches; inside diameter, about 2 inches; inside depth, 1⅛ inches.

Southeastern Montana, Black Hills in eastern Wyoming and western South Dakota, and northwestern Nebraska.

White-winged Junco

11. Of dry grasses, rather loosely put together; lined with cow hair.* In a hollow of the ground under a low bush, the nest being built flush with the surface; also in a hole along the roots of bushes and trees; sometimes under woodpiles.

    Northwestern Montana, northern Idaho, Washington, Oregon, and California.

    Oregon Junco
    (Shufeldt's Junco)
    (Montana Junco)
    (Thurber's Junco)
    (Point Pinos Junco)

12. Of coarse, dry grass, with an inner lining of fine yellow straw and hair (of the mountain sheep).*

    Canadian border to southern Idaho, south-central Montana, and northern Wyoming.

    Pink-sided Junco

13. Similar to nest of Pink-sided Junco. See above.

    Rocky Mountains in southern Wyoming, Colorado, Utah, Nevada, and northern New Mexico.

    Gray-headed Junco

14. Of bark and dead grass; slight lining of hair; under a small pine; well concealed.*

    High mountains of New Mexico and eastern Arizona.

    Red-backed Junco
    (Arizona Junco)

15. Of grass, moss, fine twigs, and a few leaves; lined with fine grass and feathers; for the most part placed on the ground and usually concealed by the drooping

* Measurements of nest similar to those of the White-winged Junco.

branches of evergreens, but sometimes placed in a bush or low tree. See also Nests Above the Ground VI A a(2) 7 and VI B b(1) 16. Evergreen forests of high mountains.

Canadian border south to western Colorado (rare) and southern California and from Rocky Mountains west to Sierras, Cascades, and islands off coast of northwestern Washington.

Fox Sparrow

a(2). *In or under tussocks of grass or weeds*

1. For description of nest see Part One, page 24. See also II A a(3) 1 and II A a(4) 1.

    Local or rare in Great Basin and Rocky Mountain region.

    Red-breasted Merganser

2. A slight depression in the ground; thinly lined with dry grass or pine needles; sometimes placed under grass, at other times in bushes or beside a log. See also II A a(3) 2. Evergreen forests.

    Rocky Mountains from Canadian border south to central New Mexico and central Arizona and west to eastern Washington and eastern Oregon.

    Dusky Grouse
    (Richardson's Grouse)

3. The eggs are deposited on the ground in a bed of dead leaves under the shelter of a tuft of weeds, grass, small bush, rock, or log. Inside diameter, 4½ inches; inside depth, 1 inch. See also II A a(1) 6.

    Mountains of southwestern Washington, Oregon, southern Idaho, western Nevada, and California.

    Mountain Quail
    (Plumed Quail)

4. Loosely built; of fine fibrous weed stalks; lined with fine grass, rootlets, plant fibers, and a few hairs. Outside diameter, 5 inches; outside height, 3 inches; inside diameter, 2½ inches; inside depth, 1½ inches. Usually placed beneath a tuft of grass on a hillside.

    High mountains of southeastern Arizona and southwestern New Mexico.

    Red-faced Warbler

5. See I A a(1) 7 and Nests Above the Ground VI A a(2) 8 and VI B b(1) 17.

    Song Sparrow

a(3). *In or beneath dense underbrush or shrubbery*

1. See II A a(2) 1 and II A a(4) 1.

    Red-breasted Merganser

2. See II A a(2) 2.

    Dusky Grouse

3. A hollow in the ground; lined with a few leaves; very well concealed. Inside diameter, about 12 inches; inside depth, about 3 inches.

    Mountains of southern Colorado, Arizona, New Mexico, and western Texas.

    Merriam's Turkey

4. Eggs usually deposited on the bare ground, although a slight hollow may sometimes be scraped in the bare earth; sometimes the eggs are laid on a flat rock, or in full sunlight, but generally they are laid where they may be partially shaded, as in the thick growth at the edge of timber or at the roots of a bunch of bushes or briers upon the prairies. See also I A a(4) 1.

    Western United States east of the Cascades and Sierras south to Mexico and west of the Cascades and Sierras from southern Oregon south to Lower California.

    Poor-will

5. Eggs laid on ground among bushes.

    Gulf Coast of Texas and Lower Rio Grande Valley.

    Merrill's Pauraque

6. Loosely made of dry grass, rootlets, bark strips, and moss; lined with a few horsehairs and fine vegetable fibers. Outside diameter, 4 inches; outside height, about 1⅝ inches; inside diameter, 1⅞ inches; inside depth, about 1⅛ inches. Chaparral hillsides and brushy open woods.

    Canadian border south to southern California, Arizona, and New Mexico, and from Rockies west to Coast.

    Orange-crowned Warbler
    (Lutescent Warbler)
    (Dusky Warbler)

7. Of a loosely intricate interweaving of fine bark strips, fine stems of grasses, roots, and mosses; lined with the same material but sometimes fur and hair are added; sometimes embedded in deposits of dead or decaying leaves with the rim just even with the surface. Inside diameter, 3½ inches; inside depth, 2 inches. Shrubbery and scrub oak on mountainsides and foothills.

    Southern Rocky Mountain region from southern Arizona and northeastern New Mexico north to Nevada, Utah, and northern Colorado.

    Virginia's Warbler

8. Bulky; of dry grass, shreds of bark, leaves, and twigs; lined with rootlets and grass stems; usually well concealed by dense growth of low bushes. Outside diameter, 5½ inches; outside height, 3 inches; inside diameter, 2¼ inches; inside depth, 1½ inches. Open woodlands.

    Mountains from central Oregon and south-central Montana, south to southern California, southeastern New

Mexico, and central-western Texas, west to Cascades and Sierras.

Green-tailed Towhee

9. In a depression in the ground, just large enough to contain the nest, the rim flush with the level of the ground; strongly built of bark strips, blades of grass, pine needles, and twigs; lined with grass or straw. Outside diameter, about 5⅛ inches; outside height, about 2½ inches; inside diameter, 3 inches; inside depth, 1½ inches. Beneath a bush or shrubbery, a favorite place being growths of cherry shrubbery; often near water. Open woodlands.

Western United States south to Mexico.

Spotted Towhee
(Arctic Towhee)
(Spurred Towhee)
(Nevada Towhee)
(Oregon Towhee)
(Sacramento Towhee)
(San Francisco Towhee)
(San Diego Towhee)
(San Clemente Towhee)

a(4). *In woods clear of dense undergrowth*

1. See II A a(2) 1 and II A a(3) 1.

Red-breasted Merganser

2. Merely a slight depression in the ground, sometimes containing a few dead leaves on which the eggs are laid; usually placed under a bush but sometimes under the edge of a boulder. See also I A a(3) 1.

Mountains of southern Arizona, southern New Mexico, and western Texas.

Stephens's Whip-poor-will

a(5). *Among rocks or in hollow logs*

1. See Nests Above the Ground VIII A a(3) 5.

    (Western) Harlequin Duck

2. For description of nest see Part One, page 29. See also VII A 1 and Nests Above the Ground VIII A a(3) 8.

    Western United States south to Mexico.

    Turkey Vulture

3. No nesting material, the eggs being deposited in a recess among rocks or on the floor of a cave in the most inaccessible mountains. See also VII A 3.

    Southern California (very rare).

    California Condor

4. See VI B 11.

    Dipper

5. Rather large and loosely made; foundation of sticks and trash; on this foundation the true nest of grasses, pine needles, and weed stalks is built; but the whole carelessly made and loosely constructed; the mass of material hanging below frequently betrays the nest, especially when placed among rocks. Inside diameter, about 2⅞ inches; inside depth, 1½ inches.

    High mountains from Canadian border through Sierras to San Bernardino Mountains in southern California and through Rockies and adjacent high range to central Arizona and New Mexico.

    Townsend's Solitaire

a(6). *In swampy woods or bogs*

1. For description of nest see Part One, page 30. See also Nests Above the Ground VI B b(1) 5.

Possibly breeding in mountains of northwestern Montana.

Tennessee Warbler

a(7). *On a steeply sloping bank or the rocky side of a canyon*

1. Rather large, flat, and shallow; loosely constructed of grasses and fine shreds of vegetable bark; lined with horsehair. Outside diameter, 5 inches or more; outside height, 1½ inches; inside diameter, about 2 inches; inside depth, 1 inch. In a cavity in a bank or beneath a projecting stone; often in the vicinity of a spring or waterfall.

   High mountains of central and southern Arizona, southwestern New Mexico, and western Texas.

   Painted Redstart

B. Arched Nest

b(1). *At foot of tree, bush, stump, rock, or log; among roots of fallen tree, etc.*

1. Of grass stems and sunken in the ground, entrance concealed and partially arched over. Inside diameter, about 5 inches; inside depth, about 2 inches.

   Arid regions from central Arizona, central New Mexico, and western Texas south to Mexico.

   Mearns's Quail

2. Of twigs, leaves, and moss; lined with fine rootlets, feathers, fur, or hair, with a small circular opening in one side only, just large enough to admit the little owner. Outside diameter, 4¼ inches; outside height, 6 inches; inside diameter, 2¼ inches; inside depth, 1¼ inches. May be built in cavity of low stump or tree. See also Nests Above the Ground VIII A a(3) 33. Evergreen forests.

Canadian border south to central California and north-ern Colorado.

(Western) **Winter Wren**

b(2). *Among dead leaves of forest floor*

1. For description of nest see Part One, page 31.

    Black Hills section of northwestern Wyoming and extreme southeastern Montana and locally in central Colorado.

Ovenbird

III

/////////////////////

In Marshes, Bogs, Wet
Meadows, and Swamps

A. Open Nest

a(1). *In or among reeds, flags,* rushes, or sedges*

1. For description of nest see Part One, page 33.
   Northern Washington and Montana.

   Holboell's Grebe

2. For description of nest see Part One, page 33.
   Northern Montana.

   Horned Grebe

3. A floating, flimsy, careless platform of reeds and vegetation. Outside diameter, 12 to 14 inches; inside diameter, 5 to 6 inches. On shallow lagoon, pond, or lake.

   Locally, chiefly east of Cascades and Sierras from
   Canadian border to eastern California, northern Arizona,
   and New Mexico.

   Eared Grebe

4. Of water plants and pieces of reeds heaped into a cone-
   shaped mass, slightly fastened to one or two tule stalks

* Note: As in Part One the word "flag" refers to cattails.

and forming a wet floating mass. Outside diameter, 14 to 24 inches; outside height, 4 to 6 inches, tapering to 6 to 8 inches at the top. Freshwater ponds, marshes, and resacas of southern Texas.

Southern Texas.

Mexican, or Least, Grebe

5. For description of nest see Part One, page 34.

    East of Cascades and Sierras from Canadian border to northern California, Utah, and Colorado.

    Western Grebe

6. For description of nest see Part One, page 34. Freshwater ponds and marshes.

    Western United States south to Mexico.

    Pied-billed Grebe

7. For description of nest see Part One, page 34. See also III B b(1) 1. Often in wet meadows over almost dry ground.

    Western United States south to southern California, central Arizona, and northern New Mexico (probably).

    American Bittern

8. For description of nest see Part One, page 34. See also Nests Above the Ground I A 1.

    California and eastern Oregon, occasionally in Rocky Mountain States and on Great Plains in eastern Wyoming and eastern Colorado.

    (Western) Least Bittern

9. For description of nest see Part One, page 35. See also III B b(1) 2.

    Eastern Washington and Montana south to northeastern California, Nevada, northwestern New Mexico, and southern Colorado.

    Redhead

10. For description of nest see Part One, page 35.

Locally or occasionally from Canadian border south to eastern Oregon, northern Utah, and Colorado.

Canvas-back

11. For description of nest see Part One, page 35. See also III B b(1) 3 and IV B 2.

Locally from Canadian border south to southern California, northern Arizona, and New Mexico.

Ruddy Duck

12. For description of nest see Part One, page 36. See also III B b(1) 4.

Western United States south to southern California, Utah, and northern New Mexico.

Sora

13. For description of nest see Part One, page 36.

Marshes from central California and Arizona south to Mexico.

Florida Gallinule

14. For description of nest see Part One, page 36.

Western United States south to Mexico.

Coot

15. See IV A 5.

Black-necked Stilt

16. For description of nest see Part One, page 37.

Utah.

Franklin's Gull

17. For description of nest see Part One, page 37. See also IV A 12.

Eastern Washington and Wyoming south to eastern California, Nevada, Utah, and Colorado.

Forster's Tern

18. For description of nest see Part One, page 38.

> Locally inland from Canadian border south to California, Nevada, and Colorado.

> **Black Tern**

a(2). *In weeds or grass*

1. Of twigs, grasses, reeds, and leaves; lined with down; usually placed on a mound in marshes; sometimes a hollow in the sand of a lake beach and at times, though rarely, an old nest of a hawk or eagle may be appropriated, repaired, and lined with down. Inside diameter, 11 inches; inside depth, 3 inches. See also IV A 4. Marshes and sloughs.

> Canadian border south to northeastern California, northern Nevada, northern Utah, and Wyoming.

> **Canada Goose**

2. For description of nest see Part One, page 38.

> Central and southern California, central Nevada, southwestern Arizona, and southern Texas.

> **Fulvous Tree Duck**

3. For description of nest see Part One, page 38. See also I A a(1) 1.

> Western United States south to California and New Mexico.

> **Mallard**

4. See I A a(2) 1 and I A a(5) 3.

> **Cinnamon Teal**

5. For description of nest see Part One, page 39.

> Occasionally in western states ("colonies" in southwestern Montana and White Mountains of eastern Arizona).

> **Ring-necked Duck**

6. A hollow scooped in the ground, lined with dark down mingled with a little dry grass; or of weeds and grass, lined with fine grass and down; on a dry shore a little back from the water's edge or in a firm tussock of meadow grass, at the margin of a boggy slough.

   Locally in eastern Oregon, Idaho, Montana, Wyoming, and northern Colorado.

   Lesser Scaup Duck

7. For description of nest see Part One, page 39.

   Western United States south to southern California and New Mexico, except in northwestern coast belt.

   Marsh Hawk

8. For description of nest see Part One, page 40. See also III A a(3) 7.

   Northeastern California, eastern Oregon, northern Nevada, southern Idaho, southwestern Montana, western Wyoming, and northwestern Colorado.

   Sandhill Crane

9. Of Salicornia, dry marsh grass, or weeds. Outside diameter, 7 inches; outside height, 1¼ inches; inside diameter, 5 inches; inside depth, ½ inch. Saltwater marshes.

   San Diego to San Francisco, California (casually farther north), also lower Colorado River from Yuma to Laguna Dam and Imperial Valley marshes south of Salton Sea.

   California Clapper Rail
   (Light-footed Rail)

10. For description of nest see Part One, page 40.

    Western United States south to southern California, Utah, and Colorado.

    Virginia Rail

11. For description of nest see Part One, page 41.

   East-central California.

                                              Yellow Rail

12. For description of nest see Part One, page 48. Black
   Rail.

   Locally in coastal marshes of California and occasionally inland.

                                      California Black Rail

13. A shallow platform or rim of grass and weed stems,
   hidden in the grass of marshes.

   Eastern Washington and Montana south to southern
   California, New Mexico, and southern Texas.

                                                    Avocet

14. Of weed stalks, with a little grass and a few feathers,
   arranged in a careless manner, about 6 inches above
   the ground. Outside diameter, about 3 inches; outside
   height, 1⅝ inches; inside diameter, 1¾ inches; inside
   depth, about 1 inch.

   Salt marshes of southern California.

                                        Belding's Sparrow

a(3). *In the ground*

  1. See IV B 1.

                                              Common Loon

  2. For description of nest see Part One, page 42. See
    also I A a(5) 1.

   Eastern Washington and Montana south to northeastern California, northern Nevada, northern Utah, and
   Colorado.

                                                   Gadwall

  3. For description of nest see Part One, page 43. See
    also III A a(4) 1.

Canadian border south to eastern Oregon, central California (probably), northern Nevada, northern Utah, and northern New Mexico.

Green-winged Teal

4. For description of nest see Part One, page 43.

Eastern Washington and Montana south to northeastern California, Nevada, northern Utah, and New Mexico.

Blue-winged Teal

5. For description of nest see Part One, page 43.

Eastern Washington and Montana south to northeastern California, northern Utah, and northern Colorado.

Baldpate

6. For description of nest see Part One, page 44. See also I A a(5) 4 and III A a(4) 2.

Eastern Washington and Montana south to southern California, northwestern Nevada, Utah, and New Mexico.

Shoveller

7. See III A a(2) 8.

Sandhill Crane

8. For description of nest see Part One, page 44.

Locally from Canadian border south to eastern California, northern Nevada, northern Utah, and northern Colorado.

Wilson's Snipe

9. For description of nest see Part One, page 44. See also III A a(4) 4.

East-central Oregon, northeastern California, northern Nevada, Utah, eastern Montana, Wyoming, and Colorado (occasionally).

(Western) Willett

10. See III A a(4) 5.

Short-eared Owl

a(4). *Beneath bushes or grass clumps*
1. See III A a(3) 3.

Green-winged Teal

2. See III A a(3) 6 and I A a(5) 4.

Shoveller

3. For description of nest see Part One, page 45. See also III A a(5) 1 and VII A 2.
   Western Texas and southern Arizona.

Black Vulture

4. See III A a(3) 9.

(Western) Willett

5. For description of nest see Part One, page 46. See also III A a(3) 10.
   Western United States south to Colorado and north-eastern California.

Short-eared Owl

6. For description of nest see Part One, page 46. See also III B b(1) 6 and Nests Above the Ground VI A a(1) 2.
   Western United States south to southern Texas, New Mexico, southern Arizona, and southern California.

Yellow-throat

7. For description of nest see Part One, page 47.
   High mountains from Canadian border south to southern California, central Arizona, and New Mexico.

Lincoln's Sparrow

a(5). *Among rocks and in hollow logs*

   1.   See III A a(4) 3 and VII A 2.

Black Vulture

B. Arched Nest

b(1). *Beneath bushes or in clumps of grass*

   1.   See III A a(1) 7.

American Bittern

   2.   See III A a(1) 9.

Redhead

   3.   See III A a(1) 11 and IV B 2.

Ruddy Duck

   4.   See III A a(1) 12.

Sora

   5.   For description of nest see Part One, page 48.

      Eastern Washington and Montana south to central California, Nevada, Utah, and Colorado.

Wilson's Phalarope

   6.   See III A a(4) 6 and Nests Above the Ground VI A a(1) 2.

Yellow-throat

IV

////////////////

On or Near Seashore and Lake Beaches

A. Nesting in Colonies

1. A shallow platform of sticks, reeds, and grass, about a foot in diameter, on a base of sandy soil about 6 inches high, scraped together by the bird; sometimes a mere depression in sand or pebbles.

   Locally on inland lakes from Canadian border south to southern California, western Nevada, northern Utah, and Wyoming (Yellowstone).

   White Pelican

2. For description of nest see Part One, page 50. (Eastern) Brown Pelican.

   See also Nests Above the Ground VII B b(3) 1.

   Along coast of southern California and on ocean islands.

   California Brown Pelican

3. Of grass, stalks, leaves, and feathers; placed on an elevated knoll near water.

   Yellowstone Park, Wyoming, Red Rock Lake, Montana, and neighboring lakes.

   Trumpeter Swan

4. A hollow in the sand, surrounded with a few sticks and twigs; lined with gray down. See also III A a(2) 1.

    Canadian border south to northeastern California, northern Nevada, northern Utah, and Wyoming.

    Canada Goose

5. For description of nest see Part One, page 51. See also III A a(1) 15.

    South-central Oregon, northern Utah, and southern Colorado south to southern California, southern New Mexico, and southern Texas.

    Black-necked Stilt

6. Well-made; of seaweed, rockweed, kelp, and straws; sometimes decorated with feathers or fishbones; on ledges and niches in rocks. See also VI A 5.

    Along coast of Washington.

    Glaucous-winged Gull

7. Rather bulky; of dry, rank weeds and grasses; placed on grassy hillside, on ledges, and the exposed summits of rocks. Outside diameter, 18 inches; inside diameter, 8 inches; inside depth, 4 inches. See also VI A 6.

    Along Pacific Coast from Washington south to southern California; also on Farallon Islands.

    Western Gull
    (Wyman's Gull)

8. Of sticks, grass, weeds, rubbish, straw, and a few feathers; sometimes a mere hollow surrounded by a few twigs; outer edge of nest built up from 2 to 5 inches above the ground in short grass near the beach or in the windrows of driftwood which line the shore. Outside diameter, 14 to 18 inches; inside diameter, 7 inches; inside depth, 2 inches.

Locally on inland lakes from Canadian border south to Mono Lake, California, Great Salt Lake, Utah, and Yellowstone Lake, Wyoming.

California Gull

9. Of dried grasses and weeds, sometimes of small sticks; lined with finer grasses; occasionally decorated with feathers. Outside diameter, 10 to 16 inches; inside diameter, 9 inches; inside depth, 2 inches. On the ground along the upper edges of the beach and among rocks and boulders.

Inland lakes from Canadian border south to southern Oregon, Utah, and Colorado.

Ring-billed Gull

10. For description of nest see Part One, page 51.

Salton Sea in southern California.

Laughing Gull

11. For description of nest see Part One, page 52. See also IV B 5.

Salton Sea in southern California.

Gull-billed Tern

12. For description of nest see Part One, page 52. See also III A a(1) 17.

Eastern Washington and Wyoming south to eastern California, Nevada, Utah, and Colorado.

Forster's Tern

13. For description of nest see Part One, page 52.

Locally or occasionally in Washington and Montana.

Common Tern

14. For description of nest see Part One, page 53.

Northern to central California, along North Platte River in Wyoming, and occasionally in Colorado.

Least Tern
(Brown's Tern)

15. For description of nest see Part One, page 54.

    Coast of California from San Francisco Bay south.

    Royal Tern

16. For description of nest see Part One, page 54.

    Locally inland from Canadian border south to southern Oregon, eastern California, Utah, and Wyoming.

    Caspian Tern

B. Nesting Singly

1. For description of nest see Part One, page 55. See also III A a(3) 1.

    About shores of inland lakes from Canadian border south to Wyoming, eastern Oregon, and northeastern California.

    Common Loon
    (Lesser Loon)

2. See III A a(1) 11 and III B b(1) 3.

    Ruddy Duck

3. No nesting material, the eggs being laid directly upon the gravel on the beach.

    Rocky shores and islands along the Pacific Coast.

    Black Oyster Catcher

4. Eggs laid in depression in the sand, frequently on a mound.

    Along Pacific Coast and locally inland in Pacific states and in Utah and New Mexico.

    (Western) Snowy Plover

5. See IV A 11.

    Gull-billed Tern

6. See I A a(6) 1 and Nests Above the Ground IX A a(1) 1.

    Nighthawk

V

ⵏ ⵏ ⵏ ⵏ ⵏ ⵏ ⵏ ⵏ ⵏ ⵏ ⵏ ⵏ ⵏ ⵏ

In Burrows in the Ground

A. Nesting in Colonies

1. A hole or burrow about a foot deep, terminating in an enlarged gallery, in a steep bank; thinly lined with fine roots and dry grass.

    On islands off northern California and Oregon.

    Fork-tailed Petrel

2. A burrow in a bank; lined with grass, pieces of bark, or chips of wood.

    On islands off Washington, Oregon, and California (Farallon Islands).

    Beal's Petrel

3. At the end of a burrow about 3 feet long; no nesting material.

    On Coronados Islands off San Diego, California.

    Black Petrel

4. Eggs laid at the end of a burrow about 3 feet long; the tunnel slightly enlarged at end where a flimsy platform is built of bits of twigs and rootlets.

    Coronados Islands off San Diego, California.

    Socorro Petrel

177

5. At end of short burrow in a bank or mountainside or in a hole in rocks. See also VI A 9.

   Along coast of Washington and Oregon.

   Marbled Murrelet

6. Eggs usually deposited in a burrow in the ground but sometimes in a crevice in rocks. Opening of burrow located about the roots of trees or beneath partially buried logs or stones. Burrow 2 to 4 feet long. See also VI A 11.

   Islands along Pacific Coast.

   Cassin's Auklet

7. Eggs deposited in a burrow in the ground, burrow 5 to 15 feet in length, about 5 inches in diameter, and terminating in a dome-shaped chamber; chamber lined with a few dead leaves or dried grasses.

   Islands off coast of Washington.

   Rhinoceros Auklet

8. For description of nest see Part One, page 58.

   Western United States south to southern California, Arizona, and New Mexico.

   Bank Swallow

9. See VI A 12.

   Tufted Puffin

B. Nesting Singly

1. For description of nest see Part One, page 59. Burrowing Owl.

   Open country of western United States from Pacific east through Great Plains.

   (Western) Burrowing Owl

2. Eggs merely deposited in a hole in a bank, about 18 inches deep; also in natural cavities of trees or in cavities excavated by woodpeckers. See also Nests Above the Ground VIII A a(2) 13.

    Mountains of southern Arizona.

    Coppery-tailed Trogon

3. For description of nest see Part One, page 59. (Eastern) Belted Kingfisher.

    Western United States south to southern California and New Mexico.

    (Western) Belted Kingfisher

4. In a hole about 2 inches in diameter; in a sandy, clay, or gravelly bank; the nesting chamber slightly larger than the tunnel leading to it; about 2 feet from the mouth of the hole and containing fish bones and scales.

    Southern Texas.

    Texas Kingfisher

5. See Nests Above the Ground VIII A a(1) 2 and IX A a(5) 2.

    Red-shafted Flicker
    (Northwestern Flicker)

6. For description of nest see Part One, page 60. See also Nests Above the Ground VI C 2 and VI D 1.

    Washington and Montana south to southern California, Arizona, and northern New Mexico.

    Rough-winged Swallow

7. See VI B 13.

    Rock Wren

VI

𝍌𝍌𝍌𝍌𝍌𝍌𝍌𝍌𝍌𝍌𝍌𝍌𝍌𝍌

On Rocks or Rocky Ledges

A. On Ledges of Rocks on Islands off Coast, or Along Mainland

1. Eggs deposited beneath stone piles on the ground but sometimes in a cavity under boulders.

   On Farallon Islands and Santa Cruz Island, off coast of California.

   Ashy Petrel

2. For description of nest see Part One, page 61. See also Nests Above the Ground VII B b(3) 2.

   Along Pacific Coast and locally on large bodies of water inland in California, Oregon, Utah, Arizona, and western Nevada, and along Great Plains.

   Double-crested Cormorant
   (Farallon Cormorant)
   (White-crested Cormorant)

3. A compact, circular structure of eelgrass or seaweed, cemented with guano.

   On rocky islands along Pacific Coast.

   Brandt's Cormorant

4. Of dry grass with occasionally a few feathers in the lining. On the narrowest and most inaccessible little shelves or crannies of a steep, rocky cliff.

   On rocky islands along Pacific Coast.

   Baird's Cormorant

5. See IV A 6.

   Glaucous-winged Gull

6. See IV A 7.

   Western Gull

7. Eggs merely laid on rock of cliffs, without any attempt at nest building.

   Chiefly on islands from Washington to central California.

   California Murre

8. Eggs merely laid in the crevices of rocks, in open situations on flat rocks or shelves, or in dark nooks under boulders, often near water's edge; sometimes small stones are gathered together for a nest.

   On islands and shore cliffs from Washington south to Santa Barbara Islands, California.

   Pigeon Guillemot

9. See V A 5.

   Marbled Murrelet

10. Eggs laid in a cranny among loose boulders in a cliff or under a rock.

    Islands off southern California.

    Xantus's Murrelet

11. See V A 6.

    Cassin's Auklet

12. Eggs deposited in a crevice of rocks or in a cavity in a granite cliff, the cavity varying in length from 2 to 5 feet; sometimes a few pieces of weeds are found in the cavity, but often no material is used as a nest lining. See also V A 9.

Islands along Pacific Coast from Washington south to Santa Barbara Islands, California.

Tufted Puffin

B. On Rocky Ledge of Cliff

1. See Nests Above the Ground VII B b(1) 5.

Swainson's Hawk

2. See Nests Above the Ground VII B b(1) 8.

Ferruginous Rough-leg

3. For description of nest see Part One, page 62. See also Nests Above the Ground VII A 3.

Mountainous regions of western United States.

Golden Eagle

4. Of sticks; lined with grass; usually on cliffs and ledges of rocks, frequently on the tops of the massive sandstone columns that stand solitary like huge chimneys in the rocky canyons of Colorado, but sometimes in the cavities of trees. See also Nests Above the Ground VIII A a(3) 9.

Arid regions of western United States south to Mexico.

Prairie Falcon

5. For description of nest see Part One, page 63.

Locally throughout western United States south to Mexico.

Duck Hawk

6. See Nests Above the Ground VII B b(1) 10 and VIII A a(3) 10.

(Western) Pigeon Hawk

7. A flimsy, cup-shaped, shallow structure of grass, moss, rootlets, and possibly some mud, snugly tucked away in a niche of the rocks.

In crevices of sea cliffs at scattered points along Pacific Coast and inland on inaccessible mountain walls.

Black Swift

8. Small and shallow; saucer-like; about 4 inches in diameter and ¾ inch in depth, but varying in size and shape to suit the crack and crevice where built; sometimes round and well-cupped; of vegetable fibers and feathers; glued to cliff or cave sides or in holes in limestone cliffs. See also VII B 1.

Locally and chiefly in mountains throughout western United States south to Mexico.

White-throated Swift

9. See Nests Above the Ground VIII A a(3) 19 and IX A a(3) 2.

Violet-green Swallow

10. See Nests Above the Ground VII B b(2) 5.

Raven

11. A beautiful sphere of soft green moss, 7 inches or more in diameter, sometimes dome-shaped with a neatly arched opening near the bottom; in a crevice of rocks, on a rock in midstream, or on some narrow ledge of a rocky cliff; always placed near running water; often where spray keeps the outside damp, and sometimes behind a cascade. See also II A a(5) 4.

Mountain streams of western United States south to southern California, northern Arizona, and New Mexico.

Dipper

12. Cup-shaped; of twigs, moss, bits of leaves, catkins, and bud scales, thickly felted; lined with wool, down, and feathers. Outside diameter about 8 inches; outside height, about 3 inches; inside diameter, 2½ inches; inside depth, 2 inches. In a crevice or hole in a cliff or on a shelf or projecting ledge in a cave. See also VII B 3. Rocky canyons.

Western United States from southeastern Washington, Idaho, and Wyoming south to southern California, Mexico, and western Texas.

Canyon Wren

13. Of a large variety of materials but principally of small twigs, moss, wool, hair, grass, weeds, bark strips, and rootlets, the ground around entrance paved with small pebbles, pieces of glass, or rock. Outside diameter, 4½ inches; outside height, 3 inches; inside diameter, 2½ inches; inside depth, 1 inch. Usually placed in a cavity or small crevice under or among loose rocks of a cliff; sometimes in a niche in a cliff and sometimes in a burrow. See also V B 7. Dry rocky regions.

Western United States south to Mexico except in northwestern Coast Belt.

Rock Wren

14. Cup-shaped; of grasses, weed stems, and mosses; lined with fine grass and a few feathers. Outside diameter, 4½ inches; outside height, 2 inches; inside diameter, 2½ inches; inside depth, 1½ inches. In a rocky crevice or cliff niche or under a boulder. Above timberline on mountains.

Canadian border south to northwestern Montana and south in Cascades to northern California and to central Sierras, California.

Gray-crowned Rosy Finch
Hepburn's Rosy Finch
Sierra Nevada Rosy Finch

15. Similar to nest of Gray-crowned Rosy Finch.

Salmon River Mountains of Idaho, mountains of northern Utah, and mountains of western Wyoming.

Black Rosy Finch

16. Compactly woven of dry grass and flower stems with a quantity of fine moss; lined with fine grass and a few feathers. Outside diameter, 4¾ to 5½ inches; outside height, 3 inches; inside diameter, 2½ inches; inside depth, 1½ inches. In a cavity of a cliff.

High mountains of Colorado and probably in northern New Mexico.

Brown-capped Rosy Finch

VII

↗↗↗↗↗↗↗↗↗↗↗↗↗↗

In Caves

A. On the Floor

1. See II A a(5) 2 and Nests Above the Ground VIII A a(3) 8.

   Turkey Vulture

2. See III A a(4) 3 and III A a(5) 1.

   Black Vulture

3. See II A a(5) 3.

   California Condor

B. In or On a Shelf of the Wall

1. See VI B 8.

   White-throated Swift

2. See Nests Above the Ground VI C 1, VIII A a(3) 17, IX A a(2) 2, and IX A a(3) 1.

   Say's Phoebe

3. See VI B 12.

   Canyon Wren

VIII

✔✔✔✔✔✔✔✔✔✔✔✔✔✔

In Deserts

A. In a Depression in the Sand

1. A hollow in the sand sparsely lined with grass or leaves. Inside diameter, 4½ to 5½ inches; inside depth, ½ to 3½ inches. Beneath a creosote bush, mesquite, cactus, yucca, or a tuft of grass.

   Deserts of southern California, southern Nevada, southwestern Utah, Arizona, central and southwestern New Mexico, and extreme western Texas.

   Gambel's Quail

2. See Nests Above the Ground VI A a(1) 11.

   Sage Sparrow

IX

ff ff ff ff ff ff ff ff

On Alpine Summits

A. In Open Situations

1. Sometimes a mere depression in the ground, at others a well-built structure of grass, leaves, and weed stalks; lined with feathers. Inside diameter 6 inches or more.

   Cascade Mountains of Washington and Rockies from Montana to northern New Mexico.

   White-tailed Ptarmigan

*Nests of Birds West of the
One-Hundredth Meridian*

✔✔✔✔✔✔✔✔✔✔✔✔✔✔✔

Nests Above the Ground

I

↑↑↑↑↑↑↑↑↑↑↑↑↑↑

Hanging or Semihanging

A. Attached to Reeds or Bushes in Marshes

1. See Nests On or In the Ground III A a(1) 8.

    (Western) Least Bittern

2. For description of nest see Part One, page 67.

    Eastern Oregon, northern Utah, and Wyoming south to Mexico.

    White-faced Glossy Ibis

3. For description of nest see Part One, page 68.

    Canadian border south to New Mexico and northeastern California and from Great Plains to Coast.

    Long-billed Marsh Wren (Tule Wren)

4. For description of nest see Part One, page 69.

    Canadian border south to southern California, northern Arizona, and New Mexico, and from Great Plains west to eastern Washington, eastern Oregon, and interior of California.

    Yellow-headed Blackbird

5. For description of nest see Part One, page 70. See also I B 2.

     Western United States south to Mexico.

     Red-winged Blackbird

6. Of straw, mud, and coarse sedges and grasses; lined with finer similar material; in alders, willows, and flags. See also I B 3. Nesting in colonies.

     Southern Oregon and valleys of California (west of Sierras).

     Tricolored Red-winged Blackbird

B. Attached to Bushes in Wet Meadows or Swampy Thickets

1. For description of nest see Part One, page 71.

     Western United States south to Mexico west of the Rockies, and south to northeastern Colorado east of the Rockies.

     Alder or Traill's Flycatcher (Little Flycatcher)

2. See I A 5.

     Red-winged Blackbird

3. See I A 6.

     Tricolored Red-winged Blackbird

C. Attached to Upland Trees and Bushes

c(1). *Fully suspended*

d(1). Less than 2 inches deep inside

1. For description of nest see Part One, page 72.

     Central and central-western Texas.

     Black-capped Vireo

2. A neat, cup-shaped, compact structure; of fine vege-table fibers, bits of paper, and grasses, covered on the outside with green and gray mosses; lined with fine grasses. Outside diameter, 3 inches; outside height, 2¾ inches; inside diameter, 2 inches; inside depth, 1¾ inches. In low-hanging limbs, usually of live oaks.

   Pacific States (west of Cascades and Sierras) and oak belt of mountains of southeastern Arizona, southwestern New Mexico, and western Texas.

   Hutton's Vireo
   (Stephens's Vireo)

3. For description of nest see Part One, page 73.

   California, southern Arizona, southwestern New Mex-ico, western Texas, and eastern Colorado.

   Bell's Vireo
   (Texas Vireo)
   (Arizona Vireo)

4. In forks of trees and bushes; rarely higher than 15 feet above the ground; of coarse, dry grasses, shreds of bark, plant fibers, and cocoons; sometimes of mesquite bark and loosely woven coarse grass; lined with fine grass and vegetable fibers; often decorated with sage-bush leaves. Outside diameter, 2¾ inches; outside height, 2 inches; inside diameter, 2¼ inches; inside depth, 1¾ inches. In chaparral.

   Southern California, southern Nevada, and southwest-ern Colorado south to Mexico.

   Gray Vireo

5. In fork of horizontal or descending bough of sapling 5 to 30 feet above the ground; cup-shaped; compactly woven of bark shreds, grasses, and bits of plant down; decorated with pieces of white cocoons, sometimes paper and string; bound with webs, plant blossoms, and feathers. Outside diameter, about 3⅝ inches; out-

side height, 2 inches; inside diameter, 2 inches; inside depth, 1½ inches. In low trees of lower mountain slopes of forested lowlands.

Pacific States and Rocky Mountain region from northern Nevada, northern Utah, southern Montana, and southeastern Wyoming south to Mexico.

Solitary Vireo
(Plumbeous Vireo)
(Cassin's Vireo)

6. For description of nest see Part One, page 74.

Eastern United States west to eastern Colorado, eastern Wyoming, and in northwest to Portland, Oregon, and Seattle, Washington.

Red-eyed Vireo

7. For description of nest see Part One, page 75. (Eastern) Warbling Vireo.

Western United States south to Mexico.

(Western) Warbling Vireo

d(2). Over 2 inches deep inside

1. For description of nest see Part One, page 76.

West to eastern Montana, eastern Wyoming, and eastern Colorado, east of Rocky Mountains.

Baltimore Oriole

2. Suspended from branches of poplars, cottonwoods, mesquites, or other trees; sometimes in a cluster of mistletoe, from 5 to 40 feet up; a woven structure of vegetable fibers, inner bark, and horsehair; lined with wool, down, horsehair, or cow hair. Outside diameter, 4½ inches; outside height, 5 to 9 inches; inside diameter, 2¾ inches; inside depth, 4 inches. Orchards and woodlands.

Western United States south to Mexico.

Bullock's Oriole

c(2). *Partly suspended*

d(1). Less than 2 inches deep inside

1. See V B (2) 5.

   Gray Flycatcher

2. For description of nest see Part One, page 78. (Eastern) Golden-crowned Kinglet.

   In high mountains of western United States south to northern New Mexico, Arizona, and southern California and in evergreen forests along coast south to central California.

   (Western) Golden-crowned Kinglet

3. Placed almost invariably near or at end of a branch of a coniferous tree, usually within 25 feet of the ground; neatly and compactly built with soft, thick walls of moss, fine strips of bark, grasses, and cocoons; lined warmly with feathers and hair. Outside diameter, 3¼ inches; outside height, 3¼ inches; inside diameter, about 2 inches; inside depth, about 1½ inches. In evergreen forests.

   High mountains of western states south to southern California, central Arizona, and central New Mexico.

   Ruby-crowned Kinglet

d(2). Over 2 inches deep inside

1. A large, gourd-shaped structure, flaring at the bottom, entrance near top at side; from 8 to 10 inches long and 4 or 5 inches in diameter; the walls are three times as thick at bottom as at top, where they are about ½ inch thick and 4½ inches deep; exteriorly of dry sage leaves, plant down, moss, lichens, and cobwebs; thickly lined with small feathers. Placed in low oaks, in bunch of mistletoe, or mesquite from 5 to 20 feet up.

Western Washington, western and southern Oregon, southern Idaho, Utah, and western Wyoming south to Mexico and from Rockies and central-western Texas to coast.

Bush-tit

2. For description of nest see Part One, page 78.

Eastern United States west to western Texas.

Orchard Oriole

3. Attached to upright terminal branches; firmly constructed of dried grasses woven among the growing twigs and leaves so as to form a light and firm matting. Usually in mesquite trees, thickets, or heavy timber, from 6 to 14 feet up.

Lower Rio Grande Valley, Texas.

Audubon's Oriole

4. A perfectly wrought, cup-shaped structure; placed in clumps of Spanish moss, or in a sycamore, oak, fig, palm, or yucca; constructed mainly of materials of tree or bush in which located; typical nests composed almost entirely of Spanish moss; others, fastened to bayonet yucca points, built of fibers from edges of leaves; lined with wool, vegetable down, feathers, or hair. Outside diameter, 3 inches; outside height, 3½ inches; inside diameter, 2½ inches; inside depth, 2 inches. Woods and groves.

Southern and south-central California, southern Arizona, southwestern New Mexico, and lower Rio Grande Valley, Texas.

Hooded Oriole
(Sennett's Oriole)

5. Of grass, yucca threads, horsehair, and cotton waste; lined with fine grass and a feltlike down. Outside diameter, 5 inches; outside height, 3 inches; inside diam-

eter, 3 inches; inside depth, about 2½ inches. Usually in a yucca about 5 feet up, near water. Desert country where tree yuccas or agaves predominate.

Southern California, southern Nevada, southwestern Utah, Arizona, southern and central New Mexico, and western Texas.

Scott's Oriole

II

ꞗꞗꞗꞗꞗꞗꞗꞗꞗꞗꞗꞗꞗꞗ

Covered on Outside with Lichens and Saddled on Branch

A. Less than 2 Inches, Outside Diameter

1. See III C 2 and III A 2.

   Costa's Hummingbird

2. See III A 3, III B 1, and III C 3.

   Anna's Hummingbird

3. See III B 2 and III C 4.

   Broad-tailed Hummingbird

4. See III C 5, III A 4, and III B 3.

   Rufous Hummingbird

5. See III B 4, III A 5, and III C 6.

   Allen's Hummingbird

6. Cup-shaped, neatly built; of shreds of vegetable fiber, thistledown, or downy blossoms, covered exteriorly with flower blossoms, shreds of bark, and light-colored lichens, fastened in place with spiders' webs; lined with thistledown. Outside diameter, 1⅓ inches; outside height, 1¼ inches; inside diameter, about ¾ inch;

inside depth, about ½ inch. Usually saddled on a small, drooping branch, but sometimes placed on a fork of a horizontal twig.

Rio Grande Delta, Texas.

Buff-bellied Hummingbird

7. A hollow sphere with the upper quarter cut away; of plant down; covered exteriorly with mosses and lichens, held in place with spiders' webs. Outside diameter, 1¾ inches; outside height, 1½ inches; inside diameter, 1 inch; inside depth, 1 inch. Usually saddled on the twig of a bush or small tree but sometimes placed in an upright crotch.

Mountains of southeastern Arizona.

White-eared Hummingbird

B. Over 2 Inches, Outside Diameter

1. Cup-shaped; of soft, silky plant fibers; thickly coated exteriorly with small pieces of lichens, securely bound on by a network of the finest silk from spiders' webs; lined with soft, fluffy feathers. Outside diameter, 2¼ inches; outside height, 2 inches; inside diameter, 1½ inches; inside depth, 1¼ inches. In maples, sycamores, and other trees, from 10 to 50 feet above the ground.

Mountains of southeastern Arizona and southwestern New Mexico.

Rivoli's Hummingbird

2. Cup-shaped; compact; of fine grasses, fine weed stems, shreds of weed stalks, a few bits of dry leaves, flowering grass, and weed tops; deeply hollowed; lined with the finest of bright yellow grasses; the exterior profusely decorated or camouflaged with pieces of lichens, often selected to match those growing on the branch; the upper rim firmly and smoothly finished, forming

an almost perfect circle; a beautiful nest, uniform in pattern and materials, suggesting a glorified Wood Pewee's nest. Outside diameter, 4 to 5 inches; outside height, 2 to 3 inches; inside diameter, 2¾ inches; inside depth, 1½ inches. Placed in a horizontal fork or on a horizontal branch to which it is firmly plastered with spiders' webs. Usually in conifers some distance from the ground.

Mountains of central and southeastern Arizona and southwestern New Mexico.

Coues's Flycatcher

3. A flat, well-made structure, usually sunk well down into the fork, so that its rim projects very little above the supporting branch; of short pieces of dead twigs, shreds, and pieces of weed stalks, fine grasses, rootlets, plant fibers, bits of dry leaves and lichens, fine strips of inner bark, cocoons, and spiders' webs; lined with fine pieces of similar material, plant down, horsehair, fur, and feathers; the exterior is often profusely decorated with lichens; the whole structure firmly bound together and anchored to the branch with spiders' webs. Outside diameter, 2½ to 3 inches; outside height, 1 to 2 inches; inside diameter, 1¾ to 2 inches; inside depth, 1 inch. In horizontal forks or crotches, generally on rather small limbs. Semiarid or desert regions.

Southern and western Texas, southern New Mexico, southern and western Arizona, southwestern Utah, southern Nevada, and southeastern California.

Vermilion Flycatcher

4. Cup-shaped, gracefully contracted at brim; composed of soft, silky milkweed or cattail down, withered blossoms, or other dainty material, pinned together with fine grasses, old leaf stems, and horsehair; exteriorly

decorated with lichens held by spiders' webs. Outside diameter, about 2 inches; outside height, 2¾ inches; inside diameter, 1¾ inches; inside depth, 1½ inches. Usually saddled on a horizontal limb in tall trees, rarely in sapling; from 10 to 75 feet above the ground; if saddled on a limb, resembles a knot. In chaparral.

Colorado, southern Utah, southern Nevada, and northern California south to Mexico.

Western Gnatcatcher

5. A neat, beautiful affair of weed stalks, moss, vegetable down, and lichens, tied with spiders' webs; lined with fine rootlets. Outside diameter, from 3 to 4 inches; outside height, from 1¾ to 2½ inches; inside diameter, 2 inches; inside depth, 1¼ inches. Usually saddled on a branch but sometimes placed in a fork, generally in a conifer from 30 to 50 feet above the ground.

Pine forests of high mountains of southeastern Arizona and southwestern New Mexico.

Olive Warbler

III

⌇⌇⌇⌇⌇⌇⌇⌇⌇⌇⌇⌇⌇⌇

Felted Nests of Cottony Materials

A. In Forks of Bushes, Saplings, or Large Trees

1. See III C 1.

> **Black-chinned Hummingbird**

2. See III C 2 and II A 1.

> **Costa's Hummingbird**

3. Cup-shaped; of plant down put together with spiders' webs and occasionally lined with feathers and bits of flower stems; covered exteriorly with moss, spiders' webs, and here and there bits of lichens; similar to that of Costa's Hummingbird but slightly larger, with fibers and stemmy materials in the walls and feathers in the lining. Outside diameter, 1¾ inches; outside height, 1½ inches; inside diameter slightly less than an inch; inside depth, ½ inch. See also II A 2, III B 1, and III C 3.

   California, west of Sierras.

> **Anna's Hummingbird**

4. See III C 5, II A 4, and III B 3.

> **Rufous Hummingbird**

5. See III B 4, II A 5, and III C 6.

    Allen's Hummingbird

6. A handsome and rather bulky structure; of fine mosses
    smoothly quilted together with spiders' webs; lined
    with down of willow catkins. Outside diameter, 2¾
    inches; outside height, 3 inches; inside diameter, 1¼
    inches; inside depth, ¾ inch. Usually placed in the
    fork of a shrub or sapling but sometimes placed on a
    fern, a vine, or hanging wire.

    Southwestern Texas (Chisos Mountains), southwestern
    New Mexico (San Luis Mountains), and mountains of
    southern Arizona.

    Blue-throated Hummingbird

7. Of plant fibers and vegetable down; lined with down;
    ornamented on the outside with bits of leaves and
    down, bound together with spiders' webs. Usually
    placed in the fork of a drooping twig of a bush or
    small tree within 10 feet of the ground.

    Mountains of southern Arizona and southwestern New
    Mexico; also southwestern Texas (rare).

    Broad-billed Hummingbird

8. A delicate, cup-shaped structure; of soft bark strips
    and hemplike vegetable fibers; lined with plant down,
    a few feathers, and hair. Outside diameter, 2½ inches;
    outside height, 2 inches; inside diameter, 1½ inches;
    inside depth, about 1⅜ inches. Placed low in bushes.

    Deserts of southeastern California, southern Nevada,
    Arizona, New Mexico, and Rio Grande Valley of western
    Texas.

    Plumbeous Gnatcatcher
    (Black-tailed Gnatcatcher)

9. For description of nest see Part One, page 81.

    Western United States south to southern California,

southern Arizona, southern New Mexico, and western Texas.

Yellow Warbler

10. For description of nest see Part One, page 82.

   Eastern United States and diagonally northwest through Colorado, northern Utah, Wyoming, and Montana to eastern Oregon and eastern Washington.

American Redstart

11. For description of nest see Part One, page 82.

   Canadian border south to Colorado, Nevada, and southern California.

American Goldfinch
(Eastern Goldfinch)
(Pale Goldfinch)
(Willow Goldfinch)

12. Similar to nest of Common Goldfinch but slightly smaller. See above.

   Oregon, Utah, and Colorado south to Mexico.

Arkansas Goldfinch
(Greenbacked Goldfinch)

13. Of wool, fine grasses, down, and feathers, closely matted together; lined with feathers or long hair; sometimes made entirely of grass. Outside diameter, 3 inches; outside height, 2 inches; inside diameter, about 2 inches; inside depth, 1 inch.

   Central and southern California, west of Sierras.

Lawrence's Goldfinch

B. On Horizontal Branch or in Upright Crotch of Small Tree

1. See III A 3, II A 2, and III C 3.

Anna's Hummingbird

2. A beautiful, cup-shaped structure of soft vegetable down; covered externally with lichens or bark fiber; variable in shape, size, and makeup; usually placed on low, horizontal branches of willows, alders, and cottonwoods, at no great distance from the ground, or overhanging small streams, but sometimes saddled on boughs or limbs of pine, fir, spruce or aspens; from 4 to 5 feet above the ground. See also II A 3 and III C 4.

    Montana and southern Idaho south to Mexico and west to eastern Washington (rare), eastern Oregon (rare), and western Arizona.

    Broad-tailed Hummingbird

3. See III C 5, II A 4, and III A 4.

    Rufous Hummingbird

4. Cup-shaped; well and compactly built of moss, decorated with flakes of lichens bound on with spiders' webs; lined with plant down. Outside diameter, 2½ inches; outside height, 2½ inches; inside diameter, about 1 inch; inside depth, ¾ inch. Usually saddled on a small limb growing away from the main stem of a sapling but also placed in large trees and on small twigs of bushes or vines; better built than those of most hummingbirds. See also II A 5, III A 5, and III C 6.

    Along coast of California.

    Allen's Hummingbird

5. For description of nest see Part One, page 83.

    Southern Great Plains west to southeastern New Mexico and western Texas.

    Scissor-tailed Flycatcher

6. Large, dome-shaped or globular, with an entrance on one side; of dead grass and any other soft material at

hand, such as rags, plant fibers, and feathers; lined with finer materials of the same kind. Outside diameter, 10 inches; outside height, 8 inches; outside length, 18 inches; inside diameter, 5 inches; inside depth, 5 inches; inside length, 7 inches. Usually in thorny trees or bushes.

Lower Rio Grande Valley, Texas.

Derby Flycatcher

7. For description of nest see Part One, page 83.

Eastern and central United States west to central Montana and eastern Wyoming.

Least Flycatcher

C. On Horizontal Branch or in Upright Crotch of Large Tree

1. An exquisite structure; semiglobular in shape; deeply hollowed with the rim curved inward at the top; of plant down of various colors (sycamore, willow, milkweed, thistle), firmly felted and reinforced and bound on the supporting twigs with spiders' webs; often resembles a small, round yellow sponge. Outside diameter, about 1½ inches; outside height, 1 inch; inside diameter, 1 inch; inside depth, ½ inch. Usually saddled on the small horizontal branches of oaks and sycamores but sometimes resting lightly in the forks of slender twigs. See also III A 1.

Western United States north to eastern Washington (rare) and northwestern Montana; common in southern parts of California, Arizona, New Mexico, and western Texas.

Black-chinned Hummingbird

2. Rather shallow; of soft, downy, yellowish or grayish vegetable substances; here and there bits of flower stems; the whole covered exteriorly with spiders' webs,

with occasionally bits of lichens. Outside diameter, 1½ inches; outside height, 1¼ inches; inside diameter, about ¾ inch; inside depth, ½ inch. Sometimes placed almost at the extremity of the branches of large trees; at other times built on the twigs or in the forks of small bushes. See also II A 1 and III A 2.

Southern California, southern Utah, southern Nevada, and Arizona.

Costa's Hummingbird

3. See III A 3, II A 2, and III B 1.

Anna's Hummingbird

4. See III B 2 and II A 3.

Broad-tailed Hummingbird

5. A firm, compact, handsome, cup-shaped structure; of willow floss and soft plant down, profusely covered externally with moss so that it seems entirely made of this material, but often more or less decorated externally with leaf or bud scales, shreds of inner bark, lichens, and various other plant fibers, securely bound on with spiders' webs. Outside diameter, 1½ inches; outside height, 1¼ inches; inside diameter, about ¾ inch; inside depth, ½ inch. Usually placed on the drooping branch of a conifer but also placed in deciduous trees, bushes, and vines; often near creeks and embankments. See also II A 4, III A 4, and III B 3.

Oregon and southwestern Montana north to Canadian border.

Rufous Hummingbird

6. See III B 4, II A 5, and III A 5.

Allen's Hummingbird

7. Cup-shaped; of thin strips of bark held together with spiders' webs; lined with plant down. Outside diam-

eter, 1¼ inches; outside height, 1¼ inches; inside diameter, ¾ inch; inside depth, ½ inch. Sometimes saddled on a branch but usually placed on or against a dead pine cone, which the nest so much resembles as to almost defy detection; generally placed on a small branch or twig directly under a larger branch or under a canopy of foliage which serves to conceal or protect the nest from overhead.

High mountains of western United States south to southern California and northern New Mexico and from Rockies west to eastern Washington, eastern Oregon, and Sierras of California.

Calliope Hummingbird

8. A delicate, cup-shaped structure; of fine vegetable materials, weathered leaves, fibers, and grasses, carefully inwrought; lined with hair, fine grass, and bits of moss. Outside diameter, 3½ inches; outside height, 2¼ inches; inside diameter, 1 inch; inside depth, 2 inches. Usually in a conifer.

Coniferous forests of mountains of western United States south to central California and Colorado.

Hammond's Flycatcher

9. A flat, saucer-shaped, compactly made structure; of soft vegetable matter, small twigs, plant fibers, blossoms, and cottony fibers, bound together with cobwebs. Outside diameter, about 3¾ inches; outside height, about 2¼ inches; inside diameter, 2½ inches; inside depth, 1 inch. Usually placed in oaks, elders, or mesquite trees from 8 to 25 feet above the ground.

Arid lowlands of California, southern Nevada, southern Utah, Arizona, southwestern New Mexico, and western Texas.

Phainopepla

10. Cup-shaped and compact; of vegetable fibers, straws, string, bud scales, and insect webs. Outside diameter, 3 inches; outside height, 1½ inches; inside diameter, 1¾ inches; inside depth, 1¼ inches. High in pine trees, 50 to 60 feet above the ground.

> Pine forests in high mountains of southwestern Colorado, central and eastern Arizona, and New Mexico.

Grace's Warbler

D. Inside the Loose Bark of Trees

1. See VIII A a(3) 15.

Ash-throated Flycatcher

IV

✓✓✓✓✓✓✓✓✓✓✓✓✓✓

Containing a Layer of Mud

A. Built in Trees

a(1). *Under 4 Inches, Inside Diameter*

1. For description of nest see Part One, page 85. See also IV B b(3) 1 and IX A a(2) 3.

   Western United States south to Mexico.

   Robin

2. For description of nest see Part One, page 86.

   Canadian border south to California, northern Arizona, and New Mexico.

   Brewer's Blackbird

a(2). *Over 4 Inches, Inside Diameter*

1. A large, bulky structure of large sticks and twigs, moss and grass, cemented together with mud; lined with fine grasses, rootlets, and hair. Outside diameter, 7 inches; outside height, 4 inches; inside diameter, 4⅜ inches; inside depth, 2¾ inches. Usually located in firs but sometimes in other trees and bushes, from 10 to 50 feet above the ground. Coniferous forests.

   210

Canadian border south to Mexico in mountains and along the coast to northern California.

Steller's Jay
(Coast Jay)
(Blue-fronted Jay)
(Black-headed Jay)
(Long-crested Jay)

2. A large, bulky bowl of mud and grass, surrounded and arched by a rustic latticework of sticks, with the sticks pointing in all directions; a formidable-appearing nest; entrance on one side; lined with a few grasses and roots. Outside diameter, 12 to 18 inches; outside height, 2 to 3 feet. In bushes and trees from 5 to 60 feet above the ground (in the mountains the black pine is a favorite nesting site).

    Canadian border south to northern Arizona and northern New Mexico and west to eastern Washington, eastern Oregon, and eastern California (eastern slope of Sierras).

    American Magpie

3. Nest similar to that of American Magpie but slightly smaller; usually high in oaks and sycamores. See above.

    Valleys of central California.

    Yellow-billed Magpie

4. A strongly built structure of straws, leaves, grasses, and mud, and, where Spanish moss is plentiful, almost entirely of it. Usually placed near the top of one of the main upright branches of a young mesquite tree.

    Locally in southern and western Texas and southern New Mexico.

    Great-tailed Grackle

5. For description of nest see Part One, page 87. See also IV B b(3) 2.

Eastern United States, west of foothills of Rockies in Montana, eastern Wyoming, and eastern Colorado.

Bronzed Grackle

B. Built on or in Buildings, on Bridges, or Against Rocks

b(1). *Outer layer of mud with strengthening of grass or straw*

1. Cup-shaped; of small pellets of mud mixed with bits of dry grass, weed fibers, or hair; lined with weed fibers, fine roots, strips of bark, grass tops, hair, wool, and occasionally feathers; outer wall carried up to rim; resembles nest of Barn Swallow. Outside diameter, 5 inches; outside height, 3½ inches; inside diameter, 2¾ inches; inside depth, 1¼ inches. Sometimes built in wells. See also IX A a(4) 2. Along streams and near human habitation.

Western Texas, southern New Mexico, Arizona, southern Utah, southern Nevada, and north through California.

Black Phoebe

2. For description of nest see Part One, page 88. See also IX B b(1) 2.

Western United States south to Mexico.

Barn Swallow

3. For description of nest see Part One, page 88. See also IX A a(3) 3.

Western United States south to Mexico.

Cliff Swallow

b(2). *Outer layer of mosses*

1. For description of nest see Part One, page 89. See also IX A a(4) 1.

Locally in southeastern Colorado and eastern New Mexico.

Eastern Phoebe

b(3). *Outer layer of grasses*

   1.   See IV A a(1) 1 and IX A a(2) 3.

Robin

   2.   See IV A a(2) 5.

Bronzed Grackle

C. In a Cave

   1.   Eggs laid on a balcony of mud plastered in a hole in the rocks.

      South-central Texas.

Coahuila Cliff Swallow

V

Made Chiefly of Bark, Fibers, Twigs, and Rootlets

A. Less than 2 Inches, Inside Diameter

a(1). *Usually in conifers*

1. A rather bulky structure for a warbler; sometimes well-built, at other times loosely constructed; of strips of bark, twigs, or pine needles; lined with rootlets, hair, and feathers. Outside diameter, 3½ inches; outside height, 2½ inches; inside diameter, 2 inches; inside depth, 1½ inches. Usually saddled on the limb of a coniferous tree.

   Canadian border south to mountains of southern California, Arizona, and southeastern New Mexico.

   Audubon's Warbler
   (Black-fronted Warbler)

2. Cup-shaped; chiefly of cedar-bark strips, with a few weed stalks and fibers, woven with spiders' webs and cocoons; lined with fine grass tops, hair, and feathers. Outside diameter, 3½ inches; outside height, 3½ inches; inside diameter, 1½ inches; inside depth, 2 inches. Usually placed in perpendicular forks of the main limbs of cedar trees, from 10 to 18 feet above

Photographs by courtesy of Olin S. Pettingill and Torrey Jackson

Ruby-throated Hummingbird

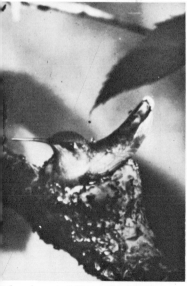

Ruby-throated Hummingbird, Michigan

Yellow Warbler

Common Redpoll

A Long-billed Marsh Wren

Brown-capped Chickadee

Clapper Rail

Common Nighthawk

Belted Kingfisher

American Woodcock

Slate-colored Junco

Olive-sided Flycatcher

Downy Woodpecker

Yellow-bellied Flycatcher

Least Flycatcher

Traill's Flycatcher

Nest of a Cliff Swallow under the eaves of a barn

Cliff Swallow

Piping Plover

Long-billed Marsh Wren on the edge of a Common Gallinule nest

Bobolink

Ovenbird

Warbling Vireo

Phoebe at Nest

Song Sparrow

Eastern Kingbird

Kildeer at Nest

Black Duck Nest

Herring Gull Nest

Eastern Phoebe

Black-Billed Cuckoo

Cedar Wax-Wing

Eastern Kingbird

Mourning Dove

Rock Dove (Pigeon)

Double-crested Cormorant

Spotted Sandpiper

Pair of Green Herons

Red-Shouldered Hawk

Red-phased Screech Owl

Male Marsh Hawk

Peregrine Falcon (Duck Hawk)

Young Barn Owls

Least Bittern

Immature Black-crowned Night Hero

Great Horned Owl

Snowy Egret (Brewsters)

Common Tern

Adult Saw-Whet Owl

the ground; average about 15 feet. In cedar growth.

Timbered parts of the Edwards Plateau in south-central Texas.

Golden-cheeked Warbler

3. Cup-shaped; neat and nicely constructed; of weed stems, fibrous stalks of plants, pine needles, and small twigs, bound together with cobwebs; lined with soft, fine strips of bark and hair. Outside diameter, 4 inches; outside height, about 2¾ inches; inside diameter, 2 inches; inside depth, 1 inch. Usually well concealed in conifers, generally pitch pines, from 25 to 40 feet above the ground. Coniferous forests.

Pacific States from western Washington south through California to Mt. Whitney.

Hermit Warbler

4. For description of nest see Part One, page 94.

Evergreen forests of mountains of western United States south to southern California, Arizona, and New Mexico.

Pine Siskin

a(2). *In bushes or saplings*

1. Cup-shaped; of leaves, bark strips, weed stems, vegetable fibers, rootlets; lined with fine grasses. Outside diameter, 3 inches or more; outside height, 4 inches; inside diameter, 2 inches; inside depth, 1¾ inches. In bushes from 1 to 4 feet above the ground. Thick shrubbery in woodland openings.

Canadian border south in high mountains to western Texas, northern New Mexico, northern Arizona, and southern California; also in coastal belt of Washington and Oregon and along coast range south to San Diego, California.

Pileolated Warbler

B. Over 2 Inches, Inside Diameter

b(1). *Usually in conifers*

1. For description of nest see Part One, page 96.

   Western United States south to southern California, central Arizona, New Mexico, and western Texas.

   ### Olive-sided Flycatcher

b(2). *In bushes or moderately low trees*

1. For description of nest see Part One, page 96.

   Eastern and central United States west to eastern Washington, eastern Oregon, northern Nevada, Utah, and eastern New Mexico.

   ### Eastern Kingbird

2. Of small twigs, strips of bark, plant down, Spanish moss; lined with fine rootlets. Outside diameter, 6 inches; outside height, 2 inches; inside diameter, 3 inches; inside depth, 1¼ inches. Open woods.

   Lower Rio Grande River, Texas, and southern Arizona (rare and local).

   ### Couch's Kingbird

3. For description of nest see Part One, page 97. See also IX A a(5) 3.

   Western United States (except in western Washington and along coast of Oregon and northern and central California).

   ### Arkansas, or Western, Kingbird

4. Nest similar to that of Arkansas or Western Kingbird but somewhat larger and more firmly built; of small twigs, rootlets, weed stalks, strips of inner bark, and other plant fibers mixed with bits of string, rags, and dry leaves; the sides and rim often decorated with feathers, dry blossoms of the sage, or the dry flower

clusters of other plants; lined with finer rootlets, fine grass, and, perhaps, a few small feathers; sometimes profusely lined with the cottony seeds of the cottonwood. Outside diameter, 8 inches; outside height, 3 inches; inside diameter, 3½ inches; inside depth, about 1⅝ inches. Almost invariably placed near the end of a horizontal branch in positions not easily reached. In foothills and lower mountain regions.

Central California, Utah, and southern Wyoming south to Mexico.

Cassin's Kingbird

5. Cup-shaped; bulky and rather loosely constructed externally with many loose ends projecting, giving the nest a ragged appearance; of bark, plant fibers, and grasses, quilted together; lined with wool and fine feathers; usually in the crotch of a juniper or sage bush. Sagebrush plains or semiarid flats overgrown with desert underbrush or juniper. See also I C c(2) d(1) 1.

Great Basin from western Colorado to extreme eastern California and eastern Oregon.

Gray Flycatcher

6. Cup-shaped; compact; of bark fibers, bark strips, grasses, and plant fibers, hairs, grasses, and bits of lichens. Outside diameter, 4 inches; outside height, 3½ inches; inside diameter, about 2⅛ inches; inside depth, 2 inches. Placed in a group of horizontal or vertical twigs built into or lashed to the nest; sometimes in a crotch and usually placed so that the leafy twigs screen it from view. Shrubbery ravines and solitary canyons.

Coast belt and interior valleys of California and coast belt of Oregon.

Wren-tit

7. A loose, bulky, and inartistic structure of bark strips, small twigs, coarse grasses; lined with fine stems and rootlets. Outside diameter, about 5½ inches; outside height, 3½ inches; inside diameter, 3½ inches; inside depth, 2 inches. In low bushes, especially sage, from 10 inches to 3 feet above the ground. Arid sagebrush country.

    Eastern Washington and Montana south to south-central California and northern New Mexico.

    Sage Thrasher

8. Compact and bulky, of closely interwoven fine grasses, moss, and lichens; built on a carefully constructed foundation of interlaced slender twigs. Outside diameter, 8 to 12 inches; outside height, 5 inches; inside diameter, about 3½ inches; inside depth, 2 inches. In low bushes, always on or near the banks of a stream. Evergreen forests.

    Northwestern California, western and northwestern Oregon, western and southeastern Washington, northern Idaho, and northwestern Montana.

    Varied Thrush

9. Cup-shaped; of twigs, straws, rootlets, coarse grass, and moss; often compact with thick walls. Outside diameter, 5 inches; outside height, 2 inches; inside diameter, 2½ inches; inside depth, 1½ inches. Usually in bushes where the undergrowth is thick, particularly hillsides near sluggish water, from 3 to 10 feet above the ground.

    Canadian border south along coast to central California and in mountains throughout western United States south to southern California, Arizona, and New Mexico.

    Hermit Thrush

10. A large, compact structure; of twigs, bark strips, mosses, grass, and leaves. Outside diameter, 5 inches;

outside height, 5⅜ inches; inside diameter, 2½ inches; inside depth, 1½ inches. In bushes, saplings, and thickets, usually within a few feet of the ground and near water.

Mountains of western United States from Canadian border south to Colorado, Utah, Nevada, and southern California; also in moist woodlands east of Cascades and Sierras in the Pacific States.

Russet-backed Thrush

11. For description of nest see Part One, page 97.

Western United States south to northern California and Colorado.

Cedar Waxwing

12. For description of nest see Part One, page 98.

Western United States south to Mexico.

Loggerhead Shrike
(White-rumped Shrike)
(California Shrike)
(Island Shrike)

13. Thin, saucer-shaped; of bark strips, grass, and twigs; lined with similar, finer materials and horsehair. Outside diameter, 5 inches; outside height, 2 inches; inside diameter, 2½ inches; inside depth, 1 inch. Generally low down on horizontal branch of a conifer or oak; sometimes 30 feet above the ground. Evergreen forests.

Canadian border south to mountains of southern California, southern Arizona, New Mexico, and western Texas.

Western Tanager

14. Of grasses, weed stems, flower stalks and blossoms, leaves, and catkins; lined with finer grasses. In a pine or sycamore from 18 to 50 feet above the ground.

Mountains of Arizona, New Mexico, and western Texas.

Hepatic Tanager

15. Cup-shaped; of bark strips, rootlets, a few leaves, and grass. A firm structure but so thin and shallow that the eggs may be seen from beneath; in southern states sometimes more compactly built by the addition of moss and down. Usually near the end of a horizontal limb of a deciduous tree, from 5 to 30 feet above the ground. Generally found in woods but sometimes in villages and thickly settled towns. River bottoms.

Southeastern California, southern Nevada, southern and central Arizona, southern and central New Mexico, and western Texas.

Cooper's Tanager

16. For description of nest see Part One, page 99.

Southern Arizona, southwestern New Mexico, and central, western, and southern Texas.

Cardinal

17. Nest resembles that of Cardinal but more compactly put together and smaller; of bark strips, twigs, and grass; lined with small roots. In mesquite or in thorny thickets, from 3 to 8 feet above the ground. Mesquite and chaparral growth.

Southern Arizona, southern New Mexico, and southern and western Texas.

Pyrrhuloxia

18. A loosely put together, frail structure; of fine twigs, weed stems, and rootlets. Outside diameter, 5 inches or more; outside height, 2 inches or more; inside diameter, 3 inches; inside depth, 1½ inches. Usually in willows, live oaks, or saplings, from 5 to 20 feet above the ground. Lowlands.

Western United States south to Mexico.

Black-headed Grosbeak
(Rocky Mountain Grosbeak)

19.   For description of nest see Part One, page 100. (Eastern) Evening Grosbeak.

Canadian border south to Sierras of central California and mountains of southern Arizona and New Mexico.

(Western) Evening Grosbeak

20.   A well-built cup composed externally of interlaced twigs; internally of mosses, fine grasses, string, horsehair, and cotton waste. Outside diameter, 5 inches; outside height, 3 inches; inside diameter, 2⅛ inches; inside depth, 1⅛ inches. Wooded river bottoms and hills.

Transition zone of Pacific States from Canadian border south to Mexico and east to Cascades and Sierras.

California Purple Finch

21.   A thin, flat, saucer-shaped structure; of rootlets, twigs, grass, and weed stalks; lined with softer material together with moss and cotton. Outside diameter, 5½ inches; outside height, 2¾ inches; inside diameter, 2½ inches; inside depth, ¾ inch. Usually placed on horizontal branch of cottonwood, aspen, or pine.

High mountains from Canadian border south to northern Arizona and northern New Mexico, and from Rockies west to Cascades and Sierras.

Cassin's Purple Finch

22.   A carelessly or compactly built structure of any handy material, grass, string, paper, rags, straw, bark strips, or plant fibers. Outside diameter, 4½ inches; outside height, 3½ inches; inside diameter, 2½ inches; inside depth, 1½ inches. See also VI A a(2) 3 and VI B

b(3) 2. In trees, bushes, sagebrush, haystacks, old boxes, tin cans, usually about houses and often near water. Lowlands, deserts, open country, foothills, and towns.

Southeastern Washington, Oregon, southern Idaho, and southern Wyoming south to Mexico.

House Finch

23. Rather large, carelessly made nest; of bark strips, weed stalks, twigs, and grass; lined with fine inner bark or horsehair. Outside diameter, 6 inches; outside height, 3½ inches; inside diameter, 3 inches; inside depth, 2 inches. Usually in dense chaparral thickets, willow, canebrake, or mesquite clumps near streams, within 5 feet of the ground, rarely in trees 30 feet up.

Deserts of southeastern California, southern Nevada, southwestern Utah, southern Arizona, and southwestern New Mexico.

Abert's Towhee

24. Of fine shreds of bark, weed stems, plant fibers, and dried grasses; lined with fine blades of the last. Outside diameter, 4 inches; outside height, 2¼ inches; inside diameter, slightly more than 2 inches; inside depth, 1¾ inches. In sagebrush, cactus, or other desert shrubs near the ground.

Desert country of California, Nevada, Utah, western Colorado, Arizona, New Mexico, and western and southern Texas.

Desert Sparrow
(Black-throated Sparrow)

VI

✓✓✓✓✓✓✓✓✓✓✓✓✓✓✓

Made Chiefly of Grasses, Rootlets, Leaves, and Straw

A. In Bushes, Weeds, or Ferns

a(1). *Under 2 inches, inside diameter*

1. Small and loosely made; of dried grass; lined with fine grass, a few rootlets, and some horsehair. Outside diameter, 4¼ inches; outside height, 2 inches; inside diameter, 2 inches; inside depth, 1½ inches. Usually in briers or small bushes from 6 inches to 2 feet above the ground but sometimes in saplings or juniper trees, from 3 to 6 feet above the ground. Brushy places. See also VI B b(1) 9.

   Western United States south to central California, central Arizona, and northern New Mexico.

   Macgillivray's Warbler

2. See Nests On or In the Ground III A a(4) 6 and III B b(1) 6.

   Yellow-throat

3. Cup-shaped; of grass, leaves, strips of bark, small twigs, and rootlets; lined with fine grasses and hair.

223

Outside diameter, 3½ inches; outside height; 3½ inches; inside diameter, 2 inches; inside depth, 1¾ inches. In low willows, weeds, manzanitas, or other brush, usually near water. Dry brushy canyon slopes and hillsides.

Western United States south to southern California, northern Arizona, northern New Mexico, and western Texas.

Lazuli Bunting

4. Nest similar to that of Lazuli Bunting. See above. Mesquite thickets.

Lower Rio Grande Valley, Texas; local in southern Arizona and southeastern California.

Varied Bunting
(Beautiful Bunting)

5. For description of nest see Part One, page 101. (Eastern) Painted Bunting.
See also VI B b(1) 11.

Southeastern United States west to western Texas and southern New Mexico.

Painted Bunting

6. See Nests On or In the Ground I A a(1) 3 and Nests Above the Ground VI B b(1) 12.

Dickcissel

7. A delicate structure; of fine fibers of wiry grass, loosely interwoven; lined with similar but finer material. Outside diameter, about 2 inches; inside diameter, 1¾ inches. Usually in a bush from 2 to 6 feet above the ground.

Lower Rio Grande Valley, Texas.

Sharpe's Seedeater

8. Semi-domed, being built obliquely, the upper rim extending over, hiding the eggs from perpendicular view; of weed stalks, grasses, and leaves; lined with fine grass and hair. In open thickets and low bushes within 3 feet of the ground.

    Southern Texas north to Corpus Christi.

    Texas Sparrow

9. A compact structure of coarse grass; lined with the fine tops of the mesquite grass and not infrequently a few horsehairs. Outside diameter, 3½ to 4½ inches; outside height, 2½ to 3¼ inches; inside diameter, 1½ to 2 inches; inside depth, 2 to 2½ inches. In a fork or crotch in low bushes, preferably small mesquites, from 6 inches to 5 feet above the ground. Long grass and low mesquite.

    Southeastern Arizona (rare and local).

    Rufous-winged Sparrow

10. Of grasses, vegetable fibers, and weed stems; lined with fine grass and hair. Outside diameter, 4 inches; outside height, 2½ inches; inside diameter, 2 inches; inside depth, 1½ inches. In bushes within 3 feet of the ground. Bushy hillsides.

    California west of Sierras, north in interior to Shasta County and on coast to Marin County; also coastal islands.

    Bell's Sparrow

11. Of grasses and sagebrush bark. Outside diameter, 4 inches; outside height, 2⅝ inches; inside diameter, 2 inches; inside depth, 1½ inches. Usually in the lower branches of a bush but sometimes sunk in the ground. See also Nests On or In the Ground VIII A 2. Deserts.

    Eastern Washington, eastern Oregon, and eastern California, east of Cascades and Sierras, and central and southern Idaho, Nevada, Utah, southwestern Montana, western Wyoming, western Colorado, and northwestern New Mexico; also west of Sierras in central and southern California.

Sage Sparrow

12. For description of nest see Part One, page 102. (Eastern) Chipping Sparrow.
See also VI B b(1) 15.

Canadian border south to southern California, central Arizona, and New Mexico.

(Western) Chipping Sparrow

13. See Nests On or In the Ground I A a(4) 2.

Clay-colored Sparrow

14. Of dry grasses and rootlets; exterior of fine twigs; lined with hair. Outside diameter, 3½ inches; outside height, 1¾ inches; inside diameter, 2 inches; inside depth, 1 inch. In bushes, usually the sage, a few feet from the ground. Arid sage country and deserts.

Great Basin and Rocky Mountain sections from Canadian border south to New Mexico and Arizona and west to eastern Washington, eastern Oregon (east of Cascades), and California (east of Sierras, and local in southern California).

Brewer's Sparrow

15. Of grass and weed fibers; lined with fine grasses and cow hair. Outside diameter, 4 inches; outside height, 2½ inches; inside diameter, 2 inches; inside depth, 1½ inches. In low bushes. Dry mountain slopes covered with sage, chamise, or other low bushes, and in chaparral thickets.

Southern New Mexico, Arizona, and locally in southern California.

Black-chinned Sparrow

a(2). *Over 2 inches, inside diameter*

1. See Nests On or In the Ground II A a(1) 8 and Nests Above the Ground VIII A a(3) 36.

    Willow Thrush

2. Cup-shaped; rather large; compact; of grasses, leaves, and bark strips, well interwoven; lined with fine grasses. Outside diameter, 5 inches; outside height, 4 inches; inside diameter, 2⅝ inches; inside depth, 1¾ inches. Often well concealed in tangle of grapevine, smilax, and briers, 1 to 5 feet above the ground. In brier thickets and bushy clearings.

    Washington and northern Montana south to Mexico.

    Long-tailed Chat

3. See V B b(2) 22 and VI B b(3) 2.

    House Finch

4. Deep and large but loosely constructed; of coarse grass; lined with fine roots and hair. Outside diameter, 5¾ inches; outside height, 3⅝ inches; inside diameter, 3½ inches; inside depth, 1⅝ inches. Placed in thickets or small mesquite trees or live oaks; near ground, usually within 10 feet; sometimes in dense clumps of cholla, in sage, greasewood, or cactus, or between yucca leaves. Thickets. See also VI B b(1) 13.

    Southwestern Oregon, California, Arizona, New Mexico, southern Colorado, and western Texas.

    Brown Towhee
    (Canyon Towhee)

5. See Nests On or In the Ground I A a(5) 22 and Nests Above the Ground VI B b(1) 14.

    (Western) Lark Sparrow

6. See Nests On or In the Ground I A a(1) 6.

    White-crowned Sparrow

7. See Nests On or In the Ground II A a(1) 15 and Nests Above the Ground VI B b(1) 16.

    Fox Sparrow

8. See Nests On or In the Ground I A a(1) 7, II A a(2) 5, and Nests Above the Ground VI B b(1) 17.

    Song Sparrow

B. In Trees

b(1). *Cup-shaped*

1. A well-woven, compact structure; of fine bleached weed fibers and fine grasses; lined with very fine weed bark, grasses, hair, often bits of vegetable down, and feathers; sometimes the rim is plastered with spiders' webs. Outside diameter, 2¾ inches; outside height, 3½ inches; inside diameter, 1¾ inches; inside depth, 2 inches. High chaparral of deciduous growths on mountains.

    Western United States south to southern California, northern Arizona, northern New Mexico, and western Texas.

    Wright's Flycatcher

2. See Nests On or In the Ground II A a(1) 7 and Nests Above the Ground VIII A a(3) 18 and IX B b(1) 1.

    Western Flycatcher

3. Neatly and compactly made; deeply cupped; of various plant fibers, cottony substances, fine grasses, fine rootlets, weed blossoms, and bits of dried leaves, all bound together and to the branch with spiders' webs;

smoothly lined with the finest grasses, plant down, horsehair, and more or less feathers; decorated with broken bits of small leaves or spiders' cocoons. Outside diameter, 2½ to 3 inches; inside diameter, 1½ to 1⅝ inches; inside depth, about 1 to 1½ inches. Saddled on a branch, in a fork, in a crotch, or against the trunk.

Mountains of southeastern Arizona and southwestern New Mexico.

Buff-breasted Flycatcher

4. Cup-shaped; compact; of small pieces of plant fibers, bits of fine dry grasses, bud scales, and sometimes the exuviae of insects; the rim firmly wrought of strong wiry stems; lined with fine, bright yellow grasses and soft horsehair; exterior decorated with gray dead leaves, insect cocoons, and well camouflaged with a great profusion of spiders' webs with which it is bound to the branch. Outside diameter, 2½ to 4 inches; outside height, 1½ to 1⅝ inches; inside diameter, 2 inches; inside depth, 1 inch to slightly more than an inch. Placed on a horizontal fork, on a horizontal branch, or in an upright crotch. Open deciduous tree growth.

Western United States south to Mexico.

Western Wood Pewee

5. See Nests On or In the Ground II A a(6) 1. Nest invariably placed on ground but sometimes low in trees near the ground.

Possibly breeding in mountains of northwestern Montana.

Tennessee Warbler

6. A frail structure; of fine grass, leaves, and rootlets; lined with hair and feathers; frequently placed behind the loose bark of trees, a few feet above the ground;

similar to that of the Creeper (see VII C c(3) 1); also placed in a deserted woodpecker hole or natural cavity. See also VIII A a(3) 41. Willow and mesquite thickets in river bottoms.

Southwestern United States (from Santa Clara Valley, Utah, south through Arizona, southwestern New Mexico, and southeastern California).

Lucy's Warbler

7. Compactly constructed; of plant fibers, grasses, and a few leaf stems; lined with feathers or hair. Outside diameter, 3 inches; outside height, 2½ inches; inside diameter, 1⅝ inches; inside depth, 1½ inches. Low in dense thickets or manzanita, scrub oak, and willows, or high in a conifer.

Washington, Nevada, northern Utah, and western Colorado, south to southern California, southern Arizona, and southern New Mexico.

Black-throated Gray Warbler

8. Large, compact, and well-built; of fine plant fibers, strips of grasses, mosses, lichens, fine strips of inner bark, and spiders' cocoons firmly woven together; lined with rootlets, hair, and plant down. Outside diameter, 3 inches; outside height, 2¼ inches; inside diameter, 2 inches; inside depth, 1½ inches. Usually in firs but sometimes in other conifers a few feet above the ground.

Canadian border south to western Oregon, western Montana, and western Wyoming.

Townsend's Warbler

9. See VI A a(1) 1.

Macgillivray's Warbler

10. For description of nest see Part One, page 104. (Eastern) Blue Grosbeak.

Southern and central California, southern Nevada, southern Colorado, Arizona, New Mexico, and western Texas.

Blue Grosbeak

11. See VI A a(1) 5.

Painted Bunting

12. See Nests On or In the Ground I A a(1) 3 and Nests Above the Ground VI A a(1) 6.

Dickcissel

13. See VI A a(2) 4.

Brown Towhee

14. See Nests On or In the Ground I A a(5) 22 and Nests Above the Ground VI A a(2) 5.

(Western) Lark Sparrow

15. See VI A a(1) 12.

(Western) Chipping Sparrow

16. See Nests On or In the Ground II A a(1) 15 and Nests Above the Ground VI A a(2) 7.

Fox Sparrow

17. See Nests On or In the Ground I A a(1) 7, II A a(2) 5 and Nests Above the Ground VI A a(2) 8.

Song Sparrow

b(2). *Spherical*

1. A thick-walled, rather loosely packed, 4-inch globe; of grasses and fine weeds with the interior well padded with plant down, feathers, and fur; entrance in the side, slightly above center; sometimes with mistletoe added to the exterior; often built in a clump of mistletoe growing on the branch of a cottonwood or other tree. Low woodlands along streams.

Southeastern Arizona and Rio Grande Delta in Texas.

Beardless Flycatcher

2. For description of nest see Part One, page 105. See also VIII A a(3) 43 and IX A a(5) 7.

Distributed throughout western states; about cities, towns, farms, and ranches.

House Sparrow

b(3). *Platform-shaped*

1. A shallow structure of sticks, twigs, and leaves or of Spanish moss; on a horizontal branch a few feet above the ground.

Lower Rio Grande Valley, Texas.

Chachalaca

2. See V B b(2) 22 and VI A a(2) 3.

House Finch

C. In Buildings or Bridges

1. A cup-shaped, shallow structure; of weed stems, dry grasses, moss, plant fibers, wool, empty cocoons, spiders' webs, and hair; lined with wool and hair. Outside diameter, 5½ inches; outside height, 2½ inches; inside diameter, 2½ inches; inside depth, about 1 inch. Usually placed under the eaves or on the shelf of a building but occasionally in mine shafts, hollow trees, and in caves or shelves of rocky cliffs in uninhabited regions. See also VIII A a(3) 17, IX A a(2) 2, IX A a(3) 1, and Nests On or In the Ground VII B 2. Open country.

Western United States south to Mexico.

Say's Phoebe

2. See Nests On or In the Ground V B 6 and Nests Above the Ground VI D 1.

Rough-winged Swallow

D. On Wall Along Water

1. See Nests On or In the Ground V B 6 and Nests Above the Ground VI C 2.

Rough-winged Swallow

VII

ꜰꜰꜰꜰꜰꜰꜰꜰꜰꜰꜰꜰꜰꜰꜰ

Containing Twigs or Sticks

A. Very Large, 30 to 60 Inches, Outside Diameter

1. For description of nest see Part One, page 106.

   Shores, marshes, lakes and streams of western United States south to Mexico.

   Great Blue Heron
   (Treganza's Heron)
   (Northwestern Coast Heron)
   (California Heron)

2. For description of nest see Part One, page 107. (Eastern) Goshawk.

   Canadian border south in mountains to central California, Arizona, and New Mexico.

   (Western) Goshawk

3. See Nests On or In the Ground VI B 3.

   Golden Eagle

4. For description of nest see Part One, page 107.

   Locally throughout western United States south to Mexico.

   Bald Eagle

5. For description of nest see Part One, page 107. See also IX A a(6) 1.

    Along coast and about large streams and lakes throughout western United States south to Mexico.

    Osprey

6. For description of nest see Part One, page 108.

    Mexican border of Texas.

    Audubon's Caracara

B. Smaller, 15 to 30 Inches, Outside Diameter
b(1). *Saucer-shaped or flattened*

1. For description of nest see Part One, page 109.

    Western United States south to California, Arizona, and New Mexico.

    Sharp-shinned Hawk

2. For description of nest see Part One, page 109.

    Western United States south to Mexico.

    Cooper's Hawk

3. For description of nest see Part One, page 109.

    Throughout western United States.

    Red-tailed Hawk
    (Krider's Hawk)

4. Well-built; substantial, rather flat on top; somewhat smaller than a Red-tail's; of sticks and twigs, well-decorated with bits of white down and mixed with strips of inner bark, dry leaves, and lichens; inner cavity lined with finer shreds of inner bark, soft mosses, or lichens, and sprigs of pine, cedar, or hemlock; often decorated with leaves of deciduous trees when they become available. Usually on branches next

to trunk or in crotch of tree from 20 to 85 feet above the ground.

Valleys and lowlands of central and southern California.

Red-bellied Hawk

5. For description of nest see Part One, page 111. See also Nests On or In the Ground VI B 1.

Dry, open country of western United States south to Mexico except the coastal belt (west of Cascades) and California coast ranges.

Swainson's Hawk

6. Large, bulky; of coarse sticks and twigs; lined with leaves or Spanish moss; on the horizontal branches of tall cottonwoods, ash, sycamores, box elders, or cypress trees, from 15 to 50 feet above the ground. Along borders of streams.

Southern Arizona, southern New Mexico, and southwestern Texas.

Zone-tailed Hawk

7. A large, rough, bulky structure; of sticks and grasses; lined with leaves and grasses. Outside diameter, about 26 inches; outside height, 18 inches; inside diameter, 11 inches; inside depth, 4½ inches. In low trees or bushes within 10 feet of the ground.

Southern Texas.

Sennett's White-tailed Hawk

8. A large, bulky structure of interlaced sticks, grasses, and weeds; lined with small twigs, finer grasses, and other fibrous material well-felted together. Outside diameter, 24 inches; outside height, 12 inches; inside diameter, 9 inches; inside depth, 4 inches. Usually placed in large trees from 20 to 50 feet above the

ground but sometimes on ledges or rocky precipitous hillsides. See also Nests On or In the Ground VI B 2.

Arid country from eastern Washington and Montana south to northeastern California, Nevada, and northern New Mexico.

Ferruginous Rough-leg

9. A compactly made affair of sticks, twigs, weeds, and roots; lined with green mesquite, elm shoots, grass, moss, and roots; usually placed in cacti, Spanish bayonet, or mesquite, but often in a tree or bush from 8 to 30 feet above the ground. Nests vary in size and finish.

   Southeastern California, southern Arizona, southern New Mexico, and southern Texas.

   Harris's Hawk

10. For description of nest see Part One, page 112. (Eastern) Pigeon Hawk.

    See also VIII A a(3) 10 and Nests On or In the Ground VI B 6.

    Canadian border south in mountains to northern California and Colorado.

    (Western) Pigeon Hawk

b(2). *Cup-shaped*

1. Of large sticks; lined with leaves and grass. From 15 to 30 feet above the ground.

   Along streams near Mexican border of Arizona, New Mexico, and Texas.

   Mexican Black Hawk

2. For description of nest see Part One, page 112.

   Western United States south to Mexico.

   Horned Owl

3. Of sticks, twigs, and moss; usually lined sparingly with down but sometimes thickly with hair; usually high in a conifer but occasionally in other trees.

    Rare in northern Idaho, northern Montana, and in Cascades and Sierras to Yosemite region of California.

    Great Gray Owl

4. For description of nest see Part One, page 113.

    Western United States south to Mexico.

    Long-eared Owl

5. For description of nest see Part One, page 108. See also Nests On or In the Ground VI B 10.

    Western United States south to Mexico.

    Raven

6. Poorly constructed; of large sticks externally, inner cup deeply hollowed and compactly made; lined with strips of bark, cow hair, wool, and occasionally a few rags. Outside diameter, 20 inches; inside diameter, 8 inches; inside depth, 5 inches. Usually in solitary tree (oak, ash, or sycamore) but also in small mesquites, yuccas, and giant cacti.

    Deserts of southeastern Arizona, southern New Mexico, southeastern Colorado, southwestern Oklahoma, and western and southern Texas.

    White-necked Raven

7. For description of nest see Part One, page 117.

    Western United States south to southern California, central Arizona, and central New Mexico.

    Crow

b(3). *Like platform*

1. See Nests On or In the Ground IV A 2.

    California Brown Pelican

2. See Nests On or In the Ground VI A 2.

Double-crested Cormorant

3. For description of nest see Part One, page 114

Oregon and California.

American Egret

4. For description of nest see Part One, page 114

California, Colorado, and Utah.

**Brewster's Snowy Egret
(Western race of Snowy Egret)**

5. For description of nest see Part One, page 124.

Colorado and southern Arizona.

**Anthony's Green Heron
(subspecies of Eastern Green Heron)**

6. For description of nest see Part One, page 115.

Eastern Washington and southern Wyoming south to Mexico.

Black-crowned Night Heron

7. For description of nest see Part One, page 115.

Southern California, Arizona, and Colorado.

Wood Ibis

8. A shallow platform of small twigs; lined with small twigs and leaves; usually located in cottonwood trees, 50 to 75 feet above the ground.

Locally along Mexican border of Arizona, New Mexico, and Texas.

Mexican Goshawk

C. Small, Under 15 Inches, Outside Diameter

c(1). *Usually in evergreens*

1. For description of nest see Part One, page 117.

    Rocky Mountain region from Canadian border south to northern New Mexico and central-eastern Arizona, west to eastern Washington and eastern Oregon.

    Canada Jay
    (Rocky Mountain Jay)

2. Of sticks, twigs, and moss, loosely put together; lined with cow hair, wool, and feathers. Outside diameter, 9 inches; outside height, 3½ inches; inside diameter, 3½ inches; inside depth, 2 inches. Built close to the trunk. Mountains.

    Cascades and Pacific Slope from Washington to northern California.

    Oregon Jay
    (Gray Jay)

3. For description of nest see Part One, page 117.

    Eastern and central United States west to eastern Colorado and eastern Wyoming.

    Blue Jay

4. Nest similar to that of Crow but smaller. See VII B b(2) 7.

    Puget Sound area of western Washington.

    Northwestern Crow

5. A large, bulky, but compact structure; of sagebrush twigs, weeds, grass, and stems; lined with gray, fibrous bark broken into small fibers forming a feltlike lining. Outside diameter, 8 inches or more; outside height, 4 inches; inside diameter, 3½ inches; inside depth, 4

inches. Usually in piñon pines or junipers, 5 to 12 feet above the ground; not very well concealed.

Rocky Mountain area and eastern slope of Cascades and Sierras from Washington, Idaho, and central Montana south to southern California, Arizona, southern New, Mexico, and western Texas.

Piñon Jay

6. A rather bulky affair, the base of small sticks and twigs mostly of white sage, on which is built the true nest of dried grasses, plant fibers, moss, and fine strips of juniper bark, all deftly interwoven. Usually in pines on horizontal branches from 8 to 40 feet above the ground.

High mountains of western United States south to southern California, Arizona, and New Mexico.

Clark's Nutcracker

7. For description of nest see Part One, page 118. (Canadian) Pine Grosbeak.

Canadian border south to northern New Mexico, central-eastern Arizona, and central Sierras, California.

Pine Grosbeak

8. For description of nest see Part One, page 118.

Evergreen forests of high mountains of western United States south to central-western Texas, southern Arizona, southern New Mexico, and southern California and along coast from Washington to northern California.

Red Crossbill
(Sitka Crossbill)
(Bendire's Crossbill)
(Mexican Crossbill)

9. For description of nest see Part One, page 119.

Northern edge of western states.

White-winged Crossbill

c(2). *In chimney, inside barn wall or similar structure, and, at times, in a primitive site—a hollow tree*

1. For description of nest see Part One, page 119. See also IX B b(2) 1.

   Eastern United States rarely to eastern Montana and eastern Wyoming.

   Chimney Swift

c(3). *Inside the loose bark of trees*

1. For description of nest see Part One, page 120. See also VIII A a(3) 31.

   Western United States south to central California (along coast) and to Mexico.

   (Brown) Creeper

2. See VIII A a(3) 38.

   Western Bluebird

c(4). *In trees or bushes, vines or tangles*

1. Sometimes an insubstantial structure, scarcely more than a mere platform, the cavity being quite shallow; at other times well-built and deeply hollowed; of small twigs and larger sticks; lined with straw and grass. Inside diameter, 7 inches; inside depth, 4½ inches. In the tops of trees, usually in live oaks or sycamores.

   California.

   White-tailed Kite

2. A slight, frail platform; of small narrow twigs. Outside diameter, 6½ inches; outside height, 2½ inches; inside diameter, 4½ inches; inside depth, 1½ inches. On a horizontal limb in small trees and bushes, usually near water, from 8 to 40 feet above the ground.

   Pacific States from Cascades and Sierras to coast; also in southeastern Arizona, New Mexico, Colorado, and western Texas.

   Band-tailed Pigeon

3. A small, frail platform, sometimes cup-shaped; of small twigs, sticks, and grasses; lined with small stems and grasses. Outside diameter, 8 inches; outside height, 2⅝ inches. On large branches close to trunk of tree; sometimes in saplings.

   Lower Rio Grande Valley, Texas.

   Red-billed Pigeon

4. For description of nest see Part One, page 121. Mourning Dove.

   Western United States south to Mexico.

   (Western) Mourning Dove

5. A slight, frail structure though usually somewhat larger and bulkier than that of the Mourning Dove; of dead twigs, sticks, and weeds. Usually in mesquite but also in such trees as willow, cottonwood, and hackberry; from 4 to 25 feet above the ground.

   Southeastern California, southern Arizona, southwestern New Mexico, and southern Texas.

   White-winged Dove

6. Small and rather compact; of twigs and grasses; lined with a few straws; on the horizontal branch of a stout bush or tree, from 3 to 20 feet above the ground; often built in mesquite trees growing along dry arroyos; sometimes placed on the ground. See also Nests On or In the Ground I A a(2) 2.

   Southeastern California, southern Arizona, New Mexico, and western Texas.

   Mexican Ground Dove

7. Almost a flat platform, small, rather compact, firmly matted; of weed stems, twigs, dried grass, rootlets, a few straws with occasionally feathers, string, horsehair, or strips of cedar bark. Outside diameter, from

about 2 to 3½ inches; outside height, about 1 inch; inside depth, about ½ inch. Usually placed on a horizontal fork or flattened limb of a tree or in a bush, generally within 10 or 12 feet above the ground but varying in height from 4 to 25 feet above the ground. Frequently close to houses and barns.

Arizona, southern New Mexico (rare), and southwestern and southern Texas.

Inca Dove

8. Of dead branches, twigs, and bark of pithy weeds; flat and quite large for a pigeon's nest; in the forks of bushes or among the tendrils of a hanging vine.

Lower Rio Grande Valley, Texas.

White-fronted Dove

9. For description of nest see Part One, page 121.

Washington and Colorado south to Mexico.

**Yellow-billed Cuckoo
(California Cuckoo)**

10. For description of nest see Part One, page 122.

Eastern Montana, eastern Wyoming, and northeastern Colorado.

Black-billed Cuckoo

11. A large, coarse, compact, though not deeply cupped structure about 12 inches in diameter and 6 to 8 inches high; of sticks, but with a slight depression for the eggs; lined with leaves, grass, feathers, strips of bark, snakeskins, rootlets, and dry flakes of cattle and horse manure. In cacti, mesquite, sagebrush, thorny bushes, or low trees, from 3 to 15 feet above the ground, sometimes well hidden. Arid or semiarid regions.

North-central California, Utah, and Colorado south to Mexico.

Road-runner

12.   A bulky, flat, conspicuous structure; of black or thorny
      twigs or sticks; lined with fibrous roots or leaves. Out-
      side diameter, about 10 inches; outside height, 4
      inches; inside diameter, 4 inches; inside depth, 2½
      inches. In a tree or thorny bush but more frequently
      in an orange or lemon tree from 2 to 25 feet above
      the ground.

   Lower Rio Grande Valley, Texas; occasional in Arizona.

                                   Groove-billed Ani

13.   A bulky structure; exteriorly made of interwoven
      twigs, grass, and moss; lined with fine rootlets and
      horsehair. Outside diameter, 8 inches; outside height,
      5 inches; inside diameter, 4½ inches; inside depth, 2
      inches. Usually placed in low bushes and dense chap-
      arral but sometimes in trees 30 feet above the ground.
      Chaparral and sagebrush patches.

   Southern Washington, southern Idaho, and southern
Wyoming south to Mexico and from the Rockies and
central Texas west to Coast.

                                   California Jay
                                   (Long-tailed Jay)
                                   (Nicasio Jay)
                                   (Woodhouse's Jay)
                                   (Texas Jay)

14.   A flat, saucer-shaped, flimsy structure of small twigs
      and sticks, evenly laid in circles, supporting a woven
      interior of rootlets, otherwise unlined. Usually in a live
      oak.

   Southeastern Arizona, southwestern New Mexico, and
central-western Texas.

                                   Arizona Jay
                                   (Couch's Jay)

15. Of thorny twigs; thinly lined with grass, moss, rootlets and hair; well hidden in dense thickets or in heavy undergrowth.

   Lower Rio Grande Valley, Texas.

   Green Jay

16. A remarkable, large, bulky structure, globular or flask-shaped, with a small round entrance on one side; the outside a mass of thorny twigs and stems interwoven; the middle of flower stems; lined with feathers. Outside diameter, 6 to 7 inches; entrance-hole diameter, ½ inch. Placed at the end of a branch of thorny tree or bush and easy to find; in brushy valleys of high, dry country away from timber and among desert thickets.

   Southeastern California, southern Nevada, southwestern Utah, western and southern Arizona, southern New Mexico, and southern Texas.

   Verdin

17. A large flask-shaped or football-shaped structure lying horizontally with entrance at one end; of sticks, thorns, straw, and grasses; lined with feathers; about 8 inches in diameter and 18 inches long. In cactus thickets, yucca, or other thorny bushes.

   Desert regions of southern California, southern Nevada, southern Utah, Arizona, New Mexico, and southern Texas.

   Cactus Wren

18. For description of nest see Part One, page 123. (Eastern) Mockingbird.

   See also VIII A a(3) 35.

   Central California, southeastern Oregon (rare), and southern Wyoming south to Mexico.

   (Western) Mockingbird

19. For description of nest see Part One, page 123.

Western United States west to eastern Washington, northeastern Oregon, and south to northern Utah, Colorado, northern New Mexico, and east-central Arizona.

Catbird

20. For description of nest see Part One, page 124.

Western United States west to base of Rocky Mountains in Montana, Wyoming, and Colorado.

Brown Thrasher

21. Nest similar to that of Curve-billed Thrasher. See VII C c(4) 23. In prickly-pear cactus, Spanish bayonet, chaparral, and in dense undergrowth from 4 to 8 feet above the ground.

Southern Texas (Lower Rio Grande Valley).

Sennett's Thrasher

22. Cup-shaped; small, daintily built in contrast to the nests of others of the genus; of sticks, twigs, and grasses; lined with soft materials—wool, feathers, horsehair, fine rootlets, and grasses. Outside diameter, 6 to 7 inches; outside height, 3 to 9 inches; inside diameter, 2¼ to 3½ inches; inside depth, 1½ to 2½ inches. In the desert trees and bushes but usually tasajo cactus, about 5 feet above the ground.

Deserts of southwestern United States (southeastern California, Arizona, and rarely southwestern New Mexico).

Bendire's Thrasher

23. Cup-shaped, 3 to 4 inches deep inside; of coarse grass and fine thorny twigs; rather loosely laid; lined with fine grasses and sometimes horsehair or rootlets. Usually in cholla from 2 to 10 feet above the ground, generally about 6 feet; in tangled thickets.

Southern Arizona, New Mexico, and western and
southern Texas.

Curve-billed Thrasher
(Palmer's Thrasher)
(Brownsville Thrasher)

24. A coarse, rudely constructed, shallow platform; of
sticks, coarse grass, and moss; lined with rootlets,
fibers, grasses, and other flexible material. Outside diameter, 6 inches; outside height, 3 inches; inside diameter, 4 inches; inside depth, 2 inches. Always well
hidden in low scrub a few feet above the ground. Scrub
oaks and greasewood brush.

California, west of deserts and Sierras and north along
coast to northern part of state.

California Thrasher
(Sonoma Thrasher)

25. A remarkable, bulky, loose, and deep affair of thorny
twigs, dried weeds, and stems, and grasses; lined with
finer material and feathers. Outside diameter, 9 inches
or more; outside height, 7 inches; inside diameter, 4
inches; inside depth, 3 inches. Usually built in the
center of a cholla cactus or mesquite bush, from 1 to
7 feet above the ground.

Deserts of southern and western Arizona, extreme
southwestern Utah, extreme southern Nevada, and southeastern California.

Leconte's Thrasher

26. A large, bowl-shaped, loosely constructed structure;
of coarse twigs, fine withered grass, plant stems, and
shredded inner bark; lined with vegetable fibers, coarse
grass, small twigs, and a few rootlets. Outside diameter, 8 inches; outside height, 6 inches; inside diameter,
3½ inches; inside depth, 2 inches. Usually in mesquite
but also in other bushes; near the ground and rather

well concealed; dense thickets, often in the vicinity of water.

Deserts of southwestern United States (southern Nevada, southern Utah, southeastern California, Arizona, southern New Mexico, and western Texas).

Crissal Thrasher

VIII

↗↗↗↗↗↗↗↗↗↗↗↗↗↗

In Holes in Trees or Stumps, in Birdhouses or Similar Places

A. Nesting Singly

a(1). *Drilling nesting cavity but building no nest in bottom; using chips of wood only*

1. For description of nest see Part One, page 125. Flicker. See also IX A a(5) 1.

   Eastern United States west to eastern Montana, eastern Wyoming, and eastern Colorado; occasional in Pacific States.

   Northern, or Yellow-shafted, Flicker

2. The nesting habits of the Red-shafted Flicker are similar to those of the Northern Flicker except that the former will occasionally lay its eggs in a hole in the bank, the hole generally being especially prepared though sometimes the hole of a ground squirrel is used. See also IX A a(5) 2 and Nests On or In the Ground V B 5.

   Western United States south to Mexico.

   Red-shafted Flicker
   (Northwestern Flicker)

3. Opening with diameter about 3 inches, cavity from 5 to 18 inches deep, from 4½ to 6 inches across the bottom; usually in giant cactus if far from water, in cottonwood and willow if along a river or in water; if in cottonwood or willow from 5 to 25 feet above the ground; if in cactus, from 11 to 30 or 40 feet above the ground.

   In deserts of southwestern California and southern Arizona, along Colorado River and tributaries.

   Mearns's Gilded Flicker

4. For description of nest see Part One, page 125. Pileated Woodpecker.

   Heavy timber from Washington south along coast to Marin County, California, and in Sierras to Yosemite, east to Idaho and western Montana.

   (Western) Pileated Woodpecker

5. Cavity rarely over 12 inches deep, from 6 to 25 feet above the ground; preferably in live trunks of large trees, usually the mesquite, but sometimes in dead stump or limb or in a telephone pole.

   Southern Texas north to north-central Texas.

   Golden-fronted Woodpecker

6. Opening with diameter about 2 inches, cavity from 12 to 20 inches deep; average diameter, 1⅞ inches; preferably in giant cactus but also in cottonwood, willow, and oak. Low desert regions.

   Along Colorado River in southeastern California and extreme southeastern Nevada, east through southern Arizona to southwestern New Mexico.

   Gila Woodpecker

7. For description of nest see Part One, page 126. See also VIII A a(3) 12.

Canadian border south to Mexico east of the Rocky Mountains.

Red-headed Woodpecker

8. Opening about 1½ inches in diameter, perfectly circular, cavity from 8 to 24 inches in depth, 4 to 5 inches in diameter at the bottom; preferably in white-oak trees both living and dead, but also in sycamores, cottonwoods, and willows, rarely in telephone poles.

Southwestern Oregon, California, Arizona, New Mexico, and western Texas.

California, or Acorn, Woodpecker
(Mearns's Woodpecker)
(Ant-eating Woodpecker)

9. Nesting cavity usually inaccessible or difficult to reach, high above the ground in tall pines, cottonwoods, or other trees, either living or dead; in some parts of its range the bird prefers a trunk charred or blackened by fire. Timbered country.

Western United States south to central California, Arizona, and New Mexico.

Lewis's Woodpecker

10. Opening about 1 inch or slightly larger in diameter, cavity about 8 inches deep, gourd-shaped, and about 4 inches wide at the bottom; usually in a live aspen.

Mountains east of Cascades and Sierras from eastern Washington and Montana south to northeastern California, Arizona, central New Mexico, and western Texas.

Red-naped Sapsucker

11. Opening about 1¼ inches in diameter, perfectly circular, cavity from 6 to 10 inches deep, gourd-shaped, 4 to 5 inches in diameter at the bottom; in higher altitudes firs are commonly chosen, but in the lower valleys, alders, cottonwoods, and aspens are utilized.

California, southern and western Oregon, and western Washington.

Red-breasted Sapsucker

12. In a cavity about 8 inches deep and about 5 inches wide at the bottom; in a dying or partly decayed pine. Moderately thick woods or in more open clearings.

High Cascades, Sierras, Rockies, and adjacent high mountain ranges from Canadian border south to southern California, central Arizona, and New Mexico.

Williamson's Sapsucker
(Natalie's Sapsucker)

13. For description of nest see Part One, page 127.

Western United States south to Mexico.

Hairy Woodpecker
(Harris's Woodpecker)
(Cabanis's Woodpecker)
(Modoc Woodpecker)
(White-breasted Woodpecker)
(Chihuahua Woodpecker)

14. For description of nest see Part One, page 127.

Western United States south to southern California, northern Arizona, and northern New Mexico.

Downy Woodpecker
(Batchelder's Woodpecker)
(Gairdner's Woodpecker)
(Willow Woodpecker)

15. Opening about 1½ inches, cavity 7 to 10 inches deep; in rotten stubs or dead or partly decayed branches of oak, mesquite, hackberry, and willow trees but preferably mesquite, usually along a lake, river, creek, or ravine; or in telephone poles or fence posts along roadsides. Arid country.

Southeastern California, Arizona, New Mexico, southeastern Colorado, western Oklahoma, and Texas (east to 97 Meridian).

Ladder-backed Woodpecker
(Texas Woodpecker)
(Cactus Woodpecker)

16. Opening about 1¼ inches in diameter, cavity about 12 inches deep and 5 inches wide; in willows, alders, elders, cottonwoods, sycamores, live oaks, and other oaks.

Foothills of California west of Cascades and Sierras except along northwestern coast belt.

Nuttall's Woodpecker

17. Cavity similar to that of Hairy Woodpecker with opening a little smaller; in dead stubs or branches of sycamores, walnuts, maples, and oaks.

Oak belt of mountains in southeastern Arizona and southwestern New Mexico.

Arizona Woodpecker

18. Opening about 1¼ inches in diameter, perfectly circular, cavity gradually widening toward the bottom, 8 to 15 inches deep, usually located in a dead stub of a pine or fir, preferably one that is partly decayed but not rotten. Pine and fir forests.

Cascades and Sierras from Washington to south-central California, east to Idaho and western Nevada.

White-headed Woodpecker

19. For description of nest see Part One, page 128.

High mountains from Canadian border south to central California, Montana, and northern Wyoming.

Arctic Three-toed Woodpecker

20.   For description of nest see Part One, page 128.

High mountains from Canadian border south to Oregon, Arizona, and New Mexico.

(American) **Three-toed Woodpecker**

a(2).   *Using hole excavated by woodpecker, natural cavity, or birdbox; adding little or no nesting material, placing eggs on chips left by woodpecker or litter left by some previous occupant, such as mouse or squirrel*

1.   Southern Texas; accidental in Arizona and southern California.

Black-bellied Tree Duck

2.   Western United States south to Mexico.

Sparrow Hawk

3.   Occasional in mountains of southeastern Arizona.

Thick-billed Parrot

4.   Washington and Colorado south to Mexico. See also IX A a(2) 1.

Barn Owl

5.   Western United States south to Mexico.

Screech Owl

6.   Locally in high mountains from Mexico to eastern Washington and Idaho.

Flammulated Screech Owl

7.   Among oaks in canyons between 4000 feet and 6500 feet in mountains of southern Arizona.

Flammulated Screech Owl

8.   Western United States south to southern California, southern Arizona, and New Mexico.

Pygmy Owl

9. Rio Grande Delta, Texas, and low river valleys of southern Arizona.

Ferruginous Pygmy Owl

10. Southern California, southern Arizona, southwestern New Mexico, and southwestern Texas.

Elf Owl

11. Mountains from Mexico north to southern Colorado, Arizona, and Cascades of central California; also coast belt from northern California to Washington.

Spotted Owl

12. In evergreen forests of western United States south to mountains of New Mexico, Arizona, and Sierras of California.

Saw-whet Owl

13. Mountains of southern Arizona. See also Nests On or In the Ground V B 2.

Coppery-tailed Trogon

a(3). *Using woodpecker hole, natural cavity (or sometimes excavating cavity), or birdbox and building nest at bottom of cavity*

1. For description of nest see Part One, page 129.

Northern California, eastern Oregon, and eastern Washington, and locally in Idaho, Montana, and Wyoming.

Wood Duck

2. For description of nest see Part One, page 130.

Northwestern Montana.

American Goldeneye

3. Of grass, leaves, and weed stems; lined with feathers and down; sometimes cavity is lined only with down.

Canadian border south in mountains to Oregon and Colorado.

Barrow's Goldeneye

4. Hole or cavity lined with down and feathers; down small, light, and flimsy, pallid purplish-gray with small white centers. Usually in an old flicker hole.

Northern Montana.

Buffle-head

5. Of weeds, grass, and leaves; lined with down and feathers; usually near water; sometimes built in crevices of rock. See also Nests On or In the Ground II A a(5) 1.

Canadian border south in mountains to California (occasional in Sierras) and Colorado.

(Western) Harlequin Duck

6. For description of nest see Part One, page 130.

Locally from Canadian border south to Oregon and Wyoming.

Hooded Merganser

7. For description of nest see Part One, page 130. See also Nests On or In the Ground II A a(1) 1.

Western United States south to central California, northern Arizona, and northern New Mexico (rare).

American Merganser

8. See Nests On or In the Ground II A a(5) 2 and VII A 1.

Turkey Vulture

9. See Nests On or In the Ground VI B 4.

Prairie Falcon

10. See VII B b(1) 10 and Nests On or In the Ground VI B 6.

(Western) Pigeon Hawk

11.   Small, rather saucer-shaped; of twigs glued together with the bird's saliva; fastened to the inside walls of a hollow tree trunk or stub; occasionally in a chimney. Outside diameter, 3⅛ inches; outside height, 1½ inches; inside diameter, about 2 inches; inside depth, 1 inch. See also IX B b(2) 2.

    Chiefly near the coast from Santa Cruz, California, north to Canada and occasionally east to Montana and Nevada.

Vaux's Swift

12.   See VIII A a(1) 7.

Red-headed Woodpecker

13.   Nest of the stems of leaves with sometimes an admixture of pine needles or fine, stiff, weed stems; arranged in a circular shape or to conform to the shape of the cavity; no soft lining but finer leaf stems are smoothly laid in the hollow of the nest; diameter of inner cup 3 or 4 inches; outer measurements conform to the size of the cavity; if cavity is a deep one the lower part may be filled to within an inch or two of the opening with twigs, bits of bark, or rubbish. Along streams bordered with large trees, preferring to nest in holes in sycamores.

    Southeastern Arizona.

Sulphur-bellied Flycatcher

14.   Nest of hair, fur, feathers, and usually with bits or large pieces of cast snakeskin; lined with a felted mass of softer fur; usually in saguaros or giant cactus but also in other trees and fence posts. Open country.

    Lower Rio Grande Valley, Texas, and deserts of southern Arizona.

Mexican Crested Flycatcher

15.   Nest of a felted mass of hair and fur, with some dry grass, occasionally the exuviae of snakes and small

lizards; inner cup about 2½ inches in diameter by 2 inches high, but the size may vary according to the size of the cavity; if cavity is unusually large the bottom is filled with small weed stems, rootlets, grass, and bits of dry cow or horse manure; usually placed in knotholes of mesquite and other trees as well as in cavities of old stumps, in woodpecker holes, and occasionally behind loose pieces of bark in the manner of the Creepers. See also III D 1 and VII C c(3) 1. Low. Deep shady forests.

Eastern Oregon, eastern Washington, northern Utah (occasionally), and southern Wyoming south to Mexico.

Ash-throated Flycatcher

16. Nest of fine grasses, fur, straw, and weed stems; lined with rabbit's fur; sometimes made entirely of rabbit's fur. Dense thickets of hillsides and along streams.

Southeastern Arizona.

Olivaceous Flycatcher

17. See VI C 1, IX A a(2) 2, IX A a(3) 1 and Nests On or In the Ground VII B 2.

Say's Phoebe

18. See Nests On or In the Ground II A a(1) 7 and Nests Above the Ground VI B b(1) 2 and IX B b(1) 1.

Western Flycatcher

19. Nest cup-shaped; of weed stems, grasses, and straws; lined with feathers; occasionally a few horsehairs are woven into the lining; also placed beneath the eaves of buildings and in the cracks or crevices of cliffs. See also IX A a(3) 2 and Nests On or In the Ground VI B 9. In the mountains and about human habitations.

Western United States south to Mexico.

Violet-green Swallow

20.   For description of nest see Part One, page 131.

Western United States south to southern California and Colorado.

Tree Swallow

21.   For description of nest see Part One, page 132.

Canadian border south to northwestern California, eastern Oregon, northeastern Nevada, and northern New Mexico.

Black-capped Chickadee
(Long-tailed Chickadee)
(Oregon Chickadee)

22.   Of rabbit fur and wool, closely felted together in cavity excavated by the bird; usually in a dead willow stub.

Chiricahua Mountains of southeastern Arizona and mountains of extreme southwestern New Mexico.

Mexican Chickadee

23.   Nest of grasses, rootlets, sheep's wool, cattle hair, and very frequently rabbit's fur.

Mountains of western United States south to western Texas, New Mexico, Arizona, and southern California (except along humid coast belt).

Mountain Chickadee
(Grinnell's Chickadee)
(Short-tailed Chickadee)
(Bailey's Chickadee)
(Inyo Chickadee)

24.   Nest of hair, fur, feathers, and moss.

Coast belt from central California to Washington and sparingly to eastern Oregon and western Montana.

Chestnut-backed Chickadee
(Nicasio Chickadee)
(Barlow's Chickadee)

25. Nest of grasses, inner bark, feathers, moss, wool, and usually pieces of snakeskin.

    Lowlands of Texas.

                                   Black-crested Titmouse
                                   (Sennett's Titmouse)

26. Nest of fine grasses, feathers, cow hair, rabbit's fur, moss, or almost any soft material available; shape of nest conforms to the character of cavity. Outside diameter, 4⅜ inches; outside height, 1½ inches; inside diameter, 2 inches; inside depth, ½ inch. Usually in the hollow of an oak limb.

    Southern Oregon, southern Idaho, and southwestern Wyoming south to southern California, southern Arizona, southeastern New Mexico, and central-western Texas.

                                        Plain Titmouse
                                     (Oregon Titmouse)
                                   (San Diego Titmouse)
                                     (Gray Titmouse)

27. Nest of cottonwood down, fern fronds, decayed grasses, and rabbit's fur; usually in a live oak, 3 to 6 feet above the ground.

    Oak regions of mountains of southeastern and central Arizona and southwestern New Mexico.

                                       Bridled Titmouse

28. For description of nest see Part One, page 133.

    Washington and Montana south to Mexico.

                                 White-breasted Nuthatch
                             (Rocky Mountain Nuthatch)
                              (Slender-billed Nuthatch)
                                     (Inyo Nuthatch)

29. For description of nest see Part One, page 133.

    Evergreen forests of western United States south to

southern California, southern Arizona, and southern New
Mexico.

Red-breasted Nuthatch

30. Nest of feathers, plant down, bits of wood and animal
fur; usually in conifers. Coniferous forests and mountain regions.

Washington and Montana south to Mexico and from
Rockies west to eastern slope of Cascades and Sierras.
Also mountains of southern California and coast of
middle California.

Pygmy Nuthatch
(Black-eared Nuthatch)
(White-naped Nuthatch)

31. See VII C c(3) 1.

Brown Creeper

32. For description of nest see Part One, page 134. See
also IX A a(3) 4 and IX A a(5) 4.

Western United States south to Mexico and central-
western Texas.

(Western) House Wren

33. See Nests On or In the Ground II B b(1) 2.

(Western) Winter Wren

34. For description of nest see Part One, page 135. See
also IX A a(3) 5 and IX A a(5) 5.

Western Washington and Oregon (west of Cascades),
California, western and southern Nevada, southern Utah,
southwestern Wyoming, western Colorado, Arizona, New
Mexico, and Texas.

Bewick's Wren
(Baird's Wren)
(Seattle Wren)
(San Clemente Wren)
(Nicasio Wren)

(Vigor's Wren)
(San Joaquin Wren)
(San Diego Wren)
(Santa Cruz Wren)
(Catalina Wren)

35. See VII C c(4) 18.

(Western) Mockingbird

36. See Nests On or In the Ground II A a(1) 8 and Nests Above the Ground VI A a(2) 1.

Willow Thrush

37. For description of nest see Part One, page 136.

Eastern United States west sparingly to eastern Montana, eastern Wyoming, and eastern Colorado; occasionally in high mountains of southeastern Arizona.

Eastern Bluebird
(Azure Bluebird)

38. Nest of sticks, straw, hay, or any similar material; occasionally placed between the trunk and loose bark. See also VII C c(3) 2. In foothills and pine forests.

Pacific states and in northern Idaho and western Montana; also in Rocky Mountain section from Utah and Colorado south to Mexico; occasional in Wyoming.

Western Bluebird
(Chestnut-backed Bluebird)

39. Nest entirely of dried grass but sometimes lined with a few feathers and fine strips of cedar or other tree bark; usually in a tree cavity but frequently beneath the eaves and cornices of buildings. See also IX A a(3) 6 and IX A a(5) 6.

Mountain sections from eastern slope of Cascades and Sierras to Great Plains and from Canadian border south to southern California, central Arizona, and New Mexico.

Mountain Bluebird

40. For description of nest see Part One, page 136.

Eastern United States spreading westward.

Starling

41. See VI B b(1) 6.

Lucy's Warbler

42. Cavity excavated in an orchid, growing on the small branches of trees; lined with short cottony wood fibers on which the eggs are laid; cavity about 2 inches in diameter and entrance hole 1¼ inches in diameter; sometimes a nesting cavity is fashioned in hanging moss and lined with hair. Woodlands where hanging moss is prevalent.

Lower Rio Grande Valley, Texas.

Sennett's Warbler

43. See VI B b(2) and IX A a(5) 7.

House Sparrow

B. Nesting in Colonies, Usually in Martin-houses

1. For description of nest see Part One, page 137.

Western United States south to Mexico.

Purple Martin

IX

🗲🗲🗲🗲🗲🗲🗲🗲🗲🗲🗲🗲🗲🗲🗲🗲

In or on Buildings

A. Outside

a(1). *On flat roofs*

1. See Nests On or In the Ground I A a(6) 1 and IV B 6.

    Nighthawk

a(2). *On shelf or projection*

1. See VIII A a(2) 4.

    Barn Owl

2. See VI C 1, VIII A a(3) 17, IX A a(3) 1, and Nests On or In the Ground VII B 2.

    Say's Phoebe

3. See IV A a(1) 1 and IV B b(3) 1.

    Robin

a(3). *Beneath eaves*

1. See VI C 1, VIII A a(3) 17, IX A a(2) 2, and Nests On or In the Ground VII B 2.

    Say's Phoebe

2. See VIII A a(3) 19 and Nests On or In the Ground VI B 9.

    Violet-green Swallow

3. See IV B b(1) 3.

Cliff Swallow

4. See VIII A a(3) 32 and IX A a(5) 4.

(Western) House Wren

5. See VIII A a(3) 34 and IX A a(5) 5.

Bewick's Wren

6. See VIII A a(3) 39 and IX A a(5) 6.

Mountain Bluebird

a(4). *On wall*

1. See IV B b(2) 1.

Eastern Phoebe

2. See IV B b(1) 1.

Black Phoebe

a(5). *In a corner or cornice*

1. See VIII A a(1) 1.

Northern, or Yellow-shafted, Flicker

2. See VIII A a(1) 2 and Nests On or In the Ground V B 5.

Red-shafted Flicker

3. See V B b(2) 3.

Western, or Arkansas, Kingbird

4. See VIII A a(3) 32 and IX A a(3) 4.

(Western) House Wren

5. See VIII A a(3) 34 and IX A a(3) 5.

Bewick's Wren

6. See VIII A a(3) 39 and IX A a(3) 6.

Mountain Bluebird

7. See VI B b(2) and VIII A a(3) 43.

House Sparrow

a(6). *On chimney*

1. See VII A 5.

Osprey

B. Inside

b(1). *On a rafter*

1. See Nests On or In the Ground II A a(1) 7 and Nests Above the Ground VI B b(1) 2 and VIII A a(3) 18.

Western Flycatcher

2. See IV B b(1) 2.

Barn Swallow

b(2). *In a chimney*

1. See VII C c(2) 1.

Chimney Swift

2. See VIII A a(3) 11.

Vaux's Swift

PART THREE

/////////////////

NESTS OF MAMMALS EAST OF THE ONE-HUNDREDTH MERIDIAN

/////////////////

Introduction

ィィィィィィィィィィィィィィ

When we speak of nests we usually think of those made by birds, since we are better acquainted with them. Yet other animals, such as mammals, also build nests. To be sure, many mammal nests are merely collections of leaves, grasses, and other materials that serve mainly as bedding, but some nests are woven structures and a few are rather elaborate. Mammals cannot match birds in weaving, although squirrels show considerable skill in making nests of interwoven plant materials.

The nests of mammals often vary in construction according to the sites where they are built. Squirrels fashion a somewhat complicated nest in a crotch of a tree, but for a nest in a woodpecker's hole or natural cavity in a tree, squirrels merely gather a few leaves or other similar material to make a soft bed. The white-footed mouse also builds a more compact nest in tangled herbage above the ground than when it makes its nest in a fallen log.

In the choice of nesting materials, mammals do not exhibit as wide a range as birds. Mostly they use grasses, leaves, sticks, feathers, and fur, the last two from the remains of their victims. An exception is the cottontail rabbit that lines her nest with fur from her breast and belly.

Mammals show less diversity in their choice of nesting sites than the birds. They make their nests in some secluded or protected spot such as in or under a fallen log, in a hollow tree, in a tussock of grass, in a burrow in the ground, or beneath the leaf cover of the woodland floor.

In using the guide to mammals' nests much the same procedure should be followed as that for birds' nests. As the nests of mammals in general are not as well defined as those of birds, it must be admitted that the best way to identify a nest is to see the maker or the animal itself. This is particularly true of such mammals as shrews, ground squirrels, and mice, which have several species whose habits are much alike, and which build nests following a pattern common to the genus.

It must be said that in some cases the external characteristics of two or more species are so similar that they cannot be distinguished; only by a study or comparison of internal characteristics can a positive species determination be made, and often only by an expert mammalogist. For these reasons only the nests of the more widely distributed and the more common species of those mentioned above are included.

In spite of these limitations, it is hoped that the guide to mammals' nests may serve a purpose and lead to a greater interest in these animals. Perhaps it may also encourage a study of some of the lesser-known species, and develop more information about them.

Nests of Mammals East of the
One-Hundredth Meridian

✔✔✔✔✔✔✔✔✔✔✔✔✔✔✔

Nests In the Ground or In Burrows

I

↗↗↗↗↗↗↗↗↗↗↗↗↗↗↗

In Fields, Pastures, and Hillsides

A. Burrow Indicated by a Ridge of Earth or Mounds on the Surface of the Ground

1. Nest of leaves, grasses, and small roots in a chamber about 8 inches in diameter and 5 inches in height off a burrow; from several inches to a foot or more below the surface of the ground. Nest usually located beneath a boulder, stump, or bush. Open fields, pastures, thin woods, and meadows.

   From Massachusetts south to Florida and west to the One-Hundredth Meridian.

   Eastern or Common Mole

2. Nest of dead leaves, about 6 inches in circumference, in a chamber off a burrow; 10 to 20 inches below the surface of the ground. Mounds or hills smaller than those of the common mole. Pastures and upland wooded country.

   Northeastern United States south to the mountains of western North Carolina.

   Hairy-tailed Mole

3. See I B b(1) 20.

   Pine Mouse

B. Burrow Not Indicated by a Ridge of Earth or Mounds on the Surface of the Ground

b(1). *Entrance to burrow in the open or more or less exposed to view*

1. Nest a dainty, ball-shaped affair of leaves and grass in a shallow burrow near the surface of the ground. Outside diameter of nest, 6 to 8 inches; inside diameter, 2 to 3 inches. Entrance a small hole in the side. Also built in or beneath a fallen log and stump. Grassy fields, woodlands, swamps, meadows, and marshes.

   Maine west to North Dakota south through Illinois, northern Kentucky, and in the east south to New Jersey and the mountains of North Carolina and Tennessee.

   Common or Masked Shrew *

2. Nest a ball of shredded leaves and grasses in a shallow tunnel. Also built on the ground beneath a rock slab, stump, or fallen log. Dry fallow fields, marshy woods, and meadows.

   New York south to Florida and westward to One-Hundredth Meridian.

   Least Shrew

3. Nest bulky for a shrew; of partly shredded leaves and grass; in a shallow burrow a few inches below the surface of the ground. Also built beneath a stump or fallen log. Weedy and dry upland fields, damp woods, and marshes.

   Eastern United States west to One-Hundredth Meridian.

   Short-tailed Shrew

* Two other shrews whose nests and burrows are similar to those of the Common Shrew are the Long-tailed Shrew and the Southeastern Shrew. The Long-tailed Shrew has a restricted range and occurs in the mountains of New York, Pennsylvania, and West Virginia. The Southeastern Shrew is found from Georgia north to the District of Columbia and west to southern Illinois.

4. Nest fairly large; sometimes of dry leaves or moss, at other times entirely of the remains of its victims. In the abandoned or deserted burrow of a woodchuck, ground squirrel, or chipmunk. See I B b(1) 9, I B b(1) 10, and II B b(2) c(1) 4. Fields, cutover brush lands, woodlands, thickets, and wooded swamps.

   Throughout eastern United States west to One-Hundredth Meridian.

   Long-tailed Weasel

5. Nest of grasses and fur. In the abandoned or deserted burrow of a woodchuck, ground squirrel, or chipmunk. See I B b(1) 9, I B b(1) 10, and II B b(2) c(1) 4. Farming country and woodlands.

   Western Pennsylvania south into the mountains of North Carolina and westward through Ohio, northern Indiana to the Dakotas.

   Least Weasel

6. Nest of grass and leaves. In the abandoned or deserted burrow of a woodchuck or badger. See I B b(1) 8 and I B b(1) 9. Also built in a hollow log or stump, in a pile of rocks, in a brush pile, or beneath the foundation of a shed. Open areas, farmlands, cultivated fields, and waste lands.

   Southeastern United States from West Virginia south to southern Florida, west to One-Hundredth Meridian, and north through central Minnesota.

   Spotted Skunk

7. Warm nest of grass and leaves in the chamber of an abandoned or deserted burrow of a woodchuck or badger, or in a burrow dug by the animal itself. See I B b(1) 8 and I B b(1) 9. Burrow dug by the skunk runs into the ground at a gentle slope for 6 to 12 feet and terminates in a small room about 2 feet below

the surface of the ground. Nest may also be built in a hollow log, in or beneath a pile of rocks, or in a building. Diverse habitats.

Throughout eastern United States west to the One-Hundredth Meridian.

Striped Skunk

8. Nest bulky; of dried grass; in an enlarged chamber at the end of a burrow. Burrow 2 to 6 feet below the surface of the ground and varies greatly in length, from 6 to 30 feet. Entrance 8 inches to a foot in diameter and elliptical in shape. Open prairie country and flat rolling farmlands.

    Northern and western Ohio westward through the greater part of Michigan, northern Indiana, northern Illinois, and most of Wisconsin.

    Badger

9. Nest bulky; of grass and leaves; in a chamber 15 to 18 inches in diameter and 7 to 10 inches high, usually at the end of a tunnel; burrow as much as 5 feet below the surface of the ground and 30 feet or more long; generally forked with several side passages from 1 to 12 feet in length. Burrow can be distinguished from the burrows of other animals by the invariable fresh mound of earth at the entrance. Sometimes entrance is located beneath a stone wall or tree stump. Open fields, hillsides, and woodland borders.

    Canadian border south to southeastern Virginia and northern Alabama west to eastern South Dakota and northeastern Oklahoma.

    Woodchuck

10. Nest bulky; of grasses and fine rootlets; in side chamber of burrow from 1 to 2½ feet below the surface of the ground; chamber about 9 inches in diameter and 6 inches in height. Burrows vary in size with the tex-

ture of the soil and the size of the maker. Large squirrels may tunnel to a depth of a foot or more and the burrow may exceed a length of 20 feet, with numerous side passages many of which lead to the surface; young squirrels usually excavate a shallow burrow of not more than 6 feet in length and with a single entrance. Although the entrance is not concealed it is difficult to detect in the grass. Fields and pastures.

Lower Peninsula of Michigan, western Ohio, western Missouri, and north-central Minnesota west through North Dakota and south through east-central Texas to Gulf Coast.

Thirteen-lined Ground Squirrel

11. Nest and burrow similar to that of Thirteen-lined Ground Squirrel but somewhat larger. Fields, preferably with some hedges and bushy borders.

North Dakota east through Wisconsin to northwestern Indiana and south to south-central Kansas.

Franklin's Ground Squirrel

12. Nest in round chamber 8 to 10 inches in diameter off burrow; lined with mats of dried grass, shredded stems of larger plants, or other similar material. Entrance to burrow from 3 to 6 inches in diameter but narrows abruptly and is usually marked by a crater-shaped dike or rim of earth which may be as much as 2 feet high and 4 feet in diameter. Entrance shaft drops almost straight down to a depth of from 3 to 16 feet, depending on the nature of the soil, level of water table, and other factors. There is usually a guardroom or listening post from 3 to 6 feet below the surface of the ground. At guardroom burrow turns horizontally and may meander about or continue in a straight line, often forking into blind passageways. Burrow sometimes has a back door.

The prairie dog has largely disappeared from the short-grass prairies and open plains it once inhabited and today may be found chiefly in the national parks and other refuges of the west.

Black-tailed Prairie Dog

13. Nest of shredded grass, leaves, vegetable fibers, and similar material; in a globular chamber just off travel route or at the end of a spur tunnel. Entrance shaft slopes and leads into a widespread labyrinth of subterranean passages about 1½ to 3 inches in diameter and many feet in extent, from a few inches to 3 feet or more below the surface of the ground. Presence of burrows indicated by fan-shaped mound of earth at entrance which may be from 2 to 4 feet in diameter and from 6 to 12 inches high. Pastureland and alfalfa and hayfields.

Northwestern Minnesota and southeastern North Dakota south to the Gulf Coast of Texas and east to the Mississippi River; also in west-central Wisconsin, central Illinois, and northwestern Indiana.

Eastern, or Plains, Pocket Gopher

14. Nest and burrow similar to that of the Plains Pocket Gopher. See above. Pastures and scrubby fields.

Southeastern United States, from central Georgia south to central Florida, westward to west-central Alabama.

Southeastern Pocket Gopher

15. Nest of seed shucks and short lengths of grass and weeds; in a globular chamber about 3 inches in diameter at end of main tunnel or at the end of a short spur; intricate network of branching burrows varies in length and may be from 6 to 8 inches to as much as 6 or 7 feet below the surface of the ground. Entrance to burrow often a small, perfectly round hole indicated

by a heap of fine soil and similar to that of the pocket gopher but not as large. Grassy areas.

Eastern South Dakota, eastern Nebraska, and eastern Kansas westward.

Plains Pocket Mouse

16. Nest of leaves, shredded bark, and similar materials at end of the burrow. Entrance 1 to 1½ inches in diameter, slopes to varying lengths then levels off into a somewhat elaborate burrow system; entrance marked by a well-defined mound of earth which at times is surprisingly large and resembles that of the Pocket Gopher. An exit tunnel is usually present. Dry neglected sandy fields, rocky hillsides, uplands, beaches, and river bottoms.

Central and northern Alabama to central Georgia and south to northern Florida.

Old-field Mouse

17. Nest small; of dry grass, fibers stripped from the stems of larger plants, and available trash; in a chamber off a shallow burrow an inch or two below the surface of the ground. Overgrown grass fields, farmlands, and thickets.

Southern Virginia south to southern Florida and west to One-Hundredth Meridian.

Cotton Rat

18. Nest semiglobular; of dried grasses and leaves; sometimes lined with fur; in a burrow several inches below the surface of the ground. Dry hillsides, fields matted with a canopy of weeds, dense woods, and swampy sphagnum bogs. Nest also built on the ground.

New England west to central Minnesota and south to western North Carolina, northern Alabama, and northeastern Arkansas.

Bog Lemming

19. Nest bulky; of dried grasses; in a chamber of a shallow burrow. Prairie country.

    From central Ohio and northern West Virginia westward through Wisconsin and northwestern Tennessee.

    Prairie Vole

20. Nest of dead grass and leaves; in a snug chamber off a burrow; burrow usually 3 to 4 inches below the surface of the ground but on occasion may be a foot or more deep. Burrows sometimes so shallow that the ground is slightly uplifted to form a ridge, as with the mole. Dry fields and woodlands.

    Central New Hampshire south to Florida and west to eastern Iowa and Louisiana.

    Pine Mouse

21. Warm nest of grass, cotton or wool, bits of cloth, and perhaps some feathers in a burrow. Fields, waste places, and orchards. Also in buildings.

    Throughout eastern United States west to One-Hundredth Meridian.

    House Mouse

22. A grass-lined nest in a burrow a few inches to a foot below the surface of the ground. This is a winter nest in which the animal hibernates. The summer nest is usually built on the ground but may also be suspended a few inches aloft in grass, shrubbery, or a brush pile. See Nests On the Ground I B b(1) 2. Dry fields and open meadows.

    Canadian border south to North Carolina and northwestern Oklahoma.

    Meadow Jumping Mouse

b(2). *Entrance to burrow concealed from view, that is, hidden by some form of plant life or an object lying on the ground*

c(1). Beneath an overhanging grass clump

1. Nest a little hollow globe of woven grasses, sedges, or other plants; frequently lined with finer, softer fibers, milkweed floss or cattail down, and moss; at the end of a shallow burrow. Subterranean nest smaller than that built on ground. See Nests On the Ground I B b(7) 1. Entrance to burrow a round hole about 2 inches in diameter; one or two openings in side walls of nest give access to tunnels. Dry fields with a protecting cover of dead grass and herbs, low meadows, swampy pastures, beaches, and salt meadows.

Maine south to South Carolina and westward to One-Hundredth Meridian.

Field Mouse or Meadow Vole *

c(2). Beneath a stump

1. See I B b(1) 2.

Least Shrew

2. See I B b(1) 3.

Short-tailed Shrew

3. Rather loosely made of fur and feathers; in a cavity beneath a stump, a pile of rocks or boulders, or bush or shrubbery. May appropriate the abandoned or deserted burrow of a chipmunk. See II B b(2) c(1) 4. Brushy fields, bordering on cultivated areas, woodlands, and woodland borders.

New England west through New York and Pennsylvania to the Dakotas.

Short-tailed Weasel

4. See I B b(1) 4.

Long-tailed Weasel

* The Prairie Vole, the typical vole of the prairies, is similar in appearance and habits. From central Ohio and northern West Virginia westward through Wisconsin and northwestern Tennessee.

5. See I B b(1) 9.

Woodchuck

6. Nest an enlarged chamber at the end of a branch burrow lined with grass, leaves of mesquite, or of other
shrubs and weeds. Burrow 7 or 8 inches in diameter
and up to 25 feet long but usually much shorter; usually straight and varies in depth from a few inches
to 4 feet; generally forks 2 or 3 times. Brushy areas
and waste lands.

Southwestern Arkansas, eastern Oklahoma, and Louisiana southwest through Texas.

Armadillo

c(3). Beneath a bush or shrubbery
1. See I B b(2) c(2) 3.

Short-tailed Weasel

c(4). Beneath a rock or rock slab
1. See I B b(1) 2.

Least Shrew

2. See I B b(2) c(2) 6.

Armadillo

c(5). Beneath a stone wall
1. See I B b(1) 4.

Long-tailed Weasel

2. See I B b(1) 9.

Woodchuck

c(6). Beneath a pile of boulders
1. See I B b(2) c(2) 3.

Short-tailed Weasel

c(7). Beneath a stick or similar object
  1. See I B b(2) c(1) 1.

Field Mouse or Meadow Vole

c(8). Beneath a brush pile
  1. See I B b(1) 7.

Striped Skunk

c(9). Beneath the roots of a tree
  1. See I B b(2) c(2) 6.

Armadillo

II

𝟙𝟙𝟙𝟙𝟙𝟙𝟙𝟙𝟙𝟙𝟙𝟙𝟙

In Woods, Woodland Borders, Thickets and Hedgerows

A. Burrow Indicated by a Ridge of Earth or Mounds on the Surface of the Ground

    1.   See I A 1.

                        Eastern or Common Mole

    2.   See I A 2.

                        Hairy-tailed Mole

B. Burrow Not Indicated by a Ridge of Earth or Mounds on the Surface of the Ground

    b(1).   *Entrance to burrow in the open or more or less exposed to view*

    1.   See I B b(1) 4.

                        Long-tailed Weasel

    2.   See I B b(1) 9.

                        Woodchuck

    3.   See I B b(1) 17.

                        Cotton Rat

b(2). *Entrance to burrow concealed from view, that is, hidden by some form of plant life or an object lying on the ground*

c(1). Beneath a stone wall

1. See I B b(2) c(2) 3.

Short-tailed Weasel

2. See I B b(1) 4.

Long-tailed Weasel

3. See I B b(1) 9.

Woodchuck

4. Nest bulky; of dry broken leaves and sometimes grasses; in a chamber, which may be 12 inches high and 12 inches or more wide, off a burrow. Entrance shaft, about 2 inches in diameter, descends straight down for about 4 or 5 inches, then slopes off to a depth of 3 feet where it levels off and may be as long as 30 feet, with twists and turns, several chambers, and an exit hole. Entrance and exit holes may be within 12 inches of each other. Woods, woodland borders, and hedgerows.

New England south to central Georgia and west to eastern North Dakota and southern Louisiana.

Eastern Chipmunk

5. Nest of leaves and grass; in a burrow passageway, 1¾ inches in diameter, enlarged to form an oblong chamber 4½ to 6 inches in diameter. Woodlands, sphagnum bogs, and willow-alder swamps.

Maine west to Wisconsin and south in the Appalachians to North Carolina.

Woodland Jumping Mouse

c(2). Beneath a rock or rock pile

1. See I B b(2) c(2) 3.

Short-tailed Weasel

2. See II B b(2) c(1) 4.

Eastern Chipmunk

3. Nest more bulky than that of Field Mouse or Meadow Vole; a mass of fine dry grass, moss, and other soft material. Frequently makes use of a burrow made by a mole or shrew. Cool, damp, shaded woods, meadows, and sphagnum bogs.

    New England south to northern New Jersey and in the mountains to North Carolina and Tennessee westward through the northern part of lower Michigan Peninsula and much of northern Wisconsin.

Red-backed Mouse

c(3). Beneath a stump

1. Nest of shredded leaves and grasses in a burrow. Dry open woods.

    Maine westward through New York, Michigan, and Wisconsin and south to North Carolina.

Pygmy Shrew

2. See I B b(1) 3.

Short-tailed Shrew

3. See I B b(2) c(2) 3.

Short-tailed Weasel

4. See I B b(1) 4.

Long-tailed Weasel

5. See I B b(1) 9.

Woodchuck

6. See II B b(2) c(1) 4.

Eastern Chipmunk

7. See II B b(2) c(2) 3.

Red-backed Mouse

8. See II B b(2) c(1) 5.

    Woodland Jumping Mouse

c(4). Beneath a log
  1. See II B b(2) c(3) 1.

      Pygmy Shrew

  2. See I B b(1) 3.

      Short-tailed Shrew

  3. See II B b(2) c(2) 3.

      Red-backed Mouse

  4. See I B b(1) 20.

      Pine Mouse

c(5). Beneath a bush or shrubbery
  1. See I B b(2) c(2) 3.

      Short-tailed Weasel

  2. See II B b(2) c(1) 4.

      Eastern Chipmunk

c(6). Beneath the roots of a fallen tree
  1. Nest of leaves in a burrow. See also Nests Above the Ground II A a(3) 1. Woods and woodland borders.

      South-central Wisconsin, the Upper Peninsula of Michigan, and northern Minnesota.

      Least Chipmunk

  2. See II B b(2) c(2) 3.

      Red-backed Mouse

c(7). Beneath the carpet of dead leaves or leaf mold
  1. See II B b(2) c(3) 1.

      Pygmy Shrew

  2. See I B b(1) 18.

      Bog Lemming

3. See II B b(2) c(2) 3.

Red-backed Mouse

4. See I B b(1) 20.

Pine Mouse

III

1111111111111111

In Swamps, Marshes, Meadows, Wet Lowlands, and Bogs

A. Burrow Indicated by a Ridge of Earth or Mounds on the Surface of the Ground

1. Nest of grass, dead leaves, or such material as is available; usually constructed in a rise or eminence which provides a measure of immunity from the periodic high water that often floods the animal's chosen habitat. Damp meadows, marshes, and wet ground in the vicinity of a lake or stream.

    Canadian border south through part of Minnesota, part of Wisconsin, northern Illinois, north-central Indiana, northern Ohio, and from New England and New York south to southern North Carolina.

    Star-nosed Mole

2. See I A 1.

    Eastern or Common Mole

B. Burrow Not Indicated by a Ridge of Earth or Mounds on the Surface of the Ground

b(1). *Entrance to burrow in the open or more or less exposed to view*

291

c(1).   In the open ground

   1.   See I B b(1) 3.

Short-tailed Shrew

   2.   See I B b(1) 16.

Old-field Mouse

   3.   Nest a sphere of dry grasses, leaves, and weeds loosely woven together in a shallow burrow. Nest may also be built on the ground or woven into the rushes and other emergents a foot or more above the high water level. Wet meadows, marshes, and tidal flats.

      Southern New Jersey south to Florida and west to Mississippi and north to Illinois.

Rice Rat

c(2).   In a bank

   1.   Nest of grass in an enlarged chamber at the end of a burrow. Nest also built inside a house or lodge. See Nests Above the Ground V 3. Marshy ponds, marshes, and wooded swamps.

      New England south to central South Carolina, northern Georgia, central Alabama, and southern Mississippi west to One-Hundredth Meridian.

Muskrat

   2.   See II B b(2) c(1) 5.

Woodland Jumping Mouse

b(2).   *Entrance to burrow concealed from view, that is, hidden by some form of plant life or an object lying on the ground*

c(1).   Beneath a stump

   1.   See I B b(1) 2.

Least Shrew

2. See I B b(1) 3.

Short-tailed Shrew

3. See I B b(1) 4.

Long-tailed Weasel

c(2). Beneath a log
1. See I B b(1) 2.

Least Shrew

2. See I B b(1) 3.

Short-tailed Shrew

c(3). Beneath sphagnum moss
1. See I B b(1) 18.

Bog Lemming

2. See II B b(2) c(2) 3.

Red-backed Mouse

c(4). Beneath water
1. Nest in a chamber off a burrow; chamber 2½ to 3 feet across and 1½ to 2 feet from floor to domed ceiling. Also built in a house or lodge. See Nests Above the Ground V 1.

    Generally throughout the eastern United States east of the One-Hundredth Meridian.

Beaver

c(5). Beneath an overhanging grass clump
1. See I B b(2) c(1) 1 and Nests On the Ground I B b(7) 1.

Field Mouse or Meadow Vole

IV

↗↗↗↗↗↗↗↗↗↗↗↗↗

In Beaches

A. Entrance to Burrow Concealed or Sheltered by Growing Vegetation

    1.   See I B b(1) 16.

Old-field Mouse

    2.   See I B b(2) c(1) 1.

Field Mouse or Meadow Vole

V

↑↑↑↑↑↑↑↑↑↑↑↑↑↑↑↑

In Stream and Lake Banks

A. **Nest in the Abandoned or Deserted Burrow of a Muskrat or Some Other Animal and Usually Among the Sprawling Roots of a Tree**

1. See I B b(1) 5.

   Least Weasel

2. Nest of grass or leaves. Diverse habitats but usually not far from water.

   Throughout eastern United States west to the One-Hundredth Meridian.

   Mink

3. Nest of sticks, dry leaves, and grass. In the vicinity of water, inland waterways, estuaries, and about islands.

   Throughout the United States east of the One-Hundredth Meridian.

   River Otter

4. See III B b(1) c(2) 1.

   Muskrat

VI

↗↗↗↗↗↗↗↗↗↗↗↗↗↗↗

In Buildings

A. In a Burrow Beneath a Building

1. Nest a globular cavity a foot or more in diameter in a comparatively shallow burrow rarely exceeding a depth of 17 inches beneath a building and well-lined with grasses or scraps of cloth, paper, and other soft materials. Cities and towns, grain fields, farmlands, and salt marshes.

    Throughout eastern United States west to the One-Hundredth Meridian.

    Norway Rat

VII

In Waste Land

A. Beneath a Stump

    1.   See I B b(2) c(2) 6.

                                                 Armadillo

B. Beneath a Rock

    1.   See I B b(2) c(2) 6.

                                                 Armadillo

C. Beneath the Roots of a Tree

    1.   See I B b(2) c(2) 6.

                                                 Armadillo

*Nests of Mammals East of the
One-Hundredth Meridian*

✔✔✔✔✔✔✔✔✔✔✔✔✔✔✔

Nests On the Ground

I

////////////////

In Fields, Pastures, and Hillsides

A. Open Nest

a(1). *In or beneath a pile of stones or boulders*

1. See Nests In the Ground I B b(2) c(2) 3.

Short-tailed Weasel

2. See Nests In the Ground I B b(1) 6.

Spotted Skunk

3. See Nests In the Ground I B b(1) 7.

Striped Skunk

a(2). *In a brush pile*

1. See Nests In the Ground I B b(1) 6.

Spotted Skunk

a(3). *In a stump*

1. See Nests In the Ground I B b(1) 6.

Spotted Skunk

a(4). *In a fallen log*

1. See Nests In the Ground I B b(1) 6.

Spotted Skunk

301

2. See Nests In the Ground I B b(1) 7.

Striped Skunk

a(5). *In a depression in the ground*

1. A shallow depression, about 6 or 7 inches long, 5 inches wide, and 3 to 4 inches deep, excavated by the animal or a natural cavity lined with finely shredded leaves and grass and with a good amount of fur from the mother's belly and breast. In dense grass, beneath shrubbery, and the spreading roots of an old tree. Farmlands, upland thickets, swampy woods, woodland borders, and shrubby areas.

   Throughout the United States, except New England, east of the One-Hundredth Meridian.

Eastern Cottontail

2. Nest similar to that of Eastern Cottontail. See above. Open woods, woodland borders, shrubby areas, and thickets.

   Southern Maine, northern Vermont, and western New York south in Allegheny Mountains to southeastern Alabama.

New England Cottontail

a(6). *In tangled herbage*

1. A warm nest of leaves, shredded bark, and similar materials, from a few inches to a foot in diameter. When built in the open, nest is roofed over with grasses. Grasslands, cornfields, woodlands, and sand dunes of beaches.

   New England south in the mountains to Georgia and west to One-Hundredth Meridian.

Deer Mouse °

* *Peromyscus maniculatus.*

a(7). *Beneath a grass clump*
1. See I A a(6) 1.

Deer Mouse

a(8). *Beneath a board or other litter*
1. See I A a(6) 1.

Deer Mouse

B. Closed or Covered Nest

b(1). *In a tussock of grass*
1. See Nest In the Ground I B b(1) 18.

Bog Lemming

2. Globular, well constructed; of grass and leaves; about 4 inches in diameter; small entrance at the side. Well concealed. See Nests In the Ground I B b(1) 22.

Meadow Jumping Mouse

b(2). *Beneath a rock slab*
1. See Nests In the Ground I B b(1) 2.

Least Shrew

2. Nest a globular, woven affair of the stem and roots of grasses, sedges, and other plants in a cavity scooped out in the ground. Single round entrance in the side gives access to the interior which is lined with some soft material such as thistledown or feathers. Open fields, cornfields, arable land, and sandy beaches.

Ohio, Indiana, Illinois, southern Michigan, Wisconsin, Minnesota, Iowa, Missouri, Oklahoma, eastern Kansas, eastern Nebraska, eastern North Dakota, and eastern South Dakota.

Prairie Deer Mouse

b(3). *Beneath a fallen log*

   1. See Nests In the Ground I B b(1) 3.

Short-tailed Shrew

   2. See I B b(2) 2.

Prairie Deer Mouse

b(4). *Beneath a stump*

   1. See Nests In the Ground I B b(1) 3.

Short-tailed Shrew

b(5). *Beneath a plank or similar material*

   1. See I B b(2) 2.

Prairie Deer Mouse

b(6). *Beneath a substantial clod of earth*

   1. See I B b(2) 2.

Prairie Deer Mouse

b(7). *In a depression in the ground*

   1. Strongly made; of dried grasses and fibers of weeds; loose and of coarse materials outside; compact and of finer materials inside; a small opening near the bottom; winter nests so firmly woven that the interior remains dry during prolonged storms. See Nests In the Ground I B b(2) c(1) 1.

Field Mouse or Meadow Vole

   2. See I B b(1) 2.

Meadow Jumping Mouse

b(8). *In or beneath tangled herbage*

   1. Nest a substantial globular structure about the size and shape of a baseball with only one entrance about ½ inch in diameter; of firmly woven grasses, sedges, and shredded plant fibers; lined with cattail down,

milkweed floss, fine soft grass blades, or other cottony material. Also built above the ground. Grassy fields, brushy borders, waste places, brackish meadows, and wet bottomlands.

Virginia and Ohio south to Florida and Louisiana.

Eastern Harvest Mouse *

b(9). *At the base of a clump of saplings*

1. See I B b(8) 1.

Eastern Harvest Mouse

* Includes several species with local or restricted range.

II

✓✓✓✓✓✓✓✓✓✓✓✓✓✓

In Woods, Woodland Borders, Thickets and Hedgerows

A. Open Nest

a(1). *In a fallen log*

1. Nest of leaves. Open woods, swamps, and waste lands.

   New England south to Florida and west from the Atlantic coast to Wisconsin and Texas.

   Opossum

2. See Nests In the Ground I B b(1) 4.

   Long-tailed Weasel

3. See Nests In the Ground V A 2.

   Mink

4. See Nests In the Ground V A 3.

   River Otter

5. See Nests In the Ground I B b(1) 6.

   Spotted Skunk

6. See Nests In the Ground I B b(1) 7.

   Striped Skunk

306

7. See I A a(6) 1.

    Deer Mouse

8. Warm nest of leaves and shredded bark, from a few inches to nearly a foot in diameter. Built in a variety of places. When nest is out in the open it is usually roofed over with grasses. An abandoned bird's nest is often used. Woodlands, woodland borders, and brushy areas.

    New England south to central North Carolina, central South Carolina, central Georgia, central Alabama, and west to One-Hundredth Meridian.

    White-footed Mouse *

a(2). *Beneath a fallen log*
1. See I A a(6) 1.

    Deer Mouse

2. See Nests In the Ground II B b(2) c(2) 3.

    Red-backed Mouse

a(3). *In the base of a hollow tree*
1. See Nests In the Ground V A 3.

    River Otter

2. See Nests In the Ground I B b 6.

    Spotted Skunk

a(4). *In a brush pile*
1. See Nests In the Ground I B b(1) 6.

    Spotted Skunk

a(5). *In or beneath a stump*
1. See Nests In the Ground I B b(2) c(2) 3.

    Short-tailed Weasel

* *Peromyscus leucopus.*

   2.   See Nests In the Ground V A 2.

Mink

   3.   See Nests In the Ground I B b(1) 6.

Spotted Skunk

   4.   See I A a(6) 1.

Deer Mouse

   5.   See II A a(1) 8.

White-footed Mouse *

   6.   See Nests In the Ground II B b(2) c(2) 3.

Red-backed Mouse

a(6).   *Beneath a bush or shrubbery*
   1.   See Nests In the Ground I B b(2) c(2) 3.

Short-tailed Weasel

a(7).   *In or beneath a rock, a pile of stones, or boulders*
   1.   See Nests In the Ground I B b(2) c(2) 3.

Short-tailed Weasel

   2.   See Nests In the Ground I B b(1) 6.

Spotted Skunk

   3.   See Nests In the Ground I B b(1) 7.

Striped Skunk

   4.   See Nests In the Ground II B b(2) c(2) 3.

Red-backed Mouse

a(8).   *Amid surface cover*
   1.   See Nests In the Ground II B b(2) c(2) 3.

Red-backed Mouse

a(9).   *In a depression in the ground*
   1.   See I A a(5) 1.

Eastern Cottontail

* *Peromyscus leucopus.*

2. See I A a(5) 2.

New England Cottontail

B. Closed or Covered Nest

b(1). *In a fallen log*

1. See Nests In the Ground I B b(1) 1.

Common or Masked Shrew

2. Nest of shredded leaves and grass; in the honeycombed recess of a half-rotted log. Shady, damp woods.

New England west to eastern Ohio and south in mountains to northern Georgia.

Smoky Shrew

b(2). *Beneath a fallen log*

1. See Nests In the Ground I B b(1) 1.

Common or Masked Shrew

2. See Nests In the Ground I B b(1) 2.

Least Shrew

3. See Nests In the Ground I B b(1) 3.

Short-tailed Shrew

b(3). *In or beneath a stump*

1. See Nests In the Ground I B b(1) 1.

Common or Masked Shrew

2. See II B b(1) 2.

Smoky Shrew

3. See Nests In the Ground I B b(1) 2.

Least Shrew

4. See Nests In the Ground I B b(1) 3.

Short-tailed Shrew

b(4). *In or beneath a rock, a pile of stones, or boulders*
1. See II B b(1) 2.

Smoky Shrew

b(5). *In or beneath a pile of logs or wood*
1. See Nests In the Ground I B b(1) 1.

Common or Masked Shrew

b(6). *Amid surface cover*
1. See II A a(1) 8.

White-footed Mouse

2. See Nests In the Ground I B b(1) 18.

Bog Lemming

III

ʅʅʅʅʅʅʅʅʅʅʅʅʅʅ

In Swamps, Marshes, Meadows,
Wet Lowlands, and Bogs

A. Open Nest

a(1). *In a fallen log*

1. See II A a(1) 1.

> **Opossum**

2. Nest of grass and leaves, often of cotton. Low swamp-lands, wooded swamps, and wet brushy areas.

   Dismal Swamp region of Virginia south to Florida westward through Louisiana and from the southern Smoky Mountains westward through Tennessee, Alabama, Mississippi, and north to southern Illinois.

> **Cotton Mouse**

a(2). *Beneath a fallen log*

1. See III A a(1) 2.

> **Cotton Mouse**

2. See Nests In the Ground II B b(2) c(2) 3.

> **Red-backed Mouse**

a(3). *In a stump*

1.   A large woven nest of grass or other plant material; also in a mound-shaped structure of grass or other substances gathered on the site; sometimes as large as a basketball; built on open ground or on the surface of water 1 or 2 feet deep. Two openings, on either side, lead from the single chamber to tortuous galleries below matted vegetation. Coastal marshes, weedy shores of lakes, sphagnum bogs, salt savannas, and freshwater prairies.

   Southeastern Georgia south through Florida.

   Florida Water Rat or Round-tailed Muskrat

a(4). *On the open ground*

1.   See III A a(3) 1.

   Florida Water Rat or Round-tailed Muskrat

a(5). *In a depression in the ground*

1.   See I A a(5) 1.

   Eastern Cottontail

2.   Nest similar to that of the cottontail. See above. Brackish swamps, wet bottomlands, and the borders of freshwater lakes.

   Dismal Swamp, Virginia south to northern Florida and west to Alabama.

   Marsh Rabbit

3.   Nest similar to that of the cottontail. See above. Wet bottomlands, river swamps, and jungles of cane.

   Alabama to southern Texas north to southern Illinois and southern Oklahoma.

   Swamp Rabbit

B. Closed or Covered Nest

b(1). *In a fallen log*

1. See Nests In the Ground I B b(1) 1.

   Common or Masked Shrew

2. See III A a(1) 2.

   Cotton Mouse

3. Nest a globular woven mass of fine soft grasses, shredded bark, and various other soft materials, between 6 and 10 inches in diameter. A 2-inch entrance on one side leads to the 3- to 4-inch cavity. May also be built in the crevice of a cliff or in a tree or within a house or lodge of sticks and leaves which varies in size and shape; when constructed largely of sticks and of a fair size may look like a beaver's lodge. Two to six doorways which are usually located at ground level lead into passageways that wind through the structure and connect with corridors in the ground. Low, wet ground, swamps, and rocky cliffs of mountainsides; also in caves.

   Southern Indiana and Illinois south to Georgia and west to One-Hundredth Meridian; along the coast from South Carolina to central Florida and west to One-Hundredth Meridian; also from western Connecticut and the mountains of southern New York south through northern New Jersey, Pennsylvania, western Maryland, western Virginia to northern Alabama.

   Eastern Wood Rat

b(2). *Beneath a fallen log*

1. See Nests In the Ground I B b(1) 1.

   Common or Masked Shrew

2. See Nests In the Ground I B b(1) 2.

   Least Shrew

3. See Nests In the Ground I B b(1) 3.

Short-tailed Shrew

b(3). *In or beneath a stump*

1. See Nests In the Ground I B b(1) 1.

Common or Masked Shrew

2. See Nests In the Ground I B b(1) 2.

Least Shrew

3. See Nests In the Ground I B b(1) 3.

Short-tailed Shrew

4. See III B b(1) 3.

Eastern Wood Rat

b(4). *In a tussock of grass*

1. See Nests In the Ground I B b(1) 18.

Bog Lemming

2. See Nests In the Ground I B b(2) c(1) 1.

Field Mouse or Meadow Vole

3. See Nests In the Ground I B b(1) 22.

Meadow Jumping Mouse

b(5). *In dense tangled growth*

1. See I B b(8) 1.

Eastern Harvest Mouse

2. See III B b(1) 3.

Eastern Wood Rat

b(6). *Beneath a tangle of weeds*

1. See Nests In the Ground III B b(1) c(1) 3.

Rice Rat

b(7). *Beneath a bush*

1. See Nests In the Ground III B b(1) c(1) 3.

Rice Rat

IV

𝆕𝆕𝆕𝆕𝆕𝆕𝆕𝆕𝆕𝆕𝆕𝆕𝆕𝆕

In Waste Land

A. In a Fallen Log

1. See II A a(1) 1.

Opossum

2. See Nests In the Ground I B b(1) 6.

Spotted Skunk

B. In a Stump

1. See Nests In the Ground I B b(1) 6.

Spotted Skunk

C. In a Pile of Rocks

1. See Nests In the Ground I B b(1) 6.

Spotted Skunk

D. In a Brush Pile

1. See Nests In the Ground I B b(1) 6.

Spotted Skunk

V

↑↑↑↑↑↑↑↑↑↑↑↑↑↑

On Beaches

A. Beneath a Board or Other Litter

    1.   See I A a(6) 1.

                                      Deer Mouse

    2.   See I B b(2) 2.

                           Prairie Deer Mouse

VI

✓✓✓✓✓✓✓✓✓✓✓✓✓✓✓

On Rocky Cliffs or Ledges

1. See II A a(1) 1.

   Opossum

2. See III A a(1) 2.

   Cotton Mouse

3. See III B b(1) 3.

   Eastern Wood Rat

VII

↗↗↗↗↗↗↗↗↗↗↗↗↗↗↗

In a Cave

1. See Nests In the Ground V A 3.

River Otter

2. See III B b(1) 3.

Eastern Wood Rat

*Nests of Mammals East of the
One-Hundredth Meridian*

✓✓✓✓✓✓✓✓✓✓✓✓✓✓✓

Nests Above the Ground

I

✔✔✔✔✔✔✔✔✔✔✔✔✔✔✔

In Fields, Pastures, and Hillsides

A. Closed or Covered Nest

a(1). *In a clump of weeds*
   1.   See Nests In the Ground I B b(1) 22.

                         Meadow Jumping Mouse

a(2). *In a clump of grass*
   1.   See Nests On the Ground I B b(8) 1.

                         Eastern Harvest Mouse

   2.   See Nests In the Ground I B b(1) 22.

                         Meadow Jumping Mouse

a(3). *In a small shrub*
   1.   See Nests On the Ground I B b(8) 1.

                         Eastern Harvest Mouse

a(4). *In a small tree*

   1.   See Nests On the Ground I B b(8) 1.

                         Eastern Harvest Mouse

a(5).   *In a brush pile*

    1.   See Nests In the Ground I B b(1) 22.

Meadow Jumping Mouse

a(6).   *In a knothole in a fence post*

    1.   See Nests On the Ground I B b(8) 1.

Eastern Harvest Mouse

II

↟↟↟↟↟↟↟↟↟↟↟↟↟↟

In Woods, Woodland Borders, Thickets, and Hedgerows

A. Open Nest

a(1). *In a deserted woodpecker hole or natural cavity in a tree*

    1. See Nests On the Ground II A a(1) 1.

                                     Opossum

    2. Cavity lined with grass or moss or a nest of leaves is made. Spruce and balsam forests.

        Northern Maine, northern New Hampshire, northern Vermont, and the Adirondacks.

                                     Marten

    3. Nest similar to that of marten. See above. Spruce and balsam forests.

        Northern New England and the Adirondacks.

                                      Fisher

    4. Nest of grass and bark. If cavity is not available an outdoor nest is built that is roughly globular, about

323

a foot in diameter, with an entrance in one side; of grass, fine twigs, leaves, and moss; lined with shredded bark, especially that of grape and cedar if obtainable. Nest anchored firmly on a whorl of branches. Forested areas and woodlands, preferably stands of mixed conifers and hardwoods.

New England south through Pennsylvania and in the mountains to Georgia and west through northern Illinois and Minnesota.

Red Squirrel

5. Nest of dead leaves; usually in a maple, oak, birch, or beech; 40 to 60 feet above the ground. Outdoor nest also built close to the trunk of the tree of materials that vary considerably but chiefly of twigs, bark, moss, and leaves with a lining of grass or some other material; about 16 inches across inside and 12 inches from floor to ceiling with an entrance on one side. Built on a foundation of sticks, from 30 to 50 feet above the ground. In frequented places might be mistaken for a crow's nest at a distance. Woodlands.

Throughout eastern United States west to the One-Hundredth Meridian.

Eastern Gray Squirrel

6. Nest of dry shredded leaves and bark. Outdoor nest of two kinds also built. Summer nest a loosely woven affair of leaves and twigs; the winter nest a carefully built structure. Outer shell consists of a sphere of laced twigs with leaves attached; wall several layers of damp leaves firmly pressed together to make nest that provides protection against wind, rain, and snow. Lined with soft shreds of inner bark and bits of leaves. Entrance on one side. In southern part of range nest is often built of Spanish moss. Woods, woodland groves, open borders of swamps, and thickets.

From the Atlantic Coast west to eastern South Dakota, central Kansas, and Texas; Maryland, western New York, northern Michigan (Lower Peninsula) and central Minnesota south to southern Florida and the Gulf Coast.

Eastern Fox Squirrel

7. Nest of leaves. Deciduous woods.

Eastern United States except northern New Hampshire, northern Vermont, and Maine west to the One-Hundredth Meridian.

Southern Flying Squirrel

8. Nest of shredded bark and leaves. Coniferous woods, stands of yellow birch and hemlock, less often in woods of maple and beech.

Canadian border south to central Minnesota and in the Appalachians to northeastern Tennessee.

Northern Flying Squirrel

9. See Nests On the Ground II A a(1) 8.

White-footed Mouse

a(2). *In a hollow stump or stub*

1. See Nests In the Ground V A 2.

Mink

2. See Nests On the Ground I A a(6) 1.

Deer Mouse

3. See Nests On the Ground II A a(1) 8.

White-footed Mouse

4. See Nests In the Ground II B b(2) c(2) 3.

Red-backed Mouse

a(3). *In a crotch or branch of a tree*

1. Nest of shredded bark among the foliage of a pine or spruce. See Nests In the Ground II B b(2) c(6) 1.

Least Chipmunk

B. Closed or Covered Nest

b(1). *In a hollow stump or stub*

1. See Nests In the Ground I B b(1) 1.

Common or Masked Shrew

2. See Nests On the Ground II B b(1) 2.

Smoky Shrew

3. See Nests On the Ground III B b(1) 3.

Eastern Wood Rat

b(2). *In a crotch or branch of a tree*

1. See II A a(1) 4.

Red Squirrel

2. See II A a(1) 5.

Eastern Gray Squirrel

3. See II A a(1) 6.

Eastern Fox Squirrel

4. Nest a cleverly woven round ball of soft plant materials, dead leaves, and pine needles; lined with finely shredded bark. Nests vary considerably from size of a football to some that are scarcely larger than a baseball. At various heights from a few inches to 10 feet or more above the ground. Also built in vines and shrubs. Wooded and brushy areas, thickets of honeysuckle and greenbrier, dense hemlock forests, wood-

land borders, low ground, and swampy woodland. In southern swamps nest often built of Spanish moss.

From southeastern Virginia south to central Florida and west to southern Illinois and Louisiana.

Golden Mouse

5.   See Nests On the Ground III B b(1) 3.

Eastern Wood Rat

b(3).   *In tangled herbage and vines*
1.   See Nests On the Ground II A a(1) 8.

White-footed Mouse

2.   See II B b(2) 4.

Golden Mouse

3.   See Nests On the Ground III B b(1) 3.

Eastern Wood Rat

b(4).   *In a clump of bushes*
1.   See Nests In the Ground I B b(1) 22.

Meadow Jumping Mouse

b(5).   *In a low bush or tree*
1.   See Nests On the Ground II A a(1) 8.

White-footed Mouse

2.   See II B b(2) 4.

Golden Mouse

III

↗↗↗↗↗↗↗↗↗↗↗↗↗↗↗

In Swamps, Marshes, Meadows, Wet Lowlands, and Bogs

A. Open Nest

a(1). *In a hollow tree*

   1. See Nests On the Ground II A a(1) 1.

Opossum

   2. See Nests On the Ground III A a(3) 1.

Florida Water Rat or
Round-tailed Muskrat

B. Closed or Covered Nest

b(1). *In a hollow tree*

   1. See Nests On the Ground I B b(8) 1.

Eastern Harvest Mouse

   2. See Nests On the Ground III B b(1) 3.

Eastern Wood Rat

b(2). *In a hollow stump*
  1. See Nests In the Ground I B b(1) 1.

Common or Masked Shrew

  2. See Nests On the Ground III B b(1) 3.

Eastern Wood Rat

b(3). *In grasses, rushes, and other aquatic emergents*
  1. See Nests On the Ground I B b(8) 1.

Eastern Harvest Mouse

  2. See Nests In the Ground III B b(1) c(1) 3.

Rice Rat

b(4). *In a crotch or branch of a tree*
  1. See II B b(2) 4.

Golden Mouse

b(5). *In tangled herbage and vines*
  1. See II B b(2) 4.

Golden Mouse

b(6). *In a low bush or tree*
  1. See II B b(2) 4.

Golden Mouse

IV

✓✓✓✓✓✓✓✓✓✓✓✓✓✓✓

In Waste Land

A. In a Fallen Log

    1.   See II A a(1) 1.

Opossum

V

In Houses or Lodges Above Water

1. Nest of leaves, grass, twigs, and roots in a chamber of a structure constructed primarily of large branches or the trunks of saplings and mud; sometimes as high as 7 feet and 30 or more feet in diameter. In fairly deep water. Lakes, ponds, and slow-moving streams. See Nests In the Ground III B b(2) c(4) 1.

Beaver

2. See Nests On the Ground III B b(1) 3.

Eastern Wood Rat

3. Nest of grasses in an enlarged chamber of a usually dome-shaped structure made of cattails, sedges, water plants, decayed vegetation, and mud in water not more than 2 feet deep. See Nests In the Ground III B b(1) c(2) 1.

Muskrat

VI

✓✓✓✓✓✓✓✓✓✓✓✓✓✓

In Buildings

1. See Nests In the Ground I B b(1) 6.

   Spotted Skunk

2. See Nests In the Ground I B b(1) 7.

   Striped Skunk

3. See II A a(1) 7.

   Southern Flying Squirrel

4. See II A a(1) 8.

   Northern Flying Squirrel

5. See Nests On the Ground II A a(1) 8.

   White-footed Mouse

6. See Nests In the Ground VI A 1.

   Norway Rat

7. Nest similar to that of the Norway Rat. See above. Cities and towns.

   Generally along the coast from Massachusetts south to Florida and west to Mississippi.

   Black Rat and Roof Rat

8. See Nests In the Ground I B b(1) 21.

   House Mouse

PART FOUR

/////////////

NESTS OF MAMMALS
WEST OF THE
ONE-HUNDREDTH
MERIDIAN

/////////////

Nests In the Ground or In Burrows

I

𝆑𝆑𝆑𝆑𝆑𝆑𝆑𝆑𝆑𝆑𝆑𝆑𝆑𝆑𝆑

In Fields, Pastures, Plains, Hillsides, and Mountain Slopes

A. Burrow Indicated by a Ridge of Earth or Mounds on the Surface of the Ground

1. Nest and burrow similar to those of the Eastern or Common Mole. See Part Three, page 275. Open country, woodlands, and moist places.

   Along the Pacific Coast east to the mountains and from the Canadian border south to Baja California.

   Western Mole *

B. Burrow Not Indicated by a Ridge of Earth or Mounds on the Surface of the Ground

b(1). *Entrance to burrow in the open or more or less exposed to view*

1. For a description of nest and burrow see Part Three, page 276.

* Included with the Western Mole are Townsend Mole, Pacific Mole, and California Mole.

335

Canadian border south through northern Washington to Colorado and Nebraska.

Common or Masked Shrew *

2. For description of nest see Part Three, page 277.

   Throughout western United States west of the One-Hundredth Meridian.

Long-tailed Weasel

3. For description of nest see Part Three, page 277. Plains, brushy places, forests, mountain slopes, rocky canyons and broken country.

   Generally throughout western United States west of the One-Hundredth Meridian.

Spotted Skunk

4. For description of nest see Part Three, page 277.

   Throughout western United States west of the One-Hundredth Meridian.

Striped Skunk

5. Nest and habits similar to those of the Striped Skunk. See above. Generally arid country.

   Southwestern New Mexico and southeastern Arizona south to Mexican border.

Hooded Skunk

6. Nest and habits similar to those of the Striped Skunk. See above. Semiwooded and open areas.

   Southeastern Arizona, southern Colorado, and southwestern Texas south to Mexican border.

Hog-nosed Skunk

* Several species of shrews whose nests and burrows are similar to those of the Common Shrew occur throughout the west. Some are extremely local in range; others have a wider distribution such as the Vagrant Shrew, which is the common shrew in the mountains.

7. For description of nest see Part Three, page 278.

   Throughout western United States west of the One-Hundredth Meridian except western Washington and Oregon.

   Badger

8. Nest a grass-lined chamber off a burrow; burrow system generally about 2 feet below the surface of the ground but may be as much as 5 feet or as shallow as 12 inches depending on the type of soil; burrow system rather extensive and contains on the average about 65 feet of tunnels and several chambers; nursery somewhat larger than the others. Rocky slopes with scattered trees, open valleys, grain and hay fields, and lowlands.

   Eastern Washington, eastern Oregon, Idaho, and western Montana.

   Columbian Ground Squirrel *

9. For description of nest and burrow see Part Three, page 278.

   From the One-Hundredth Meridian west to northwestern Montana, western Wyoming, and eastern Arizona.

   Thirteen-lined Ground Squirrel

10. Nest of grass, leaves, and similar material in a chamber off a burrow. Mouth of burrow oval rather than round, 2 to 3 inches in diameter, and flush with the ground; tunnel drops steeply and then levels off at a comparatively shallow depth and is quite short. Rocky foothills, mountain slopes, dry arid plains, and deserts.

---

* There are several species and geographic races of ground squirrels in western United States. They occupy diverse habitats and some species occur in large numbers. Some are rather restricted in range. As their habits are generally much alike only a few representative species are included.

Southeastern Oregon and northwestern Colorado south to Baja California and south-central Texas.

White-tailed Antelope Squirrel

11. Nest of dry leaves, shredded grass, bark, small rootlets, and similar materials in a circular chamber about 8 inches across and 4 or 5 inches deep. Entrance in the open where a carpet of grass and herbs provides some concealment but may also be located among scattered trees, under or between rocks, or beneath a stump. Inside entrance about 3 inches in diameter but tapers to 2 inches; shaft slopes down steeply at a 45° angle until about 8 inches below the surface of the ground when it levels off. Tunnel may vary in length between 10 and 15 feet, and rises again to the surface; distance between front and back entrances in a straight line about 8 to 12 feet. Dry gravelly slopes in open woods, weedy clearings, and rock slides.

Foothills and mountains from California, Arizona, and New Mexico north to the Canadian border.

Golden-mantled Ground Squirrel

12. For description of nest and burrow see Part Three, page 279. The prairie dog has largely disappeared from the short-grass prairies and open plains it once inhabited but survivors may still be found in the plains and foothills as well as in national parks and wildlife refuges.

Montana and central North Dakota south to south-central Texas and southeastern Arizona.

Black-tailed Prairie Dog

13. Nest and burrow similar to those of the Black-tailed Prairie Dog. See above. Grassy uplands and mountain areas.

Southern Montana to northeastern New Mexico and northern Arizona.

White-tailed Prairie Dog

14. Nest and burrow similar to those of the Eastern or Plains Pocket Gopher. See Part Three, page 280. Grasslands, mountains, valleys, and deserts.

    Pacific Coast west to eastern Dakotas, western Nebraska, and western Texas.

Western Pocket Gopher *

15. Nest and burrow similar to those of Plains Pocket Mouse. See Part Three, page 280. Dry and semiarid plains, prairies, valley bottoms, deserts, sandy and stony mountain slopes, and foothills.

    Throughout western United States from the Pacific Coast east to the One-Hundredth Meridian.

Pocket Mouse †

16. Nest about 4 inches in diameter; of fine soft grasses and rootlets and sometimes of seed hulls; in a roundish chamber about 7 to 10 inches in diameter at dead end of tunnel and as much as 2 feet below the surface of the ground. Burrows large, clean cut, and may be of limited extent, often quite short, or they may entwine in a complicated labyrinth that may extend to several levels. Entrance usually in a mound of earth in a clearing. Mound may have 3 to 12 round holes from 4 to 6 inches in diameter. Mounds vary in size from a few handfuls of earth to a bulky structure up to 15 feet in diameter and up to 4 feet in height which can be seen from a distance. When a mound is not built, entrance is usually located beneath a rock or

---

* Includes several species that occupy diverse habitats. Their habits are much alike.

† Includes a number of species with similar habits. The different species occupy a variety of habitats.

shrub such as prickly pear, yucca, or sagebrush. Arid or semiarid country where soil is easily worked though some species prefer rocky soil with or without scattered brush or trees.

Western United States from the Gulf Coast of Texas and southeastern Montana west to southeastern Oregon and Baja California.

Kangaroo Rat *

17. Nest of soft vegetable material in a burrow; often uses abandoned or deserted burrow of other mice, kangaroo rats, ground squirrels, prairie dogs, and other animals. Short-grass plains, weedy areas, and sandy sagebrush country in northern part of range; in the southern part grasslands, barren creosote-bush plains, mesquite areas, and limestone cliffs are occupied.

Western United States west of the One-Hundredth Meridian to the eastern foothills of the Coast Range of Oregon and California.

Grasshopper Mouse

18. For description of nest and burrow see Part Three, page 281.

Southwestern California east to the One-Hundredth Meridian.

Cotton Rat

19. For description of nest see Part Three, page 282.

Throughout western United States.

House Mouse

20. For description of nest see Part Three, page 282.

From northwestern Oklahoma northwest through northeastern Colorado, northeastern Wyoming, and Montana east to the One-Hundredth Meridian.

Meadow Jumping Mouse

* Includes a number of species, some with a limited range.

21. Nest similar to that of Meadow Jumping Mouse. See above. Essentially in the mountains.

> Washington east through Montana and south to northwestern California and northern New Mexico.

Western Jumping Mouse *

b(2). *Entrance to burrow concealed from view, that is, hidden by some form of plant life or an object lying on the ground*

c(1). Beneath an overhanging grass clump

1. For description of nest and burrow see Part Three, page 283.

> Eastern Washington east to North Dakota and south to New Mexico.

Field Mouse or Meadow Vole †

2. Nest of shredded vegetation in a subsurface cavity; usually with at least two entrances. Sagebrush plains and short-grass areas.

> Western North Dakota and Washington south to southern California and Utah.

Sagebrush Vole

c(2). Beneath a stump

1. For description of nest see Part Three, page 283.

> Washington and western Montana south to parts of California, central Nevada, central Arizona, and western New Mexico.

Short-tailed Weasel

2. See I B b(1) 2.

Long-tailed Weasel

---

* Includes several localized species.

† Several voles of the genus *Microtus* live throughout the west, and their habits are much like those of the Meadow Vole.

3. See I B b(1) 11.

Golden-mantled Ground Squirrel

4. For description of nest and burrow see Part Three, page 284.

    Southwestern Texas.

Armadillo

c(3). Beneath a bush or shrubbery

1. See I B b(2) c(2) 1.

Short-tailed Weasel

2. See I B b(1) 10.

White-tailed Antelope Squirrel

3. See I B b(1) 15.

Pocket Mouse

4. See I B b(1) 16.

Kangaroo Rat

c(4). Beneath a rock, a rock pile, or a boulder

1. See I B b(2) c(2) 1.

Short-tailed Weasel

2. See I B b(1) 10.

White-tailed Antelope Squirrel

3. See I B b(1) 11.

Golden-mantled Ground Squirrel

4. See I B b(1) 15.

Pocket Mouse

5. See I B b(1) 16.

Kangaroo Rat

6. See I B b(2) c(2) 4.

Armadillo

c(5). Beneath a stick or similar object

1. See I B b(2) c(1) 1.

Field Mouse or Meadow Vole

c(6). Beneath a brush pile

1. See I B b(1) 4.

Striped Skunk

c(7). Beneath the roots of a tree

1. See I B b(2) c(2) 4.

Armadillo

II

/////////////

In Woods, Woodland Borders, Thickets, and Hedgerows

A. Burrow Indicated by a Ridge of Earth or Mounds on the Surface of the Ground

    1.   See I A 1.

Western Mole

B. Burrow Not Indicated by a Ridge of Earth or Mounds on the Surface of the Ground

  b(1). *Entrance to burrow in the open or more or less exposed to view*

    1.   See I B b(1) 2.

Long-tailed Weasel

    2.   See I B b(1) 3.

Spotted Skunk

    3.   See I B b(1) 18.

Cotton Rat

b(2). *Entrance to burrow concealed from view, that is, hidden by some form of plant life or an object lying on the ground*

c(1). Beneath a rock or pile of rocks

1. See I B b(2) c(2) 1.

Short-tailed Weasel

2. Nest a chamber (off a burrow) about the size and shape of a small coconut, lined with shredded grass and chewed and frayed pieces of bark and moss. Wooded areas.

Pacific Coast east to central Wisconsin, western South Dakota, eastern Colorado, and extreme western Texas.

Western Chipmunk *

c(2). Beneath a stump

1. See I B b(2) c(2) 1.

Short-tailed Weasel

2. See II B b(2) c(1) 2.

Western Chipmunk

c(3). Beneath a bush or shrubbery

1. See I B b() c(2) 1.

Short-tailed Weasel

2. See II B b(2) c(1) 2.

Western Chipmunk

c(4). Beneath a log

1. See II B b(2) c(1) 2.

Western Chipmunk

2. For description of nest see Part Three, page 288. Cool, damp, shaded woods.

---

* Includes a number of species that occupy various habitats such as yellow pine forests, mixed woodlands, and open wooded foothills.

In the Rockies from the Canadian border south to southwestern New Mexico. Also western Washington, western Oregon, and parts of California.

Red-backed Mouse

c(5). Beneath the roots of a fallen tree

 1. For description of nest see Part Three, page 289. Brushy, semi-open areas.

Montana, Wyoming, Utah, Nevada, western Colorado, and parts of Arizona and New Mexico.

Least Chipmunk

 2. See II B b(2) c(4) 2.

Red-backed Mouse

c(6). Beneath the carpet of dead leaves or leaf mold

 1. See II B b(2) c(4) 2.

Red-backed Mouse

III

↗↗↗↗↗↗↗↗↗↗↗↗↗↗↗

In Swamps, Marshes, Meadows, Wet Lowlands, and Bogs

A. Burrow Indicated by a Ridge of Earth or Mounds on the Surface of the Ground

1. See I A 1.

    Western Mole

2. Nest similar to that of the Star-nosed Mole, see Part Three, page 291, whose habits it resembles more than those of the Common Mole (Eastern or Western Mole). Burrow often in leaf mold. Damp habitats not far from streams.

    Western Washington and Oregon to the Cascade Range and south along the coast of California.

    Shrew Mole

B. Burrow Not Indicated by a Ridge of Earth or Mounds on the Surface of the Ground

b(1). *Entrance to burrow in the open or more or less exposed to view*

347

c(1). In a bank

    1. For description of nest see Part Three, page 292. Marshy ponds, marshes, and wooded swamps.

       Throughout western United States west of the One-Hundredth Meridian but absent from California except extreme eastern and southern portions.

                        Muskrat

b(2). *Entrance to burrow concealed from view, that is, hidden by some form of plant life or an object lying on the ground*

c(1). Beneath sphagnum moss

    1. See II B b(2) c(4) 2.

                  Red-backed Mouse

c(2). Beneath a stump

    1. See I B b(1) 2.

                  Long-tailed Weasel

c(3). Beneath water

    1. For description of nest see Part Three, page 293.

       Throughout western United States west of the One-Hundredth Meridian except the southern areas of California and Nevada.

                        Beaver

c(4). Beneath an overhanging grass clump

    1. See I B b(2) c(1) 1.

              Field Mouse or Meadow Vole

c(5). Beneath a shrub

    1. Nest of dried grasses, ferns, twigs, and attached leaves in a globe-shaped chamber 16 to 20 inches in diameter, located within 2 feet of the surface and usually under a spreading stump or log, off a burrow. Size of

tunnel varies with the nature of the soil, 3 or 4 inches in diameter in hard soil but as much as 10 inches in diameter in soil that is easily worked; tunnel often 20 to 30 feet long. Nesting chamber often an enlargement of main tunnel, or it may be at the end of a blind passage. Moist rain forests of the northwest.

Northern California north through western Oregon and Washington.

Aplodontia or Mountain Beaver

c(6).   Beneath a clump of ferns
   1.   See III B b(2) c(5) 1.

Aplodontia or Mountain Beaver

IV

✔✔✔✔✔✔✔✔✔✔✔✔✔✔✔

In Beaches

A. Entrance to Burrow Concealed or Sheltered by Growing Vegetation

1. Nest and burrow similar to those of the Field Mouse or Meadow Vole. See Part Three, page 283. Seashore and grassy meadows.

Coastal regions of Washington, Oregon, and northern California.

California Vole

V

↑↑↑↑↑↑↑↑↑↑↑↑↑↑↑↑

In Stream and Lake Banks

A. **Nest in the Abandoned or Deserted Burrow of a Muskrat or Some Other Animal and Usually Among the Sprawling Roots of a Tree**

1. For description of nest see Part Three, page 295. Diverse habitats, generally not far from water.

   Throughout western United States west of the One-Hundredth Meridian except southwestern states.

   Mink

2. For description of nest see Part Three, page 295. Inland waterways, estuaries, and about islands.

   Throughout western United States west of the One-Hundredth Meridian except western Texas, southeastern New Mexico, southern California, Nevada, and western Utah.

   River Otter

3. See III B b(1) c(1) 1.

   Muskrat

VI

↑↑↑↑↑↑↑↑↑↑↑↑↑↑↑

In Buildings

1. For description of nest see Part Three, page 296.
   Throughout western United States west of the One-Hundredth Meridian.

Norway Rat

VII

✔✔✔✔✔✔✔✔✔✔✔✔✔✔✔

On Ledges, Cliffs, and in Rock Slides

A. Beneath a Ledge

1. Nest of grass and leaves in a burrow. Higher mountains.

   Canadian border south to Owens Lake, California, and east to the Black Hills and north-central New Mexico.

   Yellow-bellied Marmot

2. Nest of grass and leaves in a burrow. Near or above timberline.

   Canadian border south to central Washington and Idaho.

   Hoary Marmot

3. Nest of grasses, leaves, and similar materials in a burrow. Rocky areas, talus slopes, and rock slides.

   Northern Utah and north-central Colorado south through southern Nevada and central Texas.

   Rock Squirrel

B. In a Rock Slide

1. See VII A 1.

   Yellow-bellied Marmot

353

2.   See VII A 3.

Rock Squirrel

3.   See I B b(1) 11.

Golden-mantled Ground Squirrel

C. Beneath a Boulder

1.   See VII A 2.

Hoary Marmot

2.   See VII A 3.

Rock Squirrel

D. In a Crack or Crevice of a Cliff

1.   See VII A 1.

Yellow-bellied Marmot

VIII

𝟙𝟙𝟙𝟙𝟙𝟙𝟙𝟙𝟙𝟙𝟙𝟙𝟙𝟙𝟙

In Deserts

A. Entrance to Burrow in the Open or More or Less Exposed to View

1. See I B b(1) 3.

Spotted Skunk

2. See I B b(1) 15.

Pocket Mouse

3. See I B b(1) 16.

Kangaroo Rat

B. Entrance to Burrow Concealed from View, That Is, Hidden by Some Form of Plant Life or an Object Lying on the Ground

b(1). *Beneath a bush or shrubbery*

1. See I B b(1) 10.

White-tailed Antelope Squirrel

2. See I B b(1) 16.

Kangaroo Rat

355

IX

↗↗↗↗↗↗↗↗↗↗↗↗↗↗↗

In Waste Land

A. Beneath a Stump

    1.   See I B b(2) c(2) 4.

                                            Armadillo

B. Beneath a Rock

    1.   See I B b(2) c(2) 4.

                                            Armadillo

C. Beneath the Roots of a Tree

    1.   See I B b(2) c(2) 4.

                                            Armadillo

*Nests of Mammals West of the
One-Hundredth Meridian*

⟋⟋⟋⟋⟋⟋⟋⟋⟋⟋⟋⟋⟋⟋⟋

Nests On the Ground

I

In Fields, Pastures, Plains, Hillsides, and Mountain Slopes

A. Open Nest

a(1). *In or beneath a pile of stones or boulders*
1. See Nests In the Ground I B b(2) c(2) 1.

Short-tailed Weasel

2. See Nests In the Ground I B b(1) 3.

Spotted Skunk

3. See Nests In the Ground I B b(1) 4.

Striped Skunk

a(2). *In a brush pile*
1. See Nests In the Ground I B b(1) 3.

Spotted Skunk

a(3). *In a stump*
1. See Nests In the Ground I B b(1) 3.

Spotted Skunk

a(4). *In a fallen log*
1. See Nests In the Ground I B b(1) 3.

Spotted Skunk

2. See Nests In the Ground I B b(1) 4.

Striped Skunk

a(5). *In a depression in the ground*

1. A depression in the ground under an overhanging bush or in thick grass or weeds; lined with fur. Depression may be very shallow or as much as 8 inches deep, oval in outline, and between 4 and 9 inches across. Plains and open mountain slopes.

    Canadian border south to northern New Mexico and from western Wisconsin to central Washington and the Sierra Nevada of California.

White-tailed Jack Rabbit

2. Nest similar to that of the White-tailed Jack Rabbit. See above. Grasslands and open areas but prefers the more arid plains.

    Northern Oregon, central Nebraska, and western Missouri south to Mexican border.

Black-tailed Jack Rabbit

3. For description of nest see Part Three, page 302.

    West of the One-Hundredth Meridian to southeastern Wyoming and extreme southeastern Arizona.

Eastern Cottontail

4. Nest similar to that of Eastern Cottontail. See above. Sagebrush, timbered areas, and mountain slopes usually not below the pines. Only cottontail over most of its range.

    Western North Dakota and central New Mexico west to the Cascades and the Sierra Nevada.

Mountain Cottontail

5. Nest similar to that of Eastern Cottontail. See above. Open arid areas with scattered brush; the common cottontail of the valleys and arid southwest.

Central Oklahoma and Texas west to the Pacific Coast of California and north to Montana.

Desert Cottontail

6. Nest similar to that of Eastern Cottontail. See above. Brushy areas.

Pacific Slope from the western foothills of the Sierra Nevada to the coast and from Oregon to Southern California.

Brush Rabbit

a(6). *In tangled herbage*
1. For description of nest see Part Three, page 000.

Throughout western United States.

Deer Mouse *

a(7). *Beneath a grass clump*
1. See I A a(6) 1.

Deer Mouse

a(8). *Beneath a board or other litter*
1. See I A a(6) 1.

Deer Mouse

B. Closed or Covered Nest

b(1). *In a tussock of grass*
1. For a description of nest see Part Three, page 303. See also Nests In the Ground I B b(1) 20.

Meadow Jumping Mouse

2. Nest similar to that of Meadow Jumping Mouse. See above and also Nests In the Ground I B b(1) 21.

Western Jumping Mouse

* *Peromyscus maniculatus.* Several other related species, such as the Cactus Mouse, Canyon Mouse, and Piñon Mouse, occur in various sections of the West.

b(2). *In a depression in the ground*

1. For description of nest see Part Three, page 304. See also Nests In the Ground I B b(2) c(1) 1.

    Field Mouse or Meadow Vole

2. See I B b(1) 1.

    Meadow Jumping Mouse

3. See I B b(1) 2.

    Western Jumping Mouse

b(3). *In or beneath tangled herbage*

1. Nest similar to that of Eastern Harvest Mouse. See Part Three, page 304.

    South Dakota south to central Texas and southwestern New Mexico.

    Plains Harvest Mouse

2. Nest similar to that of Eastern Harvest Mouse. See Part Three, page 304.

    Northern North Dakota and central Washington south to Mexican border.

    Western Harvest Mouse

b(4). *At the base of a clump of saplings*

1. See I B b(3) 1.

    Plains Harvest Mouse

2. See I B b(3) 2.

    Western Harvest Mouse

b(5). *In a clump of cactus, yucca, or other brush*

1. Nest of leaves of yucca or sotol or joints of prickly pear or cholla and bark of pine, juniper, mesquite, cat-claw, or paloverde in a house 2 to 4 feet in diameter at the base and nearly as high of sticks or cactus. Also

builds nests in trees along Pacific Coast. See nest of Eastern Wood Rat, Part Three, page 313. Plains and mountain slopes.

Pacific Coast east to eastern Montana and south to Mexican border.

Western Wood Rat *

b(6). *At the base of a hollow tree*

1. See I B b(5) 1.

Western Wood Rat

---

* Includes several species such as the Southern Plains Wood Rat, the White-throated Wood Rat, the Desert Wood Rat, and the Bushy-tailed Wood Rat.

II

↑↑↑↑↑↑↑↑↑↑↑↑↑↑↑↑↑

In Woods, Woodland Borders, Thickets, and Hedgerows

A. Open Nest

a(1). *In a fallen log*

1. For description of nest see Part Three, page 306.
   Along the Pacific Coast.

   Opossum

2. See Nests In the Ground I B b(1) 2.

   Long-tailed Weasel

3. See Nests In the Ground V A 1.

   Mink

4. See Nests In the Ground V A 2.

   River Otter

5. See Nests In the Ground I B b(1) 3.

   Spotted Skunk

6. See Nests In the Ground I B b(1) 4.

   Striped Skunk

7. See Nests In the Ground II B b(2) c(1) 2.

   Western Chipmunk

8. See I A a(6) 1.

Deer Mouse

9. For description of nest see Part Three, page 307.

> Parts of Montana, South Dakota, Nebraska, Colorado, New Mexico, and Arizona.

White-footed Mouse

a(2). *Beneath a fallen log*

1. See I A a(6) 1.

Deer Mouse

2. See Nests In the Ground II B b(2) c(4) 2.

Red-backed Mouse

a(3). *In the base of a hollow tree*

1. See Nests In the Ground V A 2.

River Otter

2. See Nests In the Ground I B b(1) 3.

Spotted Skunk

a(4). *In a brush pile*

1. See Nests In the Ground I B b(1) 3.

Spotted Skunk

a(5). *In or beneath a stump*

1. See Nests In the Ground I B b(2) c(2) 1.

Short-tailed Weasel

2. See Nests In the Ground V A 1.

Mink

3. See Nests In the Ground I B b(1) 3.

Spotted Skunk

4. See I A a(6) 1.

Deer Mouse

5.   See II A a(1) 9.

White-footed Mouse

6.   See Nests In the Ground II B b(2) c(4) 2.

Red-backed Mouse

a(6). *Beneath a bush or shrubbery*

1.   See Nests In the Ground I B b(2) c(2) 1.

Short-tailed Weasel

a(7). *Beneath a rock, a pile of stones, or boulders*

1.   See Nests In the Ground I B b(2) c(2) 1.

Short-tailed Weasel

2.   See Nests In the Ground I B b(1) 3.

Spotted Skunk

3.   See Nests In the Ground I B b(1) 4.

Striped Skunk

4.   See Nests In the Ground II B b(2) c(4) 2.

Red-backed Mouse

a(8). *Amid surface cover*

1.   See Nests In the Ground II B b(2) c(4) 2.

Red-backed Mouse

a(9). *In a depression in the ground*

1.   See I A a(5) 3.

Eastern Cottontail

2.   See I A a(5) 4.

Mountain Cottontail

3.   See I A a(5) 5.

Desert Cottontail

4. See I A a(5) 6.

Brush Rabbit

B. Closed or Covered Nest

b(1). *In a fallen log*
1. See Nests In the Ground I B b(1) 1.

Common or Masked Shrew

b(2). *Beneath a fallen log*
1. See Nests In the Ground I B b(1) 1.

Common or Masked Shrew

b(3). *In or beneath a stump*
1. See Nests In the Ground I B b(1) 1.

Common or Masked Shrew

b(4). *In or beneath a pile of logs or wood*
1. See Nests In the Ground I B b(1) 1.

Common or Masked Shrew

b(5). *Amid surface cover*
1. See II A a(1) 9.

White-footed Mouse

III

↗↗↗↗↗↗↗↗↗↗↗↗↗↗

In Swamps, Marshes, Wet Lowlands, and Bogs

A. Open Nest

a(1). *In a fallen log*
  1. See II A a(1) 1.

                                             Opossum

a(2). *Beneath a fallen log*
  1. See Nests In the Ground II B b(2) c(4) 2.

                              Red-backed Mouse

a(3). *In a depression in the ground*
  1. See I A a(5) 3.

                              Eastern Cottontail

B. Closed or Covered Nest

b(1). *In a fallen log*
  1. See Nests In the Ground I B b(1) 1.

                       Common or Masked Shrew

  2. See I B b(5) 1.

                          Western Wood Rat

368

b(2). *Beneath a fallen log*
1. See Nests In the Ground I B b(1) 1.

Common or Masked Shrew

b(3). *In or beneath a stump*
1. See Nests In the Ground I B b(1) 1.

Common or Masked Shrew

2. See I B b(5) 1.

Western Wood Rat

b(4). *In a tussock of grass*
1. See I B b(2) 1.

Field Mouse or Meadow Vole

2. See I B b(1) 2.

Western Jumping Mouse

b(5). *In dense tangled growth*
1. See I B b(3) 1.

Plains Harvest Mouse

2. See I B b(3) 2.

Western Harvest Mouse

3. See I B b(5) 1.

Western Wood Rat

IV

↗↗↗↗↗↗↗↗↗↗↗↗↗↗↗

On Beaches

A. Beneath a Board or Other Litter

    1.   See I A a(6) 1.

Deer Mouse

V

✔✔✔✔✔✔✔✔✔✔✔✔✔✔

On Ledges, Cliffs, and
in Rock Slides

A. On a Rock Shelf

    1.   See I B b(5) 1.

Western Wood Rat

B. In a Crevice in a Cliff

    1.   See II A a(1) 1.

Opossum

    2.   See I B b(5) 1.

Western Wood Rat

C. In a Rock Slide

    1.   See Nests In the Ground VII A 3.

Rock Squirrel

    2.   Nest of plant material. High mountain slopes.

        From Northern New Mexico and California north and west to the Canadian border.

Pika

D. Beneath a Boulder

1. See Nests In the Ground VII A 3.

Rock Squirrel

VI

✔✔✔✔✔✔✔✔✔✔✔✔✔✔

In a Cave

1. See Nests In the Ground V A 2.

   River Otter

2. See I B b(5) 1.

   Western Wood Rat

*Nests of Mammals West of the
One-Hundredth Meridian*

✓✓✓✓✓✓✓✓✓✓✓✓✓✓✓

Nests Above the Ground

I

↑↑↑↑↑↑↑↑↑↑↑↑↑↑↑

In Fields, Pastures, Plains, Hillsides and Mountain Slopes

A. Closed or Covered Nest

a(1). *In a clump of weeds*
  1. See Nests On the Ground I B b(1) 1.

Meadow Jumping Mouse

  2. See Nests On the Ground I B b(1) 2.

Western Jumping Mouse

a(2). *In a clump of grass*
  1. See Nests On the Ground I B b(3) 1.

Plains Harvest Mouse

  2. See Nests On the Ground I B b(3) 2.

Western Harvest Mouse

  3. See Nests On the Ground I B b(1) 1.

Meadow Jumping Mouse

4. See Nests On the Ground I B b(1) 2.

Western Jumping Mouse

a(3). *In a small shrub*

1. See Nests On the Ground I B b(3) 1.

Plains Harvest Mouse

2. See Nests On the Ground I B b(3) 2.

Western Harvest Mouse

3. See Nests On the Ground I B b(5) 1.

Western Wood Rat

a(4). *In a small tree*

1. See Nests On the Ground I B b(3) 1.

Plains Harvest Mouse

2. See Nests On the Ground I B b(3) 2.

Western Harvest Mouse

a(5). *In a brush pile*

1. See Nests On the Ground I B b(1) 1.

Meadow Jumping Mouse

2. See Nests On the Ground I B b(1) 2.

Western Jumping Mouse

a(6). *In a knothole of a fence post*

1. See Nests On the Ground I B b(3) 1.

Plains Harvest Mouse

2. See Nests On the Ground I B b(3) 2.

Western Harvest Mouse

II

✔✔✔✔✔✔✔✔✔✔✔✔✔✔

In Woods, Woodland Borders, Thickets, and Hedgerows

A. Open Nest

a(1). *In a deserted woodpecker hole or natural cavity in a tree*

1. See Nests On the Ground II A a(1) 1.

   Opossum

2. For description of nest see Part Three, page 323.

   In the western mountains from the Canadian border south to extreme northern New Mexico and the southern Sierra Nevada.

   Marten

3. For description of nest see Part Three, page 323.

   South in the Rockies from the Canadian border to northwestern Wyoming, in the Sierras to Sequoia National Park, and in the Coast Range almost to San Francisco Bay.

   Fisher

4. For description of nest see Part Three, page 323.

    Montana, Wyoming, Idaho, and northeastern Washington and Oregon.

    Red Squirrel

5. Nest similar to that of Red Squirrel. See Above. Evergreen forests.

    Washington, Oregon, and Northern California.

    Chickaree or Douglas Squirrel

6. Nest similar to that of Red Squirrel. See above. Evergreen forests.

    Southern Rocky Mountain States.

    Pine or Spruce Squirrel

7. Nest similar to that of Eastern Gray Squirrel. See Part Three, page 324. Oak and pine areas.

    Extreme western United States from north-central Washington south to Baja California except the Central Valley and southeastern deserts of California.

    Western Gray Squirrel

8. For description of nest see Part Three, page 325.

    In the western mountains to the Black Hills, western Wyoming, and southern California.

    Northern Flying Squirrel

9. See Nests On the Ground II A a(1) 9.

    White-footed Mouse

a(2). *In a hollow stump or stub*

1. See Nests In the Ground V A 1.

    Mink

2. See Nests In the Ground II B b(2) c(1) 2.

    Western Chipmunk

3. See Nests On the Ground I A a(6) 1.

Deer Mouse

4. See Nests On the Ground II A a(1) 9.

White-footed Mouse

5. See Nests In the Ground II B b(2) c(4) 2.

Red-backed Mouse

a(3). *In a crotch or branch of a tree*

1. For description of nest see Part Three, page 326. See also Nests In the Ground II B b(2) c(5) 1.

Least Chipmunk

B. Closed or Covered Nest

b(1). *In a hollow stump or stub*

1. See Nests In the Ground I B b(1) 1.

Common or Masked Shrew

2. See Nests On the Ground I B b(5) 1.

Western Wood Rat

b(2). *In a crotch or branch of a tree*

1. See II A a(1) 4.

Red Squirrel

2. See II A a(1) 5.

Chickaree or Douglas Squirrel

3. See II A a(1) 6.

Pine or Spruce Squirrel

4. See II A a(1) 7.

Western Gray Squirrel

5. Nest bulky, about the size of a bushel basket; of twigs with pine needles attached; dome-shaped; lined with soft grasses and frayed bark; with one to three entrances. High in a tree. Coniferous forests of the Southwest.

   Mexican border north to the Grand Canyon region then east to central New Mexico and north in the Rockies to northern Colorado.

   Tassel-eared Squirrel

6. See Nests On the Ground I B b(5) 1.

   Western Wood Rat

b(3). *In tangled herbage and vines*

1. See Nests On the Ground II A a(1) 9.

   White-footed Mouse

2. See Nests On the Ground I B b(5) 1.

   Western Wood Rat

b(4). *In a clump of bushes*

1. See Nests On the Ground I B b(1) 1.

   Meadow Jumping Mouse

2. See Nests On the Ground I B b(1) 2.

   Western Jumping Mouse

b(5). *In a low bush or tree*

1. See Nests On the Ground II A a(1) 9.

   White-footed Mouse

2. See Nests On the Ground I B b(5) 1.

   Western Wood Rat

III

↗↗↗↗↗↗↗↗↗↗↗↗↗↗↗

In Swamps, Marshes, Meadows, Wet Lowlands, and Bogs

A. Open Nest

a(1). *In a hollow tree*

1. See Nests On the Ground II A a(1) 1.

Opossum

B. Closed or Covered Nest

b(1). *In a hollow tree*

1. See Nests On the Ground I B b(3) 1.

Plains Harvest Mouse

2. See Nests On the Ground I B b(3) 2.

Western Harvest Mouse

b(2). *In a hollow stump*

1. See Nests In the Ground I B b(1) 1.

Common or Masked Shrew

2. See Nests On the Ground I B b(5) 1.

Western Wood Rat

b(3). *In grasses, rushes, and other aquatic emergents*

1. See Nests On the Ground I B b(3) 1.

Plains Harvest Mouse

2. See Nests On the Ground I B b(3) 2.

Western Harvest Mouse

IV

✔✔✔✔✔✔✔✔✔✔✔✔✔✔

In Houses or Lodges Above Water

1. For description of nest see Part Three, page 331. See also Nests In the Ground III B b(2) c(3) 1.

   Beaver

2. For description of nest see Part Three, page 331. See also Nests In the Ground III B b(1) c(1) 1.

   Muskrat

V

ᚹᚹᚹᚹᚹᚹᚹᚹᚹᚹᚹᚹᚹᚹᚹᚹ

In Buildings

1. See Nests In the Ground I B b(1) 3.

    Spotted Skunk

2. See Nests In the Ground I B b(1) 4.

    Striped Skunk

3. See Nests Above the Ground II A a(1) 8.

    Northern Flying Squirrel

4. See Nests On the Ground II A a(1) 9.

    White-footed Mouse

5. See Nests In the Ground VI 1.

    Norway Rat

6. Nest similar to that of Norway Rat. See above. Cities and towns.

    Along the Pacific Coast.

    Black Rat

7. See Nests In the Ground I B b(1) 19.

    House Mouse

PART FIVE

////////////////////

NESTS OF INSECTS

////////////////////

Introduction

The dictionary defines a nest as a structure or place used by birds for laying their eggs and rearing their young or a place used by insects, fishes, turtles, rabbits, and the like for the same purpose. Hence, a leaf on which a female insect lays her eggs or, for that matter, any other place where she might deposit them would be a nest. Similarly, a hole excavated by a female turtle in the ground in which she lays her eggs is also a nest.

We do not intend to quibble with the dictionary's definition of a nest, but we much prefer to consider a nest as any structure, however simple, prepared by the male or female or by both for the deposition of the eggs, and where some concern, however slight, is shown by either or by both for the developing young.

Accordingly, a hole dug in the ground by a female grasshopper where she lays her eggs and then leaves them unattended, without providing for the young grasshoppers, is not a nest. On the other hand, a hole excavated by a female wasp in which she lays her eggs and stores provisions, so that the newly hatched larvae may have an accessible supply of food, is a nest.

The silken tents or webs of the tent caterpillars are not nests, though they are often called nests, since they are constructed by the young as a sort of protective covering when at rest.

That insects should be able to build a nest of any kind might at first seem surprising but, on reflection, not so surprising in view of the many different kinds of activities in which they are engaged. Most of their nests are quite simple affairs—burrows in the ground or thimble-shaped cells of mud. But some are quite elaborate, such as the waxen comb of the honeybee or the paper comb of the paper wasp. A few are even exquisitely made—the miniature water jug of the potter wasp is worthy of the potter's skill.

Of all the insects, the ants are probably the best-known, or at least the ones with which we are most familiar. As we all know, by far the greater number live in underground nests that they excavate in the soil, the excavated material being brought to the surface and often deposited in mounds or craters around the entrance—the familiar anthills. These mounds or craters may be small and consist simply of excavated particles (the corn-field ant) or they may be huge, as much as 3 or 4 feet in diameter and a foot or two high, and contain labyrinthine passages in addition to those underground (the Allegheny mound-building ant). The mounds of the mound-building ant are really elaborate structures frequently covered with twigs, dead leaves, grass, and all kinds of foreign materials and may last indefinitely.

At a casual glance the small mounds or craters may all seem more or less alike. Actually, most ants make characteristic mounds that serve as clues to their identity. Compare a few mounds at random and you will observe differences not only in the size of the mounds, but also in the size of the particles excavated and the ways in which they are arranged about the entrance.

An ant nest is quite likely to be a complex labyrinth of subterranean galleries, often with long underground passageways that extend in all directions. Unlike the social bees and wasps, ants do not have permanent brood cells. They place their young in chambers from which they can take them to other parts of the nest as the need arises.

Other than the ants, the insects that build nests in the ground are bees and wasps. Most of them merely excavate a burrow that may be simple or branched. To some of us, insect burrows may be merely holes in the ground which look more or less alike. But examine a few of them and you will detect differences. Those of the burrowing wasps show considerable variation. Thus a bembecine wasp excavates an unbranched tunnel at an angle of forty-five degrees whereas an eumenid wasp digs a vertical one that may be either branched or unbranched. Both of these wasps excavate in compact soil and both close their burrows. Some wasps build turrets of the excavated material while the burrows are being fashioned, which is later used to fill the opening when the nests have been completed.

The bees that nest in the ground are known as mining bees. Some species excavate burrows in level ground, others in banks. They are as a rule gregarious and as many as a hundred burrows may be found within a small area. Examine a burrow of *Halictus* in midsummer and you will find that side branches extend from the main tunnel and that each leads to a cell that is lined with a thin coating of firm clay. The cells may be open or closed. A closed cell contains either a mass of pollen and nectar with an egg on it, or a larva feeding on it.

An interesting facet of the nesting activities of these bees is that they use the main tunnel as a passageway to the cells they are in the process of building, but the corridor is not a public one. The corridor is constricted at the outer end and is guarded by a sentinel whose head nearly fills the opening, remaining immovable should a strange bee attempt to enter. When a bee that has the right of access appears, the guardian bee backs into the wider part of the corridor and allows it to enter, whereupon it immediately resumes its position at the opening.

Unlike the nests of *Halictus,* those of *Anthophora,* which are usually excavated in a bank, have a cylindrical tube of clay extending downward and outward from the entrance. The tube, made of small pellets of earth, is rough on the outside and smooth within. The pellets of earth are moistened with water from some nearby source and are easily molded into the desired form, and on drying become hard and firm.

It is interesting to note that some of the burrowing insects select open places devoid of grass and other herbage for their underground nests while others conceal them. The bembecine wasps, for instance, prefer open places, but some eumenid wasps conceal the openings of their nests in a clump of grass, beneath a stone, or in some similar way.

Although the vast majority of insects lay their eggs wherever they are habituated by instinct to do so and then completely forget about them, leaving their young to find their own food (though usually the eggs are laid near an accessible food supply), many insects provide food either by feeding their young day by day like the ants, honeybees, and paper wasps, or by storing food for their young so that when they emerge from the eggs they have a supply at hand, as in the case of the mud dauber and the carpenter bee.

On the basis of food supply, insects can be grouped conveniently into three classes: the non-solitary or nonsocial, the solitary,* and the social. To the nonsocial class belong the insects that do not provide for their young; to the solitary class, those that store food for their offspring (a method of feeding called mass provisioning); and to the social class the species that feed their young each day (progressive provisioning).

The solitary insects are for the most part bees and wasps. Some of them excavate burrows in the ground. Others tunnel in the pith of plants and divide the tunnel into cells by building partitions across the tunnel. Still others build simple nests of mud, clay, or vegetable matter which they attach to the trunks of trees, rocks, or other surfaces.

The solitary bees provision their nests with pollen and nectar. Some wasps use the same material, but most use food of animal origin. The spider hunters capture and paralyze a single large spider, which provides enough food for one wasp larva; the mud daubers use small spiders and place as many as twenty or more in a single cell. Other wasps provision their nests with grasshoppers, cutworms, ants, bees, beetles, and other insects. The cicada killer uses cicadas exclusively.

Most of us are familiar with the complex communities of the honey bees and ants, since much has been written about them. These insects—as well as the yellow jackets, paper wasps, ter-

* Some entomologists prefer the term subsocial.

mites, and bumblebees—live in organized groups or communities and hence are known as the social insects.

These social insects have a number of characteristics in common, such as parental care and division of labor. All build more or less elaborate nests, frequently building up large populations. Communities of some tropical species of termites may consist of several million members. Our own species of termites do not reach such proportions, nor do our other social insects. The paper wasp *Polistes* may have a community of only fifty individuals. A populous community of bumblebees may consist of three or four hundred. A single nest of the bald-faced hornet or the honey bee is much larger; that of the wasp may number as many as fifteen thousand inhabitants, of the honey bee from thirty-five to fifty thousand.

We have one species of honey bee with its characteristic nest of wax that is easy to identify. We have a number of species of bumblebees that all make the same kind of nest; therefore to identify the maker of a particular bumblebee nest it is necessary to determine the species that made it. The same can be said of the other nest-building bees as well as the wasps and ants. We have some twenty-five hundred species of bees in North America. Not all are nest-builders since some are parasitic. But the majority of them build some kind of nest, and in many cases the nests of related species are much alike or if they differ do so only slightly. Hence identifying the maker of a given nest means determining the species, obviously the task of the professional entomologist and often a specialist. For most of us, knowing that a certain mud cell was made by a mason bee would be sufficient. Similarly we have several species of the paper wasp *Polistes* whose nests are similar, so it doesn't matter much whether the nest we find was made by *Polistes fuscatus, P. annularis,* or *P. pallipes.*

Since it is obvious that it would be neither feasible nor practical to include all of our nest-building insects in the present guide, we have included only the representative species or those that would be most apt to be seen by the nature student or the amateur entomologist. Actually, the guide has been designed more as an introduction to the nests of insects, with the thought that anyone interested in the subject can pursue it further, once he has become acquainted with the nest-building species.

I

Nests In the Ground

A. Nest a Simple or Branched Burrow in the Ground

a(1). *Burrow entrance open*

b(1). In open, level places

1. A cylindrical burrow with lateral branches, each branch ending in a cell. Sides of burrow and cells plastered with a secretion that dries rapidly to form a "membrane more delicate than the thinnest goldbeater's skin and more lustrous than the most beautiful satin." Burrow from 18 to 28 inches long, lateral branches from 2 to 6 inches long. Sometimes burrow, instead of having lateral branches, may be partitioned into 6 to 10 cells. In sandy or clay-like soil.

   Throughout the United States east of the Rocky Mountains.

   Colletid Bee (*Colletes compactus*)

2. A horizontal burrow with small side branches, each branch leading to a cell the sides of which are lined with a thin coating of clay. A communal nest, each female bee having her own group of cells. Main bur-

row contracted at entrance which is guarded by a sentinel bee whose head nearly fills the opening. Gregarious, hundreds of nests being built near together.

From the Atlantic coast westward to the Rockies.

Mining Bee (*Halictus pruinosus*)

3. A vertical burrow with branching broad cells. Gregarious, many burrows being excavated close together forming large "villages." Roadsides and fields of scanty vegetation.

   Throughout the United States east of the Rockies.

Mining Bee (*Andrena carlini*)

b(2). Beneath a tuft of grass, a lichen, or moss

1. Entrance shaft short and oblique from opening to main tunnel; nursery cells in lateral clusters, barrel-shaped; about ¾ inch long; lined with clay and smooth inside.

   Generally distributed throughout the East.

Blue Digger Bee (*Augochlora humeralis*)

b(3). Beneath a stone

1. Burrow contains a series of thimble-like capsules placed end to end and made of pieces of leaves cut very neatly and either oblong or circular, the former being used for the sides and the latter for the ends. Rose leaves used more than any other.

   Throughout eastern United States.

Leaf-cutting Bee (*Megachile brevis*)

b(4). In a bank

1. See I A a(1) b(1) 1.

Colletid Bee (*Colletes compactus*)

2. See I A a(1) b(1) 2.

Mining Bee (*Halictus pruinosus*)

3. Burrow extends a variable distance and leads to a cluster of oval cells; layer of earth forms walls of cells, made firm by a cementing substance. Cylindrical tube of earth pellets compacted together extends outward and downward from entrance; tough on the outside, smooth on the inside. In an inclined or perpendicular bank, preferably of compact clay. Gregarious, hundreds of nests close together.

   Generally distributed throughout the United States east of the Rockies.

   Mining Bee (*Anthophora spp*)

a(2). *Burrow entrance closed*

  b(1). In open level places

1. Burrow enlarged at lower end to form a cell.

   Generally distributed throughout the East.

   Spider Wasp (*Psammochares atrax*)

2. Burrow similar to that of the Spider Wasp. See above.

   Southwestern United States.

   Tarantula-hawk (*Pepsis formosa*)

3. A burrow with branching short passages, each of which leads to a cell from the ceiling of which an egg is suspended by a slender thread. In a barren spot.

   Generally distributed throughout the East.

   Eumenid Wasp (*Odynerus dorsalis*)

4. Burrow similar to that of the Eumenid Wasp (*Odynerus dorsalis*). See above. While the burrow is being excavated the pellets of earth that are removed are cemented together in regular fashion in the form of a turret or tower over the entrance. When the nest has been completed and provisioned and the eggs have

been laid, the tower is torn down and the material used to close the opening.

Generally distributed throughout the United States east of the Rockies.

Eumenid Wasp (*Odynerus geminus*)

5. A deep vertical burrow with the entrance shaft sloping gently for about 6 inches and connecting with the main burrow at about a right angle; main burrow ending in a globular cell 1½ inches in diameter. Frequently a number of branches may leave the main burrow at about the same point, each terminating in a round cell. Burrow about 0.83 inch in diameter and 13 inches long. Usually in packed soil.

Throughout the East.

Cicada Killer (*Sphecius speciosus*)

6. Burrow inclined obliquely downward for about 5 inches and enlarged at the end to form a cell. A pile of pellets about 4 inches from opening of nest.

Generally throughout the eastern United States.

Golden Digger Wasp (*Chlorion ichneumoneum*)

7. Burrow rather deep; opening carefully concealed by the insertion of a stone over which dry earth is scraped.

Widely distributed.

Tool-using Wasp (*Sphex urnaria*)

8. Burrow excavated at an angle of 45°. Burrow about 0.25 inch in diameter and 10 inches long. Usually in sandy places. Gregarious, nests often close together to form a populous "village."

Throughout the East.

Sand Wasp (*Bembix spinolae*)

b(2). Beneath a clump of grass

1. A vertical burrow branching at the end into several clusters of cells.

   Throughout the United States east of the Rockies.

   Eumenid Wasp (*Odynerus annulatus*)

b(3). Beneath a stone

1. See above.

   Eumenid Wasp (*Odynerus annulatus*)

b(4). In a bank

1. Burrow more or less perpendicular to the ground with two or three side chambers.

   Generally throughout the East.

   Eumenid Wasp (*Odynerus pedestris*)

B. Nest a More or Less Complex Labyrinth of Subterranean Galleries, Frequently with Long Underground Passages that Extend in All Directions; No Permanent Brood Cells, the Young Being Kept in Chambers from Which They May be Transported to Other Parts of the Nest. Sometimes Mounds or Craters Are Built About Entrance. Mounds May be Small and Consist Simply of Excavated Particles of Earth or They May be Large, as Much as 3 or 4 Feet in Diameter and a Foot or Two High, and Contain Labyrinthine Passages in Addition to Those Underground; They May Often be Covered with Twigs, Dead Leaves, Grass, and All Kinds of Foreign Materials and May Last Indefinitely

b(1). *Nest without a mound*

c(1). In the open

1. An area about the entrance is cleared to form a disk

10 or 12 feet, sometimes 15 to 20 feet, in diameter, from which paths radiate. A southern species.

Harvesting Ant (*Pogonomyrmex barbatus*)

c(2). Beneath a stone

1. In open grassy places.

Common throughout the United States.

Thief Ant (*Solenopsis molesta*)

2. Ant often makes paper-like partitions in its nest or paper nests that are attached to the side of a log or to the branch of a shrub; frequently builds a paper nest over a herd of aphids or coccids, from which honey-dew is obtained, the so-called "cow-sheds" which may be some distance from the nest.

Northern states.

Shed-builder Ant (*Cremastogaster lineolata*)

3. Also beneath brick and flag pavements or sidewalks. Open spaces of cities and towns.

Generally throughout the United States.

Pavement Ant (*Tetramorium caespitum*)

4. In grassy places along the edges of woods.

Common in the United States.

Blood-red Slave-maker (*Formica sanguinea*)

5. Widely distributed throughout the United States.

Negro Ant (*Formica fusca*)

6. In sunny grassy fields.

Common throughout the United States.

Schaufuss Ant (*Formica pallidefulva schaufussi*)

c(3). Beneath a log

1. See I B b(1) c(2) 4.

Blood-red Slave-maker

2.   See I B b(1) c(2) 2.

Shed-builder Ant

3.   In boggy soil.

Widely distributed throughout the East.

Common Red-brown Ant (*Myrmica brevnoides*)

c(4).   Beneath a stump

1.   See I B b(1) c(2) 2.

Shed-builder Ant

c(5).   Beneath a board or some similar object

1.   See I B b(1) c(2) 2.

Shed-builder Ant

c(6).   Beneath a clump of moss

1.   See I B b(1) c(3) 3.

Common Red-brown Ant

c(7).   Beneath the foundation of a house

1.   Widely distributed throughout the United States.

Little Yellow House Ant
(*Monomorium pharaonis*)

b(2).   *Nest with a small or obscure mound or crater*

c(1).   In a sandy place

1.   Throughout the United States.

Little Black Ant (*Monomorium minimum*)

2.   Nest with many openings or craters. Often near the base of a tree.

Texas and Louisiana.

Texas Leaf-cutting Ant (*Atta texana*)

c(2).   In a cornfield

1.   In various places but especially in a cornfield. Generally throughout the United States.

Corn-field Ant (*Lasius niger*)

c(3).   Around a stump

1.   See I B b(1) c(2) 4.

Blood-red Slave-maker

2.   See I B b(1) c(2) 6.

Schaufuss Ant

c(4).   In an open place

1.   In the Southwest.

Honey Ant (*Myrmecocystus melliger*)

b(3).   *Nest with a large mound*

1.   Southern New England and New Jersey west to Ohio. Most abundant in the Allegheny Mountains of Pennsylvania.

Allegheny Mound-building Ant (*Formica exsectoides*)

C. Nest a Series of Horizontal Paper Combs Enclosed in a Paper Envelope

c(1).   *In a deserted burrow of a mouse or chipmunk or in a hole in the ground*

1.   Paper brownish in color and made from partially decayed wood. Access to nest by a single small opening that leads directly to the interior. Envelope of small overlapping sections.

Widely distributed throughout the United States.

Yellow-jacket Wasp (*Vespula pennsylvanica*)

D. Nest of Moss, Grass or Other Soft Material and Containing Cells of Wax

d(1). *In the deserted underground nest of a mouse*

1. Cells of wax in combs, sometimes of several stories.

   Widely distributed, especially abundant in the Mississippi Valley.

   Bumblebee (*Bombus americanorum*)

E. Nest a Simple Structure Extending Some 7 Inches Underground and Ending in a Chamber, Usually Containing Several Small Pulpy Balls

e(1). *In the open*

1. From the South north to Long Island, N.Y.

   Leaf-cutting Ant (*Trachmyrmex septentrionales*)

II

↑↑↑↑↑↑↑↑↑↑↑↑↑↑↑↑

Nests On the Ground

A. Nest of Paper

a(1). *In a slight hollow beneath a tuft of grass*
1. See Nests In the Ground I C c(1) 1.

Yellow-jacket Wasp

a(2). *In a slight hollow beneath a stone*
1. See Nests In the Ground I C c(1) 1.

Yellow-jacket Wasp

a(3). *Attached to the lower surface of a stone*
1. Nest a single comb of grayish, paper-like material made from weatherworn wood suspended by a pedicel and without an envelope. Resembles an open umbrella.
   Common throughout the United States.

Paper Wasp (Polistes fuscatus)

a(4). *In or beneath a stump*
1. See Nests In the Ground I C c(1) 1.

Yellow-jacket Wasp

a(5). *In a slight hollow beneath a board or some similar material*
  1. See Nests In the Ground I C c(1) 1.

Yellow-jacket Wasp

B. Nest of Moss, Grass, or Other Soft Material

b(1). *In a slight hollow beneath a tuft of grass*
  1. See Nests In the Ground I D d(1) 1.

Bumblebee

C. Nest a More or Less Complex Labyrinth of Galleries and Tunnels

c(1). *In a log*
  1. See Nests In the Ground I B b(1) c(2) 2.

Shed-builder Ant

c(2). *In a stump*
  1. See Nests In the Ground I B b(1) c(2) 2.

Shed-builder Ant

D. Nest a Rather Complicated Series of Parallel Concentric Chambers Which, in an Old Nest, Becomes a Veritable Labyrinth of Galleries, Halls, and Rooms. The Corridors Are Usually Excavated in Parallel Series of Two, Three, or More, Separated by Columns and Arches or by Thin Partitions, and the Rooms Are Somewhat Crudely Arranged in Stories and Half-Stories. Entrance to the Nest May be by a Circular or Oblong Door that Opens into Tubular Circuitous Galleries Which Communicate with the Interior; or the Entrance May be a Spacious Vestibule

d(1). *In a log*

1. Common throughout eastern United States.

Black Carpenter Ant
(*Camponotus herculeanus pennsylvanicus*)

d(2). *In a stump*

1. See above.

Black Carpenter Ant

E. Nest a Series of Galleries or Tunnels Parallel to One Another and Usually with the Grain of the Wood. They Do Not Form Such an Intricate Series of Tunnels and Chambers that Is Typical of the Nest of the Black Carpenter Ant and May Be Distinguished from Those of the Ant, and Other Tunnel-Making Insects, by the Fact that They Are Plastered with a Grayish Mortar-Like Substance Composed of Excrement

e(1). *In a log*

1. Southern Maine westward to Lake Superior and south to Florida and Texas.

Common Termite (*Reticulitermes flavipes*)

e(2). *In a stump*

1. See above.

Common Termite

F. Nest of Mud or Some Similar Material

f(1). *Beneath a stone*

1. Nest a small earthen cell of sand, earth, or clay mixed with pebbles and wood scrapings glued together. Ten to twenty usually found together.

Generally throughout the East.

Mason Bee (*Osmia spp*)

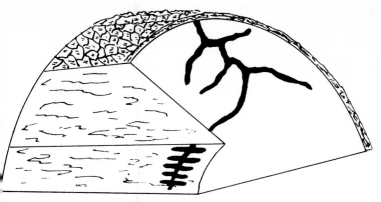

Burrow of Apple Wood Staliner

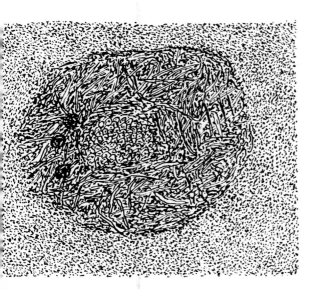

Nest of Bumblebee

Nest of Little Carpenter Bee

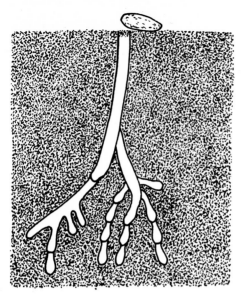

Nest of Eumenid Wasp (Odynerus annulatus)

Nest of Pemphredonid Wasp

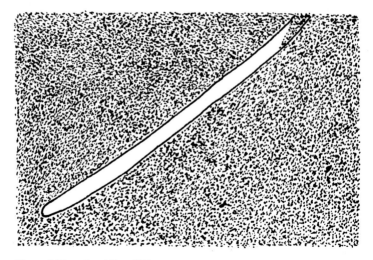

Nest of (Bembex) Sand Wasp

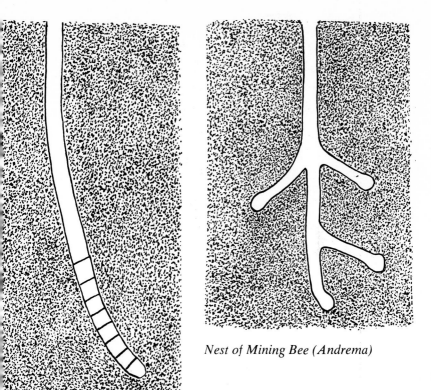

Nest of Mining Bee (Andrema)

Nest of Colletid Bee (Colletes)

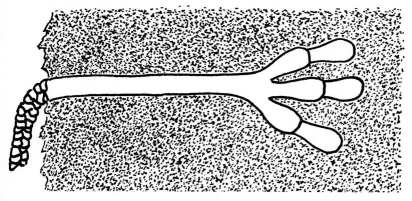

Nest of Mining Bee (Anthophora)

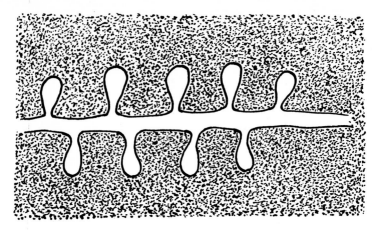

Nest of Mining Bee (Halictus)

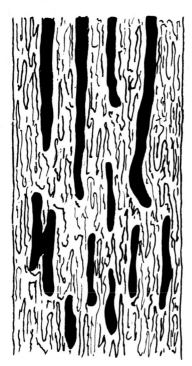

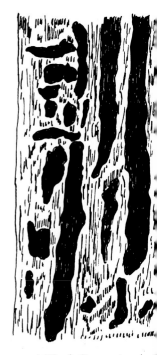

Burrows of Termites

Burrows of Black Carpenter Ant

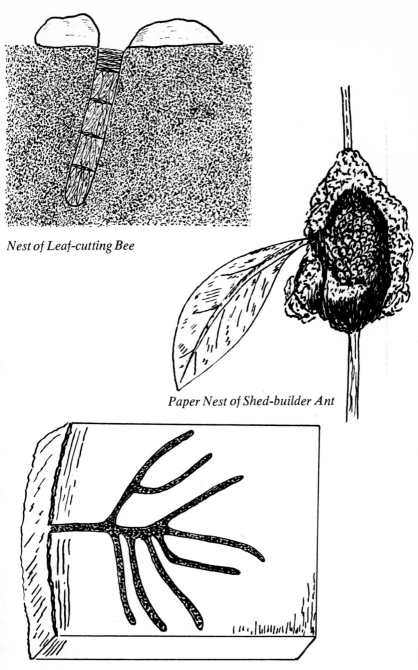

Nest of Leaf-cutting Bee

Paper Nest of Shed-builder Ant

Burrow of Hickory Timber Beetle (Xyloborus celsus)

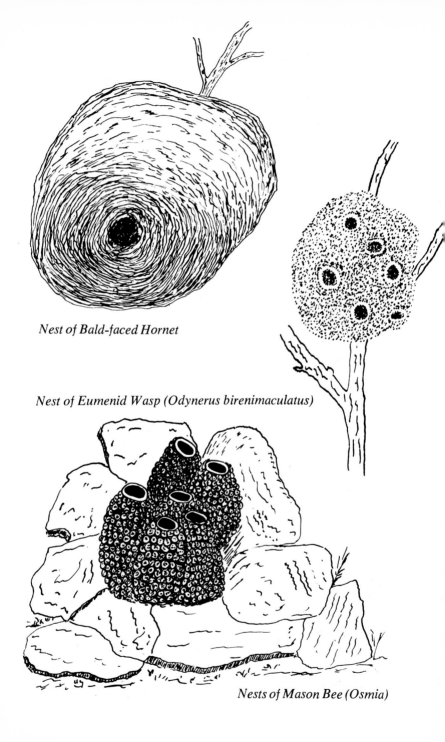

Nest of Bald-faced Hornet

Nest of Eumenid Wasp (Odynerus birenimaculatus)

Nests of Mason Bee (Osmia)

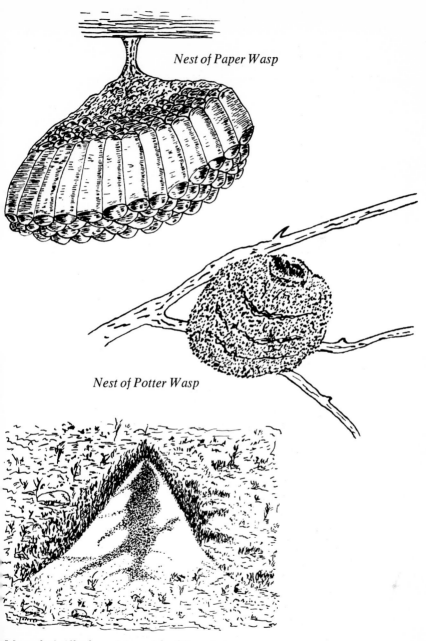

Nest of Paper Wasp

Nest of Potter Wasp

Mound of Allegheny Mound-building Ant

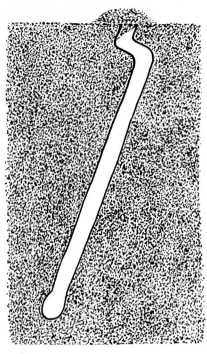

Nest of Cicada Killer

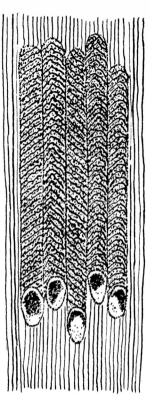

Nests of Pipe Organ Mud Dauber

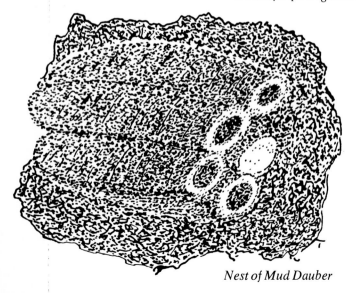

Nest of Mud Dauber

f(2). *In a log*
    1. See above.

                                    Mason Bee

f(3). *In a pile of stones*
    1. See above.

                                      Mason Bee

f(4). *Attached to the lower surface of a stone*
    1. Nest a thimble-shaped cell of mud.
        Generally throughout the East.

                    Mason Wasp (*Pseudagenia spp*)

III

Nests Above the Ground

A. Nest a Simple Burrow in a Twig or Stem

1. A tortuous burrow in the pith of (usually) sumac.
   Common in the East.

   Pemphredonid Wasp (*Stigmus fraternus*)

2. Burrow contains a series of cells separated from one another by a partition of chips of pith, the partitions serving as the roof of the cell below and the floor of the cell above. Usually in sumac and bramble.

   Widely distributed throughout eastern United States.

   Little Carpenter Bee (*Ceratina dupla*)

3. Similar to that of the Little Carpenter Bee (see above) but mostly in elder, sassafras, and rose.

   Throughout the East.

   Wasp-like Bee (*Ceratina calcarata*)

4. Burrow contains a series of cells each separated from one another by a circular disk of silk; walls of burrow coated with a glistening substance. In the stems of various pithy plants.

   In the Eastern states.

   Bifid-tongued Bee (*Prosopis ziziae*)

408

5. See Nests In the Ground I A a(1) b(3) 1.

    Leaf-cutting Bee

6. Burrow ends in a slightly enlarged nuptial chamber from which arise several egg galleries. In oak, maple, redbud, and cypress.

    Massachusetts west to Michigan and Kansas and south to Florida and Texas.

    Bark Beetle (*Micracis opacicollis*)

B. Nest a Simple Burrow in Solid Wood Such as a Porch Post, a Joist, or Timber in a Building

1. Burrow divided into a number of separate cells by partitions of cemented wood chips. Opening to burrow slightly smaller than burrow itself. Burrow about ¼ inch in diameter and continues for ½ inch to connect with main burrow at a right angle.

    Widely distributed throughout eastern United States.

    Large Carpenter Bee (*Xylocopa virginica*) *

C. Nest a Simple Burrow in a Dead Tree or Decaying and Rotten Wood

1. See above.

    Large Carpenter Bee

D. Nest a Simple Burrow in the Inner Bark of a Tree or Shrub, or at the Junction of the Bark and Sapwood

1. Entrance gallery leads directly into an irregular cavity in which the eggs are laid or in egg niches or grooves at its periphery. In red and white spruce.

    Maine and northern New York.

    Bark Beetle (*Cryphalus mainensis*)

---

* A wasp, *Monobia quadridens,* often nests in the deserted burrow of the Large Carpenter Bee.

2. Burrow irregular and elongated. Entrance gallery continued at the junction of wood and bark for a variable distance and then irregularly widened to provide a place for the eggs. In pine and spruce.

   Widely distributed throughout the United States.

   Red Turpentine Beetle (*Dendroctonus valens*)

3. Burrow longitudinal or transverse and similar to foregoing except that it is uniform in diameter. Each burrow may or may not have a turning niche or nuptial recess at the junction of entrance gallery and egg gallery. Egg niches arranged symmetrically or irregularly. In white cedar and arbor vitae.

   Northeastern United States.

   Northern Cedar Bark Beetle
   (*Phloesinus canadensis*)

4. Burrow forked longitudinal or transverse. Entrance gallery leads into a more or less enlarged chamber from which two egg galleries extend in opposite directions or diverge at a very wide angle. In spruce, larch, and fir.

   Throughout the United States westward to Montana and Colorado.

   Spruce Scolytus (*Scolytus piceae*)

5. Burrow radiate or star-shaped. Entrance gallery leads directly into an irregular chamber known as the nuptial chamber from which radiate the egg galleries. These may be systematically arranged or they may be longitudinal or transverse or irregular according to the species. In the Pine Bark Beetle they are arranged symmetrically. In pine and spruce.

   Northern States, Maine to Minnesota.

   Pine Bark Beetle (*Ips pini*)

E. Burrow Similar to Those Above but Excavated in the Wood

1. Entrance gallery leads directly through the bark into the wood where it may be continued as a simple egg gallery, or it may be branched or expanded into a nuptial chamber from which several egg galleries may arise. In hickory, pear, and maple.

   Eastern States from Massachusetts west to Iowa and south to Mississippi.

   Wood-eating Bark Beetle (*Lymantor decipiens*)

F. Nest a Simple or Branched Burrow in Wood and Stained Black from the Ambrosial Fungi on Which the Beetles Feed

1. Burrow extends into the sapwood where it is slightly widened to form a space for the eggs. In pecan.

   Southeastern states.

   Pecan Ambrosial Beetle (*Xyleborus pecanis*)

2. Burrow branched. Entrance gallery after entering the sapwood breaks up into several branches that extend in various directions in the same general plane. In hickory.

   New York westward to Minnesota and Indiana and southward to South Carolina and Mississippi.

   Hickory Timber Beetle (*Xyleborus celsus*)

3. Burrow compound and otherwise similar to the foregoing in having several egg galleries arising from the entrance gallery, but differing in having egg niches in the upper and lower sides of the galleries. In various deciduous trees, including fruit trees.

   Eastern United States south to Florida.

   Apple Wood-stainer (*Monarthrum mali*)

G. Nest a Rather Complicated Series of Parallel Concentric Chambers or Galleries

g(1). *In a dead tree*

1. See Nests On the Ground II D d(1) 1.

Black Carpenter Ant

g(2). *In a porch post or a joist of a building*

1. See Nests On the Ground II D d(1) 1.

Black Carpenter Ant

H. Nest a Series of Galleries or Tunnels Parallel to One Another and Usually with the Grain of the Wood

h(1). *In a fence post*

1. See Nests On the Ground II E e(1) 1.

Common Termite

h(2). *In a porch post, joist, or timber of a building*

1. See Nests On the Ground II E e(1) 1.

Common Termite

I. Nest a More or Less Complex Labyrinth of Galleries and Tunnels; No Permanent Brood Cells, the Young Being Kept in Chambers from Which They May be Transported to Other Parts of the Nest

i(1). *Within the walls of a house*

1. See Nests In the Ground I B b(1) c(7) 1.

Little Yellow House Ant

2. In the South.

Argentine Ant (*Iridomyrmex humulis*)

J. Nest of Wax

j(1). *A variable number of vertical combs of hexagonal cells*

  k(1). In a hollow tree

    1. Throughout the United States.

Honey Bee (Apis mellifica)

K. Nest of Paper

k(1). *A single comb of grayish paper-like material made from weatherworn wood suspended by a pedicel and without an envelope*

  l(1). In a building

    1. See Nests On the Ground II A a(3) 1.

Paper Wasp

  l(2). Attached to bushes

    See Nests On the Ground II A a(3) 1.

Paper Wasp

k(2). *A series of horizontal combs of a paper-like material made from weatherworn wood suspended one below another and enclosed within a paper envelope. Envelope consists of large sheets rather than of small sections as in the nest of the Yellow Jacket. Roughly spherical or urn-shaped. Sometimes very large.*

  l(1). Attached to a branch of a tree

    1. Widely distributed throughout the United States.

Bald-faced Hornet (Dolichovespula maculata) *

* The nest of *Brachygastra lecheguana* found along the Mexican border resembles that of the hornet but the combs are attached to the envelope instead of a central support.

k(3). *Similar to the nest of the Bald-faced Hornet except that the paper is made from the wood and bark of living trees*

l(1). In a hollow tree
1. In the East.

Giant Hornet (*Vespa crabro*)

l(2). In a building
1. See above.

Giant Hornet

l(3). Under overhanging rocks
1. See above.

Giant Hornet

L. Nest of Mud or Some Similar Material

l(1). *A jug-like structure of mud scarcely ½ inch in diameter and neatly fashioned with a delicate lip-like margin. Looks like a miniature water jug*

m(1). On the twigs and branches of trees and shrubs
1. Abundant in the eastern United States.

Potter Wasp (*Eumenes fraterna*)

l(2). *A cluster of several tubes or cells of mud, the whole smeared over with the same material. Looks like a blotch of mud*

m(1). On the walls and rafters of a building
1. Throughout the East.

Mud Dauber (*Sceliphron cementarium*) *

m(2). Attached to a twig of a low bush
1. Widely distributed through the Far West.

Masarid Wasp (*Pseudomasaris vespoides*)

* The Blue Mud Wasp (*Chalybion caeruleum*) often nests in the cells of the Mud Dauber.

l(3). *Three or four tubes of mud placed side by side, each tube divided by partitions into cells. Resembles a pipe organ*

m(1). In buildings

1. Throughout the East.

Pipe Organ Mud Dauber
(***Trypoxylon albitarsis***)

l(4). *A cluster of cells of mud or hard clay; about the size of a hen's egg*

m(1). Attached to the twig of a bush

1. Generally throughout the East.

Eumenid Wasp (***Odynerus birenimaculatus***)

l(5). *A thimble-shaped cell of mud*

m(1). In a chink in a wall

1. See Nests On the Ground II F f(4) 1.

Mason Wasp

m(2). Beneath bark

1. See Nests On the Ground II F f(4) 1.

Mason Wasp

M. Nest a Series of Thimble-Like Capsules of Pieces of Leaves

m(1). *In various places such as between the shingles of a roof, in a lead pipe, or in the nozzle of an old pump*

1. See Nests In the Ground I A a(1) b(3) 1.

Leaf-cutting Bee

PART SIX

/////////////////

NESTS OF FISHES

//////////////////

Introduction
↗↗↗↗↗↗↗↗↗↗↗↗↗↗↗↗↗↗

Except for the professional ichthyologist and the keen student of nature, few of us realize that many fishes in our streams and lakes build nests for their eggs or practice any degree of parental care. It is popularly assumed that fishes merely discharge their eggs and sperm (milt) into the water, trusting to fortuitous circumstance that the eggs will be fertilized. This is the method normally practiced by the marine species, which would not be likely to build nests anyway since there are few places in the open ocean where they could do so.

There are, of course, freshwater fishes that reproduce in this manner—pike, pickerel, carp, to name a few—but there are others that are nest-builders. Among such species the male usually prepares a nest in advance of mating, to which he lures the female. Once the eggs have been fertilized the nest may be deserted; however, in some species (sunfish) the male remains on guard until the eggs have hatched, and in a few species remains to watch over the newly hatched young (stickleback). Among the yellow catfishes both parents aerate, turn, and clean the eggs by stirring and fanning them with their fins; occasionally they take some of them into their mouths, then expel them, repeating the performance a number of times.

Most nests, as might be expected, are simple affairs. In the trout and salmon they are simply pits excavated in the bottom of the stream or lake in which the eggs are laid. Once they are fertilized they are covered with sand or gravel and forgotten. Among the sunfishes the nest is a circular depression or saucer-

419

shaped basin prepared in the bottom by the male, who clears a space a foot or so across and several inches deep by fanning the gravel away with his tail and moving the heavier stones with his mouth. Such a nest might be said to be analogous to that of the sandpipers and plovers. Some of the darters and minnows make use of a cavity or hollow beneath rocks which they clean out to serve as a nest, the eggs being attached to the lower surface of the rocks. In the brook stickleback the fishes approach the nest-building capability of the birds. The delicate nest of this tiny fish of our northern streams rivals the finest examples of avian architecture.

There are many species of freshwater fishes, even among the nest-builders. To include them all in the present guide would be neither feasible nor practical and serve no useful purpose. For instance, there are several species of salmon and trout whose nesting habits are much alike, and the same can be said of the sunfishes and others. In many instances only by identifying the fish itself can the maker of a given nest be determined.

While the present material has certain limitations, it is hoped that it may be the means of making our freshwater fishes better known to those not too well acquainted with them. Perhaps it may provide an incentive to a better understanding of these inhabitants of our streams, ponds, and lakes, which are generally viewed as providing a challenge to our manipulative skill with a fly and rod and whose sole use among fishermen is to grace our frying pans.

I

𝟏𝟏𝟏𝟏𝟏𝟏𝟏𝟏𝟏𝟏𝟏𝟏𝟏𝟏

Nests In Lakes

A. Nest a Pit or Depression in the Bottom of a Lake in Which the Eggs Are Deposited and Then Covered with Sand or Gravel

1. In clear cold waters. Introduced into western streams.

    East of the Mississippi River from the Canadian border south to northern Georgia.

    Eastern Brook Trout

B. Nest a Circular or Saucer-Shaped Depression in the Bottom of a Lake

b(1). *In mud, silt, sand, or vegetation*

1. Depression some 2½ feet in diameter; in thick vegetation at the shallow margin of a lake.

    Great Lakes and Mississippi Valley to Virginia, Florida, and Texas.

    Bowfin

2. In shallow water, at most some 6 feet deep, among water plants.

    Great Lakes and the Red River to Florida and Texas and west to Kansas and the Dakotas. Introduced in California.

    Large-mouthed Black Bass

3. Depression 2 to 4 feet in diameter, in shallow water usually where there are rocks or stumps around which the nests may be hidden.

   Lake Champlain and southward on both sides of the mountains to South Carolina and Arkansas. Introduced in Florida and California.

   Small-mouthed Black Bass

4. Depression a foot or more in diameter and 3 or 4 inches deep in the shallow part of a lake.

   Maine to Minnesota and Southward to Florida, east of the Alleghenies.

   Common Sunfish

5. Edges or bars among water plants in 5 to 15 feet of water. Nests in colonies.

   Great Lakes south to Florida and the Mexican border and east of the Alleghenies from New Jersey southward.

   Bluegill Sunfish

6. Shallow, mud-bottomed, weedy lakes.

   Great Lakes south to Florida and Texas, west to Kansas and the Dakotas.

   Warmouth

7. Nest in water varying from a few inches to several feet in depth and frequently placed adjacent to a rock, stick, or some other object. Cool, weedy lakes.

   Vermont to the Great Lakes and south to Louisiana.

   Rock Bass

b(2). *In gravel or gravelly riffle*

1. See I B b(1) 2.

   Large-mouthed Black Bass

2. See I B b(1) 3.

   Small-mouthed Black Bass

3. See I B b(1) 4.

    Common Sunfish

4. See I B b(1) 5.

    Bluegill Sunfish

5. See I B b(1) 7.

    Rock Bass

C. Nest a Pile of Stones or Gravel Heap

1. Clear lakes, along the shallow margin.

    From the Canadian border south to Virginia; common northward east of the Alleghenies.

    Fallfish or Silver Chub

II

ʔʔʔʔʔʔʔʔʔʔʔʔʔʔ

Nests In Ponds

A. Nest a Pit or Depression in the Bottom of a Pond in Which the Eggs Are Deposited and Then Covered with Sand or Gravel

1. See I A 1.

Eastern Brook Trout

B. Nest a Circular or Saucer-Shaped Depression in the Bottom of a Pond

b(1). *In mud, silt, sand, or vegetation*

1. Nest a more or less irregularly circular area in shallow water.

    Maine to the Great Lakes and Ohio Valley, south and southwestward to Florida and Texas. Introduced along the Pacific Slope.

    Horned Pout or Bullhead

2. See I B b(1) 2.

    Large-mouthed Black Bass

3. See I B b(1) 3.

    Small-mouthed Black Bass

4. Nest similar to that of Common Sunfish. See I B b(1)
   4. More abundant in small ponds.

   Great Lakes to Mexican border; not found east of the
   Alleghenies.

   Green Sunfish

5. See I B b(1) 4.

   Common Sunfish

6. See I B b(1) 5.

   Bluegill Sunfish

7. See I B b(1) 6.

   Warmouth

8. See I B b(1) 7.

   Rock Bass

9. Nest a circular depression similar to that of the sunfish. In shallow muddy water.

   Great Lakes to Texas and west to Kansas and Nebraska. Introduced along the Pacific Slope.

   Crappie

b(2). *In gravel or a gravelly riffle*

1. See I B b(1) 2.

   Large-mouthed Black Bass

2. See I B b(1) 3.

   Small-mouthed Black Bass

3. See I B b(1) 4.

   Common Sunfish

4. See I B b(1) 5.

   Bluegill Sunfish

5. See I B b(1) 7.

   Rock Bass

C. Nest a Cavity or Hollow Under Rocks, Roots, or Logs

1. Cavity prepared by the male on the lower surface of a rock or some other object, then cleaned, to which the eggs are attached. Shallow water, 2 feet or so deep.

   Canadian border south to Delaware, west to the Dakotas, and southwest to Alabama and Arkansas.

   Blunt-nosed Minnow

2. Habits similar to those of the Blunt-nosed Minnow. See above. Common in bog ponds.

   Lake Champlain west to the Dakotas and south to Kentucky and the Mexican border.

   Fathead Minnow

3. A cavity excavated beneath a rock, stick, base of water plants, and the like. See also II B b(1) 1.

   Horned Pout or Bullhead

4. Nest prepared by the male beneath a stone or some other object on the bottom, the eggs being attached to the ceiling of the breeding cavity. Usually in shallow water.

   Eastern states southward to North Carolina and westward to Pennsylvania, the Great Lakes, and the Dakotas.

   Johnny Darter or Eastern Tesselated Darter

D. Nest of Plant Material

1. Nest a delicate sphere about ¾ inch in diameter with an entrance hole in one side. Made of fine fibers, plant stems, and filaments of algae, and attached to a plant

stem or submerged twig. Practically invisible against a background of leaves and plant stems. In shallow water.

New York to Kansas and northward.

Brook Stickleback

III

✓✓✓✓✓✓✓✓✓✓✓✓✓✓

Nests In Streams, Brooks, Creeks, and Rivers

A. Nest a Pit or Depression in the Bottom of a Stream in Which the Eggs Are Deposited and Then Covered with Sand or Gravel

1. In coastal streams north of Cape Cod. Landlocked fishes that live in lakes of northern New England, ascend tributary streams to spawn.

    Atlantic Salmon

2. In clear cold brooks and rivers. See I A 1.

    Eastern Brook Trout

3. Gravelly brooks and creeks. Mississippi River drainage of Iowa, Minnesota, and Wisconsin east to New York and southward in the Ohio and Mississippi valleys to northern Alabama and Arkansas.

    Rainbow Darter

B. Nest a Shallow Pit Walled In by Small Stones

1. In riffly shallows. Rivers of the Atlantic coast from Maine to Florida. Landlocked type, known as the

    428

Lake Lamprey, that lives in northern lakes, ascends tributary streams to spawn.

Sea Lamprey

2. On gravelly riffles in brooks.

Maine to Wyoming and south to Georgia and Alabama.

Horned Dace or Creek Chub

C. Nest a Circular or Saucer-Shaped Depression in the Bottom of a Stream

c(1). *In mud, silt, sand, or vegetation*

1. See I B b(1) 1. In sluggish streams.

Bowfin

2. See II B b(1) 1. In sluggish streams.

Horned Pout or Bullhead

3. See I B b(1) 2. In sluggish streams and bayous.

Large-mouthed Black Bass

4. See I B b(1) 3. Clear cool streams of (preferably) moderate size, with pools and riffles.

Small-mouthed Black Bass

5. Nest in coarse sand close to shore in 6 inches to 2 or 3 feet of water. Various kinds of streams.

Maine to Virginia.

Long-eared Sunfish

6. See I B b(1) 4. Cool to moderately warm brooks and small streams, preferably in weedy parts.

Common Sunfish

7. Nest in shallow water, smaller and more distinct than that of the Common Sunfish. In clear brooks with quiet, deepish pools.

    Minnesota to Florida and the Rio Grande.

    Big-eared Sunfish

8. See I B b(1) 5. In the quieter pools of streams.

    Bluegill Sunfish

9. See I B b(1) 6. Sluggish streams and bayous.

    Warmouth

10. See I B b(1) 7. Rivers, creeks, and brooks of (preferably) clear, cool water.

    Rock Bass

11. See II B b(1) 9. Sluggish, somewhat turbid streams and bayous.

    Crappie

c(2). *In gravel or a gravelly riffle*

1. Nest about a foot in diameter and a couple of inches deep. Small streams, brooks, and creeks, preferably pools in streams that are clear and rapid.

    East of the Rockies except Texas and the southern Atlantic states.

    Common Shiner or Redfin

2. See III C c(1) 3 and I B b(1) 2.

    Large-mouthed Black Bass

3. See III C c(1) 4 and I B b(1) 3.

    Small-mouthed Black Bass

4. See III C c(1) 6 and I B b(1) 4.

    Common Sunfish

5. See III C c(1) 7.

    Big-eared Sunfish

6. See III C c(1) 8 and I B b(1) 5.

    Bluegill Sunfish

7. See III C c(1) 10 and I B b(1) 7.

    Rock Bass

D. Nest a Cavity or Hollow Under Rocks, Roots, or Logs

1. See II C 1. Larger creeks.

    Blunt-nosed Minnow

2. See II C 2. Small sluggish streams.

    Fathead Minnow

3. See II C 3. Slow-moving streams.

    Horned Pout or Bullhead

4. See II C 4. Both swift and sluggish streams.

    Johnny Darter or Eastern Tessellated Darter

5. Small streams, preferably riffles and shallows of gravelly creeks and brooks.

    New York west to Iowa and south to South Carolina and northern Alabama.

    Fan-tail Darter

6. Clear, rocky brooks.

    Canadian border south to Georgia and westward to Missouri and the Dakotas.

    Miller's Thumb or Fresh-water Sculpin

E. Nest a Tunnel in a Bank

1. See III C c(1) 2.

    Horned Pout or Bullhead

F. Nest a Pile of Stones or Gravel Heap

    1.   See I C 1.

Fallfish or Silver Chub

    2.   Clear gravelly creeks.

           Lake Ontario eastward and southward to Virginia.

Cut-lip Minnow

G. Nest of Plant Material

    1.   See II D 1. Shallow water of small streams.

Brook Stickleback

PART SEVEN

✦✦✦✦✦✦✦✦✦✦✦✦✦✦

OTHER NESTS

✦✦✦✦✦✦✦✦✦✦✦✦✦✦✦

I

𝟷𝟷𝟷𝟷𝟷𝟷𝟷𝟷𝟷𝟷𝟷𝟷𝟷𝟷𝟷

Nests of Turtles, Lizards, and Other Reptiles

The turtles, lizards, snakes, and other members of the reptile group generally do not build nests, unless we consider as nests the holes that many excavate in the ground as repositories for their eggs. Female turtles, as a rule, dig flask-shaped cavities in the soil or in decaying vegetable matter, the site selected varying with the species. Such aquatic turtles as the spotted and painted turtles usually select a place on the shore or bank of a stream or pond not far from water, whereas the box turtle of our woodlands prefers sandy soil of open cultivated or grassy areas. The snapping turtle may select any one of a variety of situations such as a bank, hillside, field, or meadow, the only requirements for its nest being a certain amount of moisture and sunshine. The musk turtle is even less selective and may deposit its eggs on the bare ground, beneath a fallen log, in a bundle of rushes, in a cow track, in a mass of muck, or even well above the ground such as on top of a rotten stump, though the site selected must be near water. In a few species there is a strong tendency toward gregariousness, dozens of "nests" being found under a log or similar object, and in the case of certain marine species, in a particular sandbar.

Lizards usually deposit their eggs in a sheltered situation that

435

is somewhat moist and protected from the direct rays of the sun. Commonly the female excavates a hole in the earth, beneath leaf litter, or under a log or stone, lays her eggs, and departs. Only in a few species is there any degree of parental care. The "nest" of the common western skink is an excavation beneath a rock embedded in the soil. It is flask-shaped with a fairly large cavity 2 to 3 inches in diameter at the bottom and connects to a narrow tunnel about 1 inch in diameter and about 15 inches long which passes beneath the rock and opens to the exterior at the rock's edge. The female remains with the eggs and with the hatchlings for a few days until they all disperse.

No snake has been seen to build a nest under natural conditions though in some species a number of females often lay their eggs at the same site, so a large number of eggs may be found together. The egg-laying species deposit their eggs in a variety of situations and then desert them, leaving them to hatch by themselves.

Of all the reptiles only the female alligator builds a nest in the more restricted meaning of the word. It is made of a variety of vegetable trash such as leaves, leaf litter, roots, stalks, and the like, which the female scrapes together into a large mound 6 or 7 feet in diameter and 2 to 3 feet in height. When the mound is finished the female scoops out a hole at the top in which she lays her eggs. She covers the eggs with the same material as the mound and packs it down, sometimes crawling back and forth over the top to insure a firm packing. The female may use the same nest year after year, adding a little more material each year to the top before excavating the hole.

Unlike her relative, the female American crocodile merely uses a large mound of sand in which to lay her eggs. In the United States the crocodile is found only in the extreme southern portion of the Florida Peninsula. The alligator inhabits the rivers and swamps of the low coastal region from North Carolina, throughout Florida and westward to Texas.

II

111111111111111

Nests of Frogs, Toads,
and Salamanders

Amphibians characteristically lay their eggs in water during or shortly after mating and then forget about them. A few species, however, lay their eggs in some sheltered situation on land. No species makes a real project of building a nest.

Among the salamanders, the male hellbender, in advance of mating, excavates a cavity beneath a large flat rock partially embedded in the stream bottom, with an entrance out of the direct current and usually on the downstream side. He may also take advantage of a natural cavity to which he lures his mate. The mud puppy excavates a cavity beneath a large stone or some other object, such as a board. Similarly, the four-toed salamander fashions a simple little cavity in sphagnum moss or among rhizoids and grass roots. In some instances she makes use of a natural opening in the moss or in some hollow between the roots of a bog plant. The "nest" is about 3 or 4 inches deep and usually not far from water, along the margin or pond or along the sides of a moss-covered log projecting into the water, though there are instances where the nest has been made some distance from the shore.

With the possible exception of the robber frogs none of our native frogs exercise any parental care. This is in marked con-

437

trast to some of the species found in the tropics, which have developed rather elaborate care of both the eggs and tadpoles. As for our toads, none of them show any concern for the fate of their offspring.

Much the same can be said of the salamanders, though the male hellbender remains to guard the eggs, and in the three-toed amphiuma the female remains with them until they hatch. A number of other salamanders, both terrestrial and aquatic, also stay with their eggs, the guardian parent being most often the female. However, it appears that she does little more than protect the eggs against some small predator that might destroy them.

Index

Marsh, 40, 168
Mexican Black, 237
Red-bellied, 236
Red-shouldered, 110
Red-tailed, 110, 235
Sennett's White-tailed, 236
Sharp-shinned, 109, 235
Short-tailed, 111
Sparrow, 128, 255
Swainson's, 62, 111, 182, 236
(Western) Pigeon, 183, 237, 257
Zone-tailed, 236
Hellbender, 437, 438
Hen, Sage, 148
Heron:
  Anthony's Green, 239
  Black-crowned Night, 115, 239
  California, 234
  (Eastern) Green, 124
  Great Blue, 106, 234
  Great White, 106
  Little Blue, 115
  Louisiana, 114
  Northwestern Coast, 234
  Treganza's, 234
  Yellow-crowned Night, 115
Hornet:
  Bald-faced, 413
  Giant, 414
Hummingbird:
  Allen's, 198, 203, 205, 207
  Anna's, 198, 202, 204, 207
  Black-chinned, 202, 206
  Blue-throated, 203
  Broad-billed, 203
  Broad-tailed, 198, 205, 207
  Buff-bellied, 199
  Calliope, 208
  Costa's, 198, 202, 207
  Rivoli's, 199
  Ruby-throated, 79
  Rufous, 198, 202, 205, 207
  White-eared, 199

Ibis:
  Eastern Glossy, 67
  White, 71, 116

White-faced Glossy, 67, 191
Wood, 116, 239
Ips pini, 410
Iridomyrmex humulis, 412

Jack Rabbit:
  Black-tailed, 360
  White-tailed, 360
Jay:
  Arizona, 245
  Black-headed, 211
  Blue, 117, 240
  Blue-fronted, 211
  California, 245
  Canada, 117, 240
  Coast, 211
  Couch's, 245
  Florida, 123
  Gray, 240
  Green, 246
  Long-crested, 211
  Long-tailed, 245
  Nicasio, 245
  Oregon, 240
  Pinon, 241
  Rocky Mountain, 240
  Steller's, 211
  Texas, 245
  Woodhouse's, 245
Junco:
  Arizona, 156
  Gray-headed, 156
  Montana, 156
  Oregon, 156
  Pink-sided, 156
  Point Pinos, 156
  Red-backed, 156
  Shufeldt's, 156
  Slate-colored, 24
  Thurber's, 156
  White-winged, 155

Killdeer, 15, 149
Kingbird:
  Arkansas, 97, 139, 216, 266
  Cassin's, 217
  Couch's, 216
  Eastern, 97, 216